The contributors to this volume examine current controversies about the importance of commonsense psychology for our understanding of the human mind. Common sense provides a familiar and friendly psychological scheme by which to talk about the mind. Its categories (belief, desire, intention, consciousness, emotion, and so on) tend to portray the mind as quite different from the rest of nature, and thus irreducible to physical matter and its laws.

In this volume a variety of positions on commonsense psychology, from critical to supportive, from exegetical to speculative, are represented. Among the questions posed are these: Is commonsense psychology an empirical theory, a body of analytic knowledge, a practice, or a strategy? If it is a legitimate enterprise, can it be naturalized or not? If it is not legitimate, can it be eliminated? Is its fate tied to our understanding of consciousness? Should we approach its concepts and generalizations from the standpoint of conceptual analysis or that of philosophy of science?

MIND AND COMMON SENSE

Mind and Common Sense

Philosophical Essays on Commonsense Psychology

Edited by
RADU J. BOGDAN

Tulane University

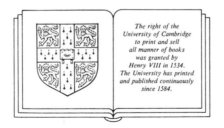

*The right of the
University of Cambridge
to print and sell
all manner of books
was granted by
Henry VIII in 1534.
The University has printed
and published continuously
since 1584.*

CAMBRIDGE UNIVERSITY PRESS

CAMBRIDGE

NEW YORK   PORT CHESTER   MELBOURNE   SYDNEY

Published by the Press Syndicate of the University of Cambridge
The Pitt Building, Trumpington Street, Cambridge CB2 1RP
40 West 20th Street, New York, NY 10011, USA
10 Stamford Road, Oakleigh, Melbourne 3166, Australia

© Cambridge University Press 1991

First published 1991

Printed in the United States of America

Library of Congress Cataloging-in-Publication Data
Mind and common sense: philosophical essays on commonsense psychology
/ edited by Radu J. Bogdan.
p.   cm.
Includes indexes.
ISBN 0-521-40201-8
1. Psychology – Philosophy.   2. Philosophy of mind.   3. Commonsense.
I. Bogdan, Radu J.
BF38.M55   1991
150–dc20   90–48289
                                           CIP

British Library Cataloguing in Publication Data
Mind and common sense : philosophical essays on commonsense
psychology.
1. Psychology. Theories
I. Bogdan, Radu J.
150.1

ISBN 0-521-40201-8 hardback

Contents

Contributors

JONATHAN BENNETT, Professor of Philosophy, Syracuse University. Author of *Rationality* (1964), *Linguistic Behavior* (1976), and *Events and Their Names* (1988).

RADU J. BOGDAN, Associate Professor, Tulane University, New Orleans. Editor of *Local Induction* (1976) and *Belief* (1986) and author of articles on philosophy of mind and epistemology.

PAUL M. CHURCHLAND, Professor of Philosophy, University of California, San Diego. Author of *Scientific Realism and the Plasticity of Mind* (1979), *Matter of Consciousness* (1984), and *A Neurocomputational Perspective* (1989).

ROBERT CUMMINS, Professor of Philosophy, University of Arizona, Tucson. Author of *The Nature of Psychological Explanation* (1983) and *Meaning and Mental Representation* (1989).

COLIN MCGINN, Professor of Philosophy, Rutgers University, New Brunswick. Author of *The Character of Mind* (1982), *The Subjective View* (1983), and *Mental Content* (1989).

ADAM MORTON, Professor of Philosophy, University of Bristol. Author of *Frames of Mind* (1980) and of articles on epistemology and philosophy of mind and language.

ALEXANDER ROSENBERG, Professor of Philosophy, University of California, Riverside. Author of *Microeconomic Laws* (1976), *Sociobiology and the Preemption of Social Science* (1980), and *The Structure of Biological Science* (1985).

KATHLEEN V. WILKES, Fellow, St. Hilda's College, Oxford. Author of *Real People* (1988) and of articles on metaphysics and philosophy of mind.

1

The Folklore of the Mind

RADU J. BOGDAN

A distinguished wise man, Emil Cioran, with whom I share a country of birth and the thought that follows, said once that the two most interesting things in life are gossip and metaphysics. I can hardly think of a more self-evident and enjoyable truth, if wisely construed. This volume combines the two pleasures, for it is an exercise in the metaphysics of wise gossip, of how we make sense of each other, and how, as a result, we interpret, explain, rationalize, and evaluate our representations and actions. The body of wisdom that allows us to do all this is currently called folk or commonsense psychology. I will also call it psychofolklore or the folklore of the mind.

The folklore of the mind has probably been around for as long as minds have. People were so used to it that they rarely asked serious questions about its nature and modus operandi. Little appeared to be at stake. Not anymore; there is now a surprising surge of interest in our psychofolklore. The stakes are high. It is not that we want to understand the mind. We always wanted *that*. It is rather that now, unlike in the past, our psychofolklore has a role to play in our understanding of the mind. Why such a role, and what could it be? It is true that common sense provides the home language in which we conceptualize the mind. It is also true that, when cleverly reconstructed by philosophers and opposed to science, commonsense psychology appears to offer ideological support and protection by portraying the mind as special, unique, and different from the rest of nature, and thus irreducible to physical matter and its laws.

But there must be more than that. The distant universe has always been of interest to ordinary people, which is why they came up with folk astronomy. In clever hands, folk astronomy too was put to useful ideological work: We are in the center of the universe, everything revolves around the earth, and other reassuring stuff like this. Folk astronomy wasn't a capricious invention. It was based on solid folksy evidence: It looked that way to most people. It still does. (One recent poll, reported in a recent *Economist,* reveals that only 34% of Britons know that the earth goes around the sun and that it takes a year to do so. One-fifth of the Britons are also reported to think the earth is hurtling around the sun once a day. Must be pretty dizzy in Britain.) And yet, folk astronomy has been effectively marginalized, mostly because its scientific counterpart works so much better, and visibly so.

So why this sudden importance of commonsense psychology? Why hasn't it been marginalized by the sciences of cognition? There are in fact two questions that we are asking here. One is about ordinary folk generally: Why is commonsense psychology a guide to *their* understanding of the mind? Another is about philosophers and perhaps some scientists: Why, in this age of science and expertise, do they cling *professionally* to a piece of folkloric wisdom? These questions need not, and are not likely to, receive the same answers. Ordinary folk must manage in life, while the philosophers and the scientists worry about the intrinsic properties of the mind. Since an introduction is not a place to provide answers to questions, the best I can offer is a sketchy map, followed by a few invited articles, to help the reader find a way to some answer.

1. Three Psychologies

Our wisdom about the mind, as about most things, is of two kinds, folkloric and scientific. The folklore of the mind, unlike the folklore of anything else, comes in two versions, one subjective and naïve, the other public and commonsensical. We can think of *subjective and naïve psychology* as based on spontaneous, unreflective, immediate, and private access to the phenomenal data of our mental life. The phenomenal data need not be only in the form of specific sensations (such as color impressions), feelings (such as pain), or generalized states (moods). They could also reveal attitudes (such as beliefs and desires) or processes (such as thinking). The phenomenal access is limited in scope and rather superficial in reach. Subjective and naïve psychology represents a natural first-person stance from where we are aware of some of the outputs of our cognition and volition. We learn our subjective and naïve psychology simply by exercising our cognitive and conative abilities such as vision, memory, language, planning, inferring, desiring, deciding, and the like. We all are natural and fairly good subjective and naïve psychologists.

Commonsense psychology appears to be a different thing altogether, even though it involves plenty of subjective and naïve psychologizing. Commonsense psychology relies on an elaborate and powerful social practice of interpersonal attribution and evaluation of cognition and behavior. The commonsense concepts appear to reflect not only properties of cognition and behavior but also environmental facts, as well as social norms and conventions. We learn how to make common sense of, or interpret, each other as part of our becoming social beings. And again, we are natural and fairly good commonsense psychologists.

The scientific psychology of cognition and behavior, a historically late development, studies mostly the information-processing mechanisms and operations that define our competence for cognition and behavior. We learn scientific psychology by going to school, taking the right classes, reading the right professional books and articles, talking to the right people, and so on. There are different ways of doing scientific psychology, some better than others, but all aspire to making psychology a science of the psyche based on operational definitions, theoretical concepts, and laws, backed by empirical evidence, careful experiment, and formal simulation. In recent years, people talk of a comprehensive alliance of the sciences of cognition, from psychology and linguistics to the neurosciences. To accommodate this development, I will talk of cognitive science as the larger class, of which scientific (cognitive) psychology is a distinguished member.

For easy reference and discussion, I will label and summarize the trilateral distinction just introduced as follows:

COGSCIENCE.   Cognition and behavior are driven by *data structures* encoded in distinct forms (*symbols, visual images, formal structures, sentences,* etc.) and processed in various patterns (*representation, computation, inference, relevance relations, etc.*) in distinct but often interacting cognitive modalities (*visual, linguistic, memory, etc.*).

SUBJECTIVITY.   We have *phenomenal access* to the outputs of our internal structures and processes in the form of *images, sensations, feelings, pains, as well as attitudes and control states.*

COMMON SENSE.   Guided by social and linguistic norms, we attribute *thoughts, beliefs, desires, and the like* to others in terms of which we then endeavor to characterize their cognitive and conative states and to explain, predict, and evaluate their cognition and behavior.

Some History

Each of these three paradigms has had its day of intellectual glory when it was thought to hold the theoretical key to the understanding of the mind. *Subjectivity* came first. Descartes, the early British empiricists, later the German psychologists inspired by Wundt and Brentano, the sense-data analysts, Husserl's phenomenologists, and many logical empiricists have all in various ways tried to fortify subjectivity into a disciplined and motivated logos of the mind. The enterprise was essentially epistemological. Mesmerized by the immediate certainty of the phenomenal data of sensation and consciousness, and suspicious of anything that is not reconstructed from such certainty, most of these philosophers were looking for a powerful method (clear and distinct ideas, internal reflection, introspection, reduction, analysis, and so on) to rigorously reassemble the human psyche from its phenomenal atoms. The mind was what the philosophically trained inner eye could see, rigorously and infallibly. The epistemological reconstruction of the psyche was thought to deliver its theoretical explanation as well.

Subjectivity ended up being challenged from two main directions. Its scientific hopes were dashed by behaviorism which pointed out, quite effectively, that the privacy and indubitability of internal experiences do not make for a good science of the psyche. Behaviorism also downgraded dramatically the psychological importance of the internal workings of cognition. At about the same time (the first decades of this century), a number of philosophers with positivist or behaviorist sympathies (Wittgenstein, Austin, Ryle, and Quine, among others) were resisting both the epistemological ideal of subjectivity and the explanatory role of the structures and mechanisms operative in cognition, and were turning toward the ordinary language and the social practices of communication, interpretation, and translation. *Common sense* was gaining ground. In the 1950s and 1960s the use of the mentalist fragment of the ordinary language and the practices of attitude attribution and meaning interpretation became prominent objects of philosophical inquiry. The result was rather deflationary: The mind is either a manner of talking about behavior, or else a manner of talking about our sociolinguistic practices and interactions.

Two largely parallel developments then started to put pressure on this deflationary common sense. One was the computational study of language and cognition, stimulated and motivated mostly by Chomsky's work in linguistics, and by advances in computer science, in general, and their applications to cognitive matters (vision, language understanding, artificial intelligence), in particular. The computer metaphor of the mind was gaining tremendous popularity, either as a heuristic frame of conceptualization, or indeed as possibly a very realistic description. *Cogscience* was taking over. The other, not unrelated, development was taking place in philosophy of mind. It came in the form of functionalism, a doctrine that encourages philosophers to construe the mind *as* a program for cognition, in terms of inputs, internal instructions and executions, and outputs. This is a construal that deliberately ignores both the hardware implementation of the program and (possibly as a consequence) the phenomenal accompaniments of the program execution.

The computer metaphor and functionalism are natural allies when it comes to understanding the mind. The computer metaphor of the mind makes functionalism not only intuitively attractive but philosophically respectable as well. Many philosophers like the detachment of program from hardware. Some even see in this detachment the latest version of the mind–body distinction. Others like any approach that frees them from the obligation to worry about hardware and other empirical matters. Yet, even more importantly, functionalism ushers in a new vision and utilization of common sense. Functionalism provides a bridge between folklore and psychology by allowing folklore to have a say in how to think of the functional construals of mental and behavioral states and, hence, of the subject matter of psychology. The assumption (or bet) is that our commonsense knowledge cannot possibly be about the bodily hardware, and, being common, cannot be about subjective and private experiences. So it must be about the functional roles of our mental states. Three options for the functionalist utilization of common sense have so far emerged: the interpretational, the heuristic, and the realist.

Both the *interpretational* and the *heuristic* options regard our commonsense attributions and explanations as approximating rationality and practicality assumptions of the deductive, inductive, decisional, and pragmatic sort. Both regard our psychofolklore as an implicit and normative (as opposed to a descriptive) paradigm of the functional program of the mind. The two options differ, however, in how they see the relation between common sense and cogscience. The *interpretational* view was notoriously articulated by Davidson (1980, 1984). It shows the influence of the earlier deflationary conception of Quine, and even reminds one of the still earlier German speculations (Dilthey, Gadamer) about hermeneutics and the human sciences. The interpretational view defends the autonomy of psychology and its irreducibility to the sciences of cognitive design and hardware. Psychology is in the business of interpretation, or explanation from representation and motive, understood commonsensically, as opposed to the explanation from natural kinds and laws, typical of the hard sciences.

The *heuristic* view [best articulated by Dennett (1978, 1987)] construes our psychofolklore as a normative guide to the functional design of the mind. The commonsense notions do not tell us how the mind works but they suggest how to look at it, if we want to find out how it works. After it shows the way, common sense is dispensable; the real conceptual and explanatory work belongs to the sciences of cognitive design and hardware. By contrast, the *realist* option construes common sense as an implicit but descriptive theory of the functional joints of the mental program (Harman 1973). The commonsense notions and attributions are fully descriptive and explanatory because the implicit functionalist theory embodied in our psychofolklore is generally true of the mind. As a result, commonsense should inspire cogscience, and end up being absorbed by and reduced to it (Fodor 1975, 1987; Pylyshyn 1984).

The opposition to any scientifically respectable treatment of common sense remains vehement, and is reminiscent in tone and intensity of the turn-of-century reaction of behaviorism against subjectivity. For what is at stake on both occasions is the very nature of the scientific enterprise. The puritanic defenders of science cannot tolerate the very thought that our folklore can have anything true to say about anything, let alone such a complex and elusive object of inquiry as human cognition. This is the ideological premise of *eliminativism*. Its position [best represented by P. M. Churchland (1979) and Stich (1983)] is that the commonsense notions and generalizations are false and capture nothing at all, least of all the functional joints of cognition. Cogscience will slowly but surely take care of everything, in its own terms, and at a level of abstraction totally incommensurate with that of folklore.

2.   Modus Operandi

Much more energy, imagination, and ink have been spent on the comparative virtues of common sense (how it fares with respect to science in general, and to cogscience in particular) than on how it works. With so much at stake, one would expect numerous speculations and analyses of how our folklore engages the mind, and how its notions, attributions, and explanations operate. In fact, such speculations and analyses are rather few and mostly traditional. Perhaps the most popular is the one (probably) initiated by Hobbes. He writes that:

[T]here is another saying . . . by which they might learn truly to read one another. . . . *Nosce teipsum, Read thyself* . . . [which was meant] to teach us that, for the similitude of the thoughts and Passions of one man to the thoughts and passions of another, whosoever looketh into himself and considereth what he doth when he does *think, opine, reason, hope, feare, &c.*, and upon what grounds, he shall thereby read and know what are the thoughts and Passions of all other men upon the like occasions. I say the similitude of *Passions*, which are the same in all men, *desire, feare, hope. &c;* not the similitude of the *objects* of the Passions, which are the things *desired, feared, hoped, &c:* For these the constitution individuall, and particular education do so vary, and they are so easie to be kept from our knowledge. . . . And though by mens actions wee do discover their designe sometimes; yet to do it without comparing them with our own, and distinguishing all circumstances, by which the case may come to be altered, is to decypher without a key. (Hobbes 1651/1979, pp. 82–3).

The Hobbesian equation is that *common sense = subjectivity + projection onto the other* under an assumption of similar design. (Hobbes was probably the first serious cognitive scientist. He is also the one who thought that cognition is mechanical computation over mental symbols.) Wisely, the Hobbesian equation covers only attitudes and operations, *not* their contents, for, given what they have to represent, mental contents can hardly be determined with any rigor and reliability. Hobbes's projection gambit has its contemporary followers (Quine 1960; Stich 1983; and many others), not only in philosophy but also in psychology. Nicholas Humphrey, for example, writes that:

Nature's solution to the problem of doing psychology has been to give to every member of the human species both the power and inclination to use a privileged picture of his own self as a model for what it is like to be another person (Humphrey 1983, p. 6).

There is a problem with the Hobbesian equation. The problem is that projection and subjectivity may fail to apply to the same entities. What is being introspected need not be what is projected onto another. How do we know, when internally scanning our phenomenal data, that what we access are states and attitudes such as beliefs, desires, and intentions, as publicly conceptualized by common sense, and not unprojectible images, feelings, or even formulae in mentalese? Saying that we *call* what we introspect "beliefs" or "passions" is not going to help. For how do we know that such commonsense concepts as belief or passion capture internal and phenomenal states in the very form in which they are accessed?

The problem faced by the Hobbesian is not that different from Hume's puzzle about personal identity. I may look inside me for my I-ness but see no separate and recognizable type of entity that the personal pronoun "I" could pick up; I only see fleeting sensations of various sorts, a headful of them. What am I going to project onto the other when I want to grasp her use of "I" from my introspective basis? The Hobbesian case for projection faces a similar puzzle. One looks inside oneself but may see no type of entity that the words "belief" and "desire" could pick up; one only sees what Hume saw. Of course, people believe and desire, for they are designed this way, and must have the required concepts to identify and attribute the attitudes. **For, when one looketh into oneself and considereth what one doth when he does think, opine, reason, fear, &c.,** *one presumably knoweth what one must look for.* **One already hath the concept of an attitude and its content.** Or else, how would one know what to look for, and how would one recognize what one has found? Those concepts must therefore come from sources *other than* introspection. The subjectivity leg of the Hobbesian equation of common sense is rather shaky.

But there is life after Hobbes. Language, a social game whose rules require some internal representation, is there to bridge the gap – to some extent. Here is Quine:

> In indirect quotation [when we describe someone's belief] we project ourselves into what, from his remarks and other indications, we imagine the speaker's state of mind to have been, and then we say what, in our language, is natural and relevant for us in the state thus feigned. . . . We find ourselves attributing beliefs, wishes and strivings even to creatures lacking the power of speech, such is our dramatic virtuosity. We project ourselves into what from his behavior we imagine a mouse's state of mind to have been, dramatize it as a belief, wish, or striving, verbalized as seems relevant and natural to us in the state thus feigned (Quine 1960, p. 219).

Quine's insight amalgamates the Hobbesian introspection of attitudes with the reconstruction of their content from linguistic and behavioral clues. Among recent attempts to develop Quine's insight, Stich's (1983) stands out as a systematic and pragmatically sensitive effort to turn projection into a set of similarity judgments based on functional (internal role), ideological (fit with other cognitive states), causal (history of the cognitive content), and social (context and prevailing norms) parameters. As in Quine's, there is in Stich's analysis less emphasis on introspection and more on what language and other general assumptions or practical guesses can do to anchor our projections.

Yet the linguistic and behavioral strategy of projection from inside faces some of the same problems we found with Hobbes's approach. Quine made them famous in the guise of problems of translation and radical interpretation. How do I, the sense maker, know that my words mean the same as those of the person I must make sense of? More generally, how do I know what the other is like, cognitively? These questions have led to the philosophically foundational project known as *radical interpretation.* It is *radical* because it starts from scratch: Very little, if anything, is either known or assumed about the person whose mental life is interpreted; and it is *interpretation* because it starts from the person's utterances, and other relevant cognitive and behavioral clues, and proceeds to determine what she means, believes, desires, and so forth. Interpretation is a reconstruction of mind from speech, with the aim of identifying the concepts, beliefs, and other attitudes that can explain or rationalize behavior. There are different strategies of radical interpretation. The best known are Quine's (1960), Davidson's (1984), and Lewis's (1983). It is not clear that these authors meant their theories of radical interpretation to be theories of commonsense psychology, although one could expect some overlap. But, given the urgent pressures of life, the commonsense psychologist can hardly afford to be a radical interpreter, and is more likely to be a pragmatic interpreter of the sort envisaged by Stich. Yet one can look at the theories of radical interpretation as attempts to make explicit, step by careful step, the various assumptions that common sense must have made to do its interpretational job.

There is finally a truly huge literature, which I do not dare even to sample, on the commonsense notions of propositional attitudes (belief, desire, thought, intention, etc.) analyzed either as linguistic forms, with plenty of logical and semantic properties, or as cognitive structures with informational and functional properties. Although they purport to tell us a good deal about how we understand and use such notions, the resulting analyses are not necessarily part of comprehensive theories of commonsense psychology, nor (therefore) are they always subject to the evidence and constraints of real-life commonsense making.

3. This Volume

This is the general background against which the reader is invited to consider the chapters written for this volume. They represent a rich variety of positions on commonsense psychology, from critical to supportive, from exegetical to speculative. Some of the papers address the matter of the intellectual identity and motivation of commonsense psychology (Bennett, Churchland, Morton, Wilkes, Bogdan): Is it an empirical theory, a body of analytic knowledge, a practice, or a strategy? If it is a legitimate enterprise, can it be naturalized (Morton, Bogdan) or not (McGinn)? If it isn't a legitimate enterprise, can it be eliminated (Churchland) or not quite (Rosenberg)? And how does commonsense psychology work – analytically (Bennett), or as a method of empirical explanation (Churchland, Rosenberg), or by various clever strategies with explanatory (Morton) or practical import (Bogdan)? And is the fate of commonsense psychology tied in with our understanding of consciousness (McGinn, Wilkes)? Should we approach the concepts and generalizations of commonsense psychology from the standpoint of conceptual analysis (Bennett) or philosophy of science (Cummins)?

That is the broad picture; now, some more details. I begin with the friends of common sense. Jonathan Bennett (Chapter 2, Analysis without Noise) is one of them. He finds commonsense psychology a good tool for social cooperation, and hence inherently worthy of study. He also finds commonsense psychology mostly made of analytic statements and generalizations, hence not much of an empirical theory, which is why his approach to it is that of conceptual analysis. But it is an analysis without noise – that is, without the bizarre thought experiments (Searle's on the Chinese Room Thinker, and variants) that challenge and check on our conceptual intuitions, yet provide no informative account of how the sources of those intuitions, our commonsense concepts, really work. Bennett's own account is teleological. It motivates the commonsense concepts of belief, desire, and the like as essentially explanatory.

Adam Morton (Chapter 6, The Inevitability of Folk Psychology) is also a friend of common sense. The thesis he is arguing for is that commonsense psychology is a natural, inevitable, and rational conceptual strategy for understanding complex cognitive systems like ours, not unlike those recently deployed in physics to explain chaos and other forms of high complexity. At the center of the commonsense strategy is the "differential explanation" in terms of which we track the perception and action of an agent. Any commonsense concept of mind we may come up with is based on this explanatory strategy. But differential or tracking explanation leaves a gap between perception and volition, a gap that (in our culture) is filled by a conception of practical reasoning in terms of beliefs and desires.

I, myself (Chapter 9, Common Sense Naturalized), am also friendly to common sense, sharing with Adam Morton the view that commonsense psychology is a natural, inevitable, and rather good device for tracking the cognitive and behavioral conditions of agents, but resisting any assimilation of commonsense policies and inferences to those of science. Far from being a theory, commonsense making is a practice whose main function is not to explain cognition and behavior but rather to represent an agent so as to obtain relevant information about the world or the agent's mind, in a context. The commonsense making practice is the exercise of a specialized cognitive competence which must have been motivated by imperative biosocial needs. The commonsense notions owe their success, not to how well they represent the mind (for they have no such theoretical function), but rather to how well they practically exploit conditions of an agent, and track the agent's cognition, volition, and behavior, in order to provide another agent with the needed information.

We now turn to the folks who would rather do without common sense. Paul Churchland (Chapter 3, Folk Psychology and the Explanation of Human Behavior) is certainly no friend of commonsense psychology. He is an all-out eliminativist. His paper reexamines the notion that commonsense psychology is an empirically false theory of human beings, a notion that he has articulated and defended over the years. Churchland still finds this notion eminently plausible but now in need of an important and consequential revision. It was wrong (Churchland argues) for him and other eliminativists, who regard common sense as a body of false empirical knowledge, to construe this knowledge linguistically, as an internally stored set of sentences. It is much more probable that, like the rest of our knowledge, the commonsense knowledge of other persons takes the form of prototypes represented by neural connectionist networks.

Alex Rosenberg (Chapter 7, How Is Eliminative Materialism Possible?) is no friend of commonsense psychology either. He is, however, a dialectical eliminativist. He thinks that eliminativism must concede a few things to save its core thesis. The reason for concessive dialectics is that Rosenberg takes seriously the charges that eliminativism may be incoherent or self defeating because its very formulation and truth depend on the existence of representational states with meaning, which are believed and acted upon, and so on, all of the latter being assumptions and categories of commonsense psychology – that is, the very framework that eliminativism charges with falsity, meaninglessness, and elimination. Rosenberg also considers the slightly weaker charge that eliminativism may be incredible because it entails the falsity of all the causal claims made in terms of commonsense psychology. His solution is to reconcile the truth of singular causal statements made by commonsense psychology with the irremediable falsity of the latter's concepts and generalizations.

Robert Cummins (Chapter 4, Methodological Reflections on Belief) seems rather neutral about commonsense psychology but urgently recommends an empirical study of it, if we want to make up our minds about what is going on. What Cummins finds, instead, in most of the fashionable philosophical literature is a misguided and fruitless attempt to turn armchair semantics and conceptual analysis into psychology. As a result, we have a notion of belief that is academic, lacks any empirical basis, and may have nothing to do with how common-sense psychology works. Cummins examines the steps that have led to this impasse. His advice to the philosophers of belief and other attitudes is: Change gears, and do philosophy of science!

Most discussions of commonsense psychology are about propositional attitudes. Colin McGinn's (Chapter 5, Consciousness and Content) is about consciousness, a topic that most philosophers of mind and common sense avoid and would rather not think about. McGinn's paper tells us why. A naturalistic account of intentionality (content) must also explain consciousness. Failure to explain the latter results in failure to understand the former, for the conscious and the intentional are two sides of the same mental coin. The trouble is that consciousness is bound to remain a mystery, forever. Whereas many philosophers have felt this way, McGinn argues for this dramatic limitation by suggesting that we are cognitively closed with respect to the phenomenon of consciousness. The phenomenon is real and determinative of intentionality but beyond our comprehension. Since the notions of content and consciousness belong to commonsense psychology, it would appear that, by a *reductio*, McGinn's thesis favors eliminativism. But McGinn's point is somewhat different. He finds consciousness a robust phenomenon, a datum, and finds its inexplicability a serious reason to doubt that commonsense psychology could ever be naturalized.

McGinn's story connects interestingly with that told by Kathleen Wilkes (Chapter 8, The Long Past and the Short History). She has argued for some time that scientific and commonsense psychology are about different and often totally incommensurate things, by having different objectives which they pursue by using different methods and making different assumptions. Why, then, the competition? Because of the stubborn Cartesian equation of mind with consciousness, an equation that favors commonsense psychology. In spite of all disclaimers, from those of early behaviorists to the more recent ones of cognitive scientists, that consciousness does not matter in scientific psychology, the Cartesian equation remains, for most philosophers, definitive of the mental, and acts as a criterion of success in understanding the mental. This cannot but place scientific and commonsense psychology on either a collision or an unnecessarily comparative course.

I conclude with a small sample of the recent literature on commonsense psychology. Like this introduction, it is meant to give the reader a first guide to the literature. I begin with the works cited above and then add a few more titles. I have generally included only those works that explicitly worry about and explore the nature and objectives of commonsense psychology. I have not included the much more numerous works in philosophy of language and philosophy of mind, epistemology and ethics, that examine, and have many interesting things to say about, our commonsense psychological concepts, such as those of belief, desire, perception, and the like, but that do not aim at either questioning and examining commonsense psychology itself or the deeper nature and functions of its concepts. Likewise, I have not included the very many books and articles that assume the position of common sense, and its truth or usefulness, but do not examine its motivation, function, psychological operation, and intellectual validity.

A BIBLIOGRAPHICAL SAMPLE

Works Cited
Churchland, Paul (1979): *Scientific Materialism and the Plasticity of Mind.* Cambridge University Press, Cambridge, England.
Davidson, Donald (1980): *Essays on Actions and Events.* Oxford University Press, Oxford.
(1984): *Inquiries into Truth and Interpretation.* Oxford University Press, Oxford.
Dennett, Daniel (1978): *Brainstorms.* The MIT Press/Bradford Books, Cambridge, MA.
(1987): *The Intentional Stance.* The MIT Press/Bradford Books, Cambridge, MA.
Fodor, Jerry (1975): *The Language of Thought.* Crowell, New York.
(1987): *Psychosemantics.* The MIT Press/Bradford Books, Cambridge, MA.
Harman, Gilbert (1973): *Thought.* Princeton University Press, Princeton.
Hobbes, Thomas (1651/1979): *Leviathan.* Penguin Books.
Humphrey, Nicholas (1983): *Consciousness Regained.* Oxford University Press, Oxford.
Lewis, David (1983): "Radical Interpretation," reprinted (1973) in *Philosophical Papers.* Vol. 1, Oxford University Press, Oxford.
Quine, W. V. O. (1960): *Word and Object.* The MIT Press, Cambridge, MA.
Pylyshyn, Zenon (1984): *Computation and Cognition.* The MIT Press/Bradford Books, Cambridge, MA.
Stich, Stephen (1983): *From Folk Psychology to Cognitive Science.* The MIT Press/Bradford Books, Cambridge, MA.

Other Works
Baker, Lynne Rudder (1987): *Saving Belief.* Princeton University Press, Princeton.

Barwise, Jon and John Perry (1983): *Situations and Attitudes.* The MIT Press/Bradford Books, Cambridge, MA.

Bogdan, Radu (1988): "Mental Attitudes and Common Sense Psychology," *Nous.* 22, 369–98.

Churchland, Paul (1981): "Eliminative Materialism and Propositional Attitudes," *Journal of Philosophy.* 78, 67–90.

Clark, Andy (1987): "From Folk Psychology to Naive Psychology," *Cognitive Science.* 11, 139–54.

Fodor, Jerry (1981): *Representations.* The MIT Press/Bradford Books, Cambridge, MA.

Gordon, Robert (1986): "Folk Psychology as Simulation," *Mind and Language.* 1, 158–71.

Horgan, Terence and James Woodward (1985): "Folk Psychology Is Here To Stay," *The Philosophical Review.* XCIV, 197–226.

Kitcher, Patricia (1984): "In Defense of Intentional Psychology," *Journal of Philosophy.* LXXI, 89–106.

Loar, Brian (1981): *Mind and Meaning.* Cambridge University Press, Cambridge, England.

Lycan, William (1988): *Judgement and Justification.* Cambridge University Press, Cambridge, England.

McGinn, Colin (1988): *Mental Content.* Blackwell, Oxford.

Millikan, Ruth (1986): "Thoughts without Laws; Cognitive Science without Content," *The Philosophical Review,* XCV, 47–80.

Morton, Adam (1980): *Frames of Mind.* Oxford University Press, Oxford.

Rosenberg, Alexander (1986): "Intentional Psychology and Evolutionary Biology," *Behaviorism.* 14, 15–28, and 125–38.

Wilkes, Kathleen (1981): "Functionalism, Psychology, and the Philosophy of Mind," *Philosophical Topics.* 12, 147–68.

2

Analysis without Noise

JONATHAN BENNETT

1. Folk Psychology and Conceptual Analysis

This paper will present some conceptual analysis, trying to command a clearer picture of how our mentalistic concepts work. I mean our untutored, workaday concepts, the ones that we employ in folk psychology. Many students of the mind these days are poised to jettison folk psychology as soon as they can, in favor of something better informed, more comprehensive, more closely in touch with the central nervous system, or the like. But given that folk psychology, whatever its defects, is not on a par with alchemy or astrology, we oughtn't to drop it until we understand more than we do about what kind of theory it is, what work it does, and how. That's one reason why even the iconoclasts should be interested in that part of the philosophy of mind that consists in old-fashioned conceptual analysis. A second reason also weighs with me: Folk psychology is a wonderful intellectual construct, an amazing tool for enabling us to get on with one another, to manipulate and predict one another, and to evade and foil such manipulations and predictions; it is an inherently worthy object of study.

The network of concepts that we use in folk psychology pretty well exhausts its content, considered as a compendium of general propositions: It is hard to find much universally received general doctrine about the human mind that doesn't qualify as highly analytic. In treating analyticity as a matter of degree, I side with Quine's view that there is a continuum between sentences that are true by virtue of their meanings and ones that are universally accepted as expressing well-entrenched truths about how the world is.[1]

That there is so little in folk psychology that counts as clearly contingent is easy to explain. Firstly, folk psychology is an old theory, so that its principal doctrines are deeply entrenched in culture, language, and literature. Secondly, it is a largely unchanging theory:

Within historical time, it seems, there has been virtually no come and go in its content. Because of this doctrinal stasis, nothing has happened to force us to distinguish the more from the less deeply entrenched parts of the theory, that is, to make discriminating decisions about *how* to accommodate facts about the mind that are seen to be recalcitrant vis-à-vis the totality of accepted doctrine. These two facts combine to produce a situation in which virtually the whole of folk psychology is considerably analytic.[2]

That makes it hard to see that folk psychology is a theory at all. A theory is presumably something that could be found to be false, and when we try to envisage discovering the falsehood of any part of folk psychology we run into a kind of absurdity: The challenged item turns out to be so deeply entrenched as to count as analytic, which makes us say that *it* couldn't be false, though we might come to use those words to express something that is false. Of course this doesn't make folk psychology invulnerable; it merely replaces the question "Might any of its theses be found to be false?" by "Might all or part of the theory be found to be inapplicable?"

2.   The Noise Problem

One way of doing conceptual analysis is to present oneself with stories using the terminology under investigation and ask oneself whether they are "intuitively" acceptable. If they are not, that fact helps us to understand our concepts by setting some limits to what they will tolerate. Consider, for example, the following two-part story:

(1) System S takes in signals from its environment and responds with physical behavior, all of this happening according to a *mind-indicating pattern,* meaning a set of (input → output) conditionals such that a system's richly conforming to that set would give it as much entitlement to count as a perceiver/thinker/wanter as input–output relations could possibly give it.

(2) S's behavior falls into a mind-indicating pattern only because it is being manipulated by someone who acts on the following plan: *I shall bring it about that* S's *behavior never conflicts with conditionals . . . ,* where the blank is filled by a list of all the conditionals that define the system's mind-indicating pattern of behavior. The manipulator thinks of the conditionals just as a list, and does not know that they constitute a mind-indicating pattern.

Is S a perceiver/thinker/wanter? Searle thinks not, and labors to get readers to agree with him.[3] These attempts of his are not arguments but appeals to intuition. The whole performance fits the schema: Tell a story and then ask whether our concepts tolerate it.

This is apt to be a risky procedure because of the *noise problem*. Why do we gag at the suggestion that S is a thinker? Is it because we have a concept of *thinker* that excludes S as described, or is it rather that this bizarre story is something for which we are not forewarned or, therefore, forearmed? Are we rejecting it in a controlled and disciplined way, or are we merely being knocked off our conceptual pins by it? Testing one's conceptual intuitions against this story about S is like testing a coin by ringing it on the counter of a busy boiler factory: There is far too much noise for a trustworthy signal to come through. We need to filter out the noise – the bizarreness reactions that are not informative about conceptual structure – if we are to know whether we have here any evidence about the limits to our concepts, that is, about the structures through which we actually think about thought.

3. The Thin End of What Wedge?

The procedure is also dubiously useful. Suppose that our mentalistic concepts really do entail that S is not a thinker because it does not satisfy some *inner-route constraint*, some conceptual requirement on how thinkers, properly so-called, must get from inputs to outputs. What makes that information worth having?

Well, it refutes those philosophers who hold that our mentalistic concepts are purely externalistic in their demands, so that the right kind of input–output pattern is enough to qualify a system as a thinker and wanter. But nothing is so boring and trivial as the information that someone has believed a falsehood. I want to know what adult reason there is for caring whether our concepts include a barrier to counting S as a thinker and wanter. What reason is there that has to do with the advancement of understanding? There may be none.

For one thing, the information that our concepts do include such a barrier is enormously thin. Look at it:

> Our concepts won't classify as a thinker something that fits the right input–output patterns only because it is caused to do so by a thinking manipulator who is guided by a list of conditionals and is not aware of the patterns as such.

Because the story about S is a rather strong, rich one, its negation is relatively thin and empty. The information that our conceptual scheme requires its negation is, therefore, correspondingly thin and empty. It's not a null result, but it comes close.

Of course, this tiny discovery might be the thin end of a wedge; perhaps we can parlay it into something larger, as Searle tries to when he infers that mentality is 'intrinsic'.[4] Of several things that he means by this, the clearest is that attributions of mentality to things are absolutely true/false and not merely acceptable/unacceptable relative to the interests of the speaker. I agree with Searle about this, but it has nothing to do with constraints on inner routes from input to output. It also has little to do with any of my themes in this paper, so I shall not pursue it. Nor shall I discuss what else Searle means by 'intrinsic'.[5]

Ned Block has considered whether something like the S result might show that our concepts don't allow that a thinker could have a part that was also a thinker. He decided against this, on the basis of a still more flabbergasting thought experiment: Suppose that the quarks composing a human brain are being separately manipulated by thinkers who have decided to make the quarks behave in accordance with what we fondly think are the laws of physics; don't you agree with Block that this is consistent with the attribution of beliefs and desires to the owner of the brain?[6] I have no answer to this. The story is so beset with noise that I can make nothing of it.

Anyway, why does it *matter* what boundaries on thinkers are set by our concepts? If for example our concepts don't allow that a thinker could be a proper part of a thinker, so what? A result along these lines would be significant only if it showed something about the central, active, operant part of our mentalistic conceptual scheme. If something in *that* won't let us classify anything both as a thinker and as a proper part of a thinker, that is interesting news. Here is the alternative:

> Our conceptual scheme has a busily active core that governs how we relate thoughts to one another and to environments and behavior. It also includes, sitting off to one side with no particular work to do in combination with the active core, a requirement that an item is not to count as a thinker unless it satisfies some condition C. Everything we know of that satisfies the core also satisfies C; the C requirement is not something we use to divide up the world of actual prima facie thinkers into Passes and Fails.

If that situation obtains, the C requirement is a wheel that turns although nothing turns with it; a negligible part of the mechanism. It's as though we had a concept of *human being* that included whatever our actual concept does include together with the requirement "was not born with purple hair." If we were foolish enough to have such a concept, that might be an interesting fact about our pathology, but it would not imply anything significant about conceptual structures.

It is unlikely that any part of our conceptual scheme does include anything like that – any large aspect to a concept that is logically detached from all its other aspects, not arising from the others or even combining with them to make itself felt in everyday thinking and talking. Why, after all, should our ancestors have conceptually fore-armed ourselves in this way? Indeed, if Quine is right about the difference between what is made true by our concepts and what is made true by how our concepts relate to the world, there cannot be a conceptual truth of the sort now in question. Quine holds that con-ceptual truth or analyticity, such as it is, results from the role the analytic sentence plays in our management of the interplay between some large class of sentences and the impingements of the world upon us. No such role, no analyticity!

If on the other hand our conceptual scheme does in a central, active way put some constraint *C* on all possible thinkers (*e.g.*, some con-straint on the inner route from their inputs to their outputs), there will be a better way of demonstrating this than by telling bizarre stories in which *C* is infringed and noting that readers aren't comfort-able with them as stories about thinkers. The better way, unhindered by the noise problem, is to show how the core works and how the *C* requirement arises out of those workings.

4. Causation and Explanation

The most popular attempt to show along those lines that our concepts imply inner-route constraints goes like this:

> *Our mentalistic conceptual scheme actively and centrally requires that we behave as we do because of our beliefs and desires. There is no non-magical way of making sense of this except by supposing that our beliefs and desires are among the causes of our conduct; this implies that beliefs and desires must be particular events or state-tokens or the like, because this is what causes are. So our conceptual scheme does make demands on the inner causal route from input to output, namely that it must run through particular items that can be rightly characterized as beliefs and desires.*

This is wrong. Folk psychology does insist that attributions of beliefs and desires must help to *explain* behavior.[7] If you like, say that they must aid in *causally explaining* behavior. Indeed, go the extra step and say that facts about behavior are caused by facts about what creatures think and want, or that facts of the former kind are causal consequences of facts of the latter kind.[8] You still haven't implied that there is any such item as a belief, or as a desire. The explanatory and perhaps causal power of attributions of beliefs and desires does not require us – perhaps it does not even permit us – to reify beliefs and desires, treating them as countable, particular items of some kind. For a simple analogy, think of the causal explanatoriness of statements about shortages ("There is a shortage of food in Ethiopia; there is no shortage of oil in Mexico"); such statements can have explanatory power without our reifying shortages, treating them as though they were particular items in the world – negative storage bins, perhaps.

The questions "What *is* a belief? and "What *is* a desire?" need have no answers, then; and I believe that they have no answers. What can be answered are such questions as "What kind of thing are we saying when we explain behavior by attributing beliefs and desires?"

A purely input–output account of intentionality may be complained of in the words "It says things about when it is all right to attribute beliefs and desires, but it doesn't say what beliefs and desires are." This could mean "The account is purely externalist; it doesn't take us into the interior," or it could mean "The account gives truth conditions for sentences using the verbs 'believe' and 'want' but doesn't give application-conditions for the nouns 'belief' and 'want'." Both complaints are misguided, I believe. But let us keep them apart: They are two complaints, not one.

What can we infer from the fact that attributions of cognitive mentality must be explanatory? In Section 9 I shall give that question an answer that does not involve any inner-route constraints. But other things have to be done first.

5. The Founding Triangle

The concepts of belief and desire are linked to one another, and to behavior, in a famous triangle: An animal will *do* what it *thinks* will lead to what it *wants*. This does not have a very long ancestry: It can be found in Braithwaite's "The Nature of Believing," which has a clear and acknowledged predecessor in Alexander Bain's work,[9] but I can't confidently run it further back than that. One might think of it as anticipated by what Hume says about beliefs as "the governing principle of our actions" combined with his remark that reason is the slave of the passions, which might mean that cognitive states can affect behavior only when desires are also at work;[10] but no careful reader of Hume could think that he had the triangle clearly in focus, and insofar as he had it at all he derived it causally from a story whose conceptual foundations were entirely different.

Although the triangle thesis has won almost complete acceptance among philosophers in a little more than a century, we are not yet at the bottom of its implications.

This triangle is deeply teleological. I think that the best way to get an entry into intentionality (*i.e.*, into the concepts of belief and desire) is through the idea of a system that seeks a goal, doing what it thinks will secure the goal. (I here rely on work that is presented more fully in my book *Linguistic Behaviour*, which develops ideas that were brought to a head in Charles Taylor's *The Explanation of Behaviour*.) Start with the suggestion that for x to have G as a long-term goal is for this to be true:

(1)   *Whenever* x *is so situated that it could get* G *by doing* F, *it does* F.

If that is right, we can analyze "x has G as a goal right now" or "x wants G" along the lines of:

(2)   x *is now in a condition such that: For as long as* x *is in that condition, (1) is true of it.*

This is too simple in many different ways (*e.g.*, what if x has more wants than it can fulfill?). But only one inadequacy needs to be paraded here, namely the fact that (1) and (2) have no chance of being true except by accident. That x could get G by doing F is a fact about how x is situated, how it relates to various kinds of objects in its environment, and at our world no such fact can modify how x behaves. What does have a chance of affecting x's behavior is its *registering* the fact that it can get G by doing F (*i.e.*, that fact's being somehow imprinted upon x). So what we need is to replace (1) by this:

(1')   *Whenever* x *registers that it could get* G *by doing* F, *it does* F.

I have coined 'registration' to name a genus of which 'belief' names the most prominent species; the differentia doesn't matter just now.

In a very tight nutshell, then, the initial launching pad for the notion of belief is a thing that conforms to a cognitive–teleological generalization of the type of (1'); and desire enters through this:

(2')   x *is now in a condition such that: Whenever* x *is in that condition, (1') is true of it.*

This way of getting the belief–desire–behavior triangle into operation (and I know of no other) implies that teleology is at the foundations of cognitive mentality. Really, that is an almost trivial result for anyone who is convinced that cognitive mentality rests on a triangle of which desire is one of the sides. But it isn't enough just to declare that teleology is foundational in psychology – one needs an understanding of what teleology is that makes clear *how* it can be harnessed to concepts of cognition. One does not, for example, want the conceptual item that Ernest Nagel offered under the label of 'teleology', for the whole point of that was to keep mentality out. Wanting to show that there could be goal-pursuits without cognition, Nagel developed a concept of teleology that resists fusion with anything cognitive.[11] That is fairly typical of what happens in the philosophy of biology. A treatment of 'teleology' by William Wimsatt, for instance, is primarily an account of the notion of *biological function,* and considered as such it is impressive; but Wimsatt does not try to develop it into something that might lie at the basis of a philosophical treatment of cognitive psychology, and I do not see how he could succeed if he did try.[12] Yet William Lycan, in an influential paper emphasizing the importance of teleological foundations for psychology, instead of offering his own account of teleology or building on Taylor's, offers only a deferential wave in the direction of "philosophers of biology," especially Popper and Wimsatt.[13] I protest that one needs to understand *how* teleological concepts might fit in with the rest, and such an understanding can be found not in the philosophers of biology but in the work of Taylor's that I have been developing.

The emphasis on evolution that dominates the work on teleology by the biologically oriented writers poses an odd problem for anyone who believes, as Lycan and I do, that teleology is at the heart of our system of cognitive concepts. Of course actual teleology evolved: That is true but irrelevant to a conceptual inquiry. There may be a sense of 'teleology' in which the existence of teleology conceptually requires evolution, but 'teleology' in that sense cannot be conceptually required for cognition. If it were, it would follow that it is absolutely, conceptually impossible that cognition should exist except as a result of evolution; presumably nobody believes a conclusion so fanciful. The one conceptual connection that *does* obtain between cognition and evolution will be presented in Section 9.

6.   The Unlikeness of Belief and Desire

A grasp of how the cognitive teleology triangle actually works shows one something that is not grasped by those who only bow to the triangle from a distance – namely, that belief and desire have almost nothing in common. Although facts about what an animal thinks and facts about what it wants collaborate to explain its behavior, the collaborators are enormously different from one another. Beliefs and desires are formally similar, in that each is a psychological propositional attitude, so that the very same propositional value of *P* could occur in "*x* thinks that *P*" and "*x* wants it to be the case that *P*"; but that is all the similarity there is, while the unlikenesses are many and striking.

For one thing, in the most fundamental story about the belief–desire–behavior triangle, the relevant beliefs are all about means to ends. The basic story goes like this (the language is a bit stilted, so as to keep the formal similarity in view):

> *The animal did* F *because it believed that* doing F was a way to bring it about that P, *and it desired that* P.

Here *P* is a dummy, which might be replaced by all sorts of things. In any unfanciful basic account, it will be a proposition about the animal's being in a certain state; in no unfanciful account will it be the proposition that something is a means to a certain end. In the ground-floor story, the animal's basic desires are never that *x* should be a means to *y*, whereas the basic beliefs are all about means to ends. Of course, a highly developed animal – such as you or I – could in principle believe anything at all (*e.g.*, that he is going to be safe and warm) and could want anything at all (*e.g.*, that eating ice cream should be a means to losing weight). But down in the simple, core situations it's not like that.[14]

For that reason, and perhaps for others, the relevant beliefs are likely to change rapidly, in lockstep with changes in the environment; desires can change, but are more likely to do so in response to internal changes (*e.g.*, levels of satiety) than in response to changes in the environment.

The differences are so great that there seems to be no way of giving a Y-shaped analysis of the concepts of belief and desire, starting with their common features and then going on with what differentiates them. A satisfactory analysis must let them stand side by side, each on its own feet, collaborating but not overlapping to any significant degree.

Searle aims to do better than that.[15] He does not try to – and does not think one can – analyze the concepts of belief and desire in terms that don't involve 'intentionality', but he does offer a Y-shaped account of them, purporting to tell a substantive part of the belief–desire (or 'intentionality') story in a general way, before dropping down to the level of detail at which belief and desire are distinguished.

The generic part of Searle's account says that an intentional state is a mental state that can be satisfied; for each such particular state there is a proposition whose truth is needed and enough for the state to be satisfied. If right now animal x is in a state S that has proposition P as its condition of satisfaction, then at this moment S *attitudes* that P, where the "attitude" is a blank verb, coined by me, that might be replaced by either "believe" or "desire."

In the differentiating part of the account, desires are said to relate to their conditions of satisfaction differently from how beliefs relate to theirs. The difference is in "direction of fit": Where beliefs are concerned, the direction runs from world to mental state, with desires it runs the other way.

Searle's account of direction of fit is not very crisp. He says that beliefs are "supposed in some way to match an independently existing world" whereas imperatives are "supposed to bring about changes in the world" (p. 7), and speaks of where the "fault" or the "responsibility" lies if fit is not achieved. He could improve upon these formulations, I think, by saying that necessarily we try to make our beliefs fit the world and necessarily we try to make the world fit our desires. This could not be part of an analysis of intentional notions in nonintentional terms, because it uses "try to," which has the concept of wanting buried in it. Searle is not looking for an analysis, however, so perhaps he is entitled to the differentiating part of his account.

That won't do much good, however, unless the generic story about beliefs and desires as states having conditions of satisfaction is all right. Is it? Well, "satisfaction" is almost Searle's favorite technical term, yet he never explains it and it does not occur in his Index. So far as I can discover, our only grip on his notion of satisfaction comes through the double thought: If P then (i) the desire that P be the case is "satisfied" in a normal sense of that word, and (ii) the belief that P is "satisfied" in the special sense of being true. The disjunctive nature of this is evidence that we don't have any unitary concept of satisfaction that does Searle's work. From that I infer that he has not succeeded in giving a useful genus-and-then-species account of belief and desire. I doubt that such an account could be given.

7. The Unity Condition

The triangle generates another line of thought, to which I now turn. The triangular conceptual structure is illustrated by the behavior of a thermostat: The thermostat "wants" the room to be warmer, "thinks" that closing the switch will bring this about, and accordingly closes the switch. But this illustration, though it is instructive, is also dangerous, as I shall now explain.

All the behavior of the thermostat that might be handled teleologically, or in intentional terms, is explained by a single mechanism, a single kind of causal chain that can be fully described without any use of intentional concepts. We can replace "The thermostat does what it can to keep the temperature of the room close to 68°" by "The thermostat's switch closes whenever its temperature falls to 66° and opens whenever its temperature rises to 70°," and we can explain the latter generalization without any mention of 68° as a goal and without mentioning beliefs and desires or anything like them.

In short, the one intentional account of the thermostat's behavior is matched by a single mechanistic account; and I submit that when that is the case, the latter account should prevail and the former, though perhaps stimulating and interesting for philosophical purposes, is false and should be rejected. For genuine teleology or intentionality, I contend, *the unity condition* must be satisfied. That is, a system x's intentionality is genuine only if

> *Some class of x's inputs/outputs falls under a single intentional account – involving a single goal-kind G such that x behaved on those occasions because on each of them it thought that what it was doing was the way to get G – and does not fall under any one mechanistic generalization.*

Where that is satisfied, applying intentional concepts to the system brings a conceptual *unity* to some set of facts about it – a set that is not unifiable under a mechanistic description.

The unity condition marks off the systems some of whose behavior falls into intentional patterns that are not coextensive with mechanistic patterns. Only if a system's behavior satisfies that condition, I contend, is it legitimate for us to exploit its intentional patterns in our thought and speech. The marking-off is of course a matter of degree. It rejects intentionality when the intentional pattern coincides with a single mechanistic one; it welcomes it when such a pattern utilizes thousands of different mechanisms; and for many intermediate cases it gives an intervening judgment: "Intentionality in this case is so-so – permissible but not very good."

The fuzzy line drawn by the unity condition matches a lot of our intuitive sense of what systems do and which ones don't have thoughts and wants. Consider a chameleon flicking out its tongue and catching a fly with it. One can plausibly think of this as goal-pursuing behavior: It wants to eat the fly and thinks that this is the way to bring that about. But suppose we find that one uniform physical mechanism controls this pattern of behavior – a relatively simple causal tie between proximity of fly and movement of tongue, and between location of fly and direction of tongue movement, with, in each case, a few parameters in the one governing a few parameters in the other. Thoughtful people will regard this as evidence that the cognitive–teleological account of the behavior was wrong because really only a single mechanism was involved. The plausibility of the response "Oh, so *that's* all it was" is evidence for the truth of the unity thesis.

But we don't have to rely on such intuitive evidence. The unity thesis also corresponds to the best *defense* there is for using intentional concepts. The question of the legitimacy of intentional explanations of behavior ought to be faced squarely. Since chemical explanations involve principles that go wider and deeper, and theoretically admit of greater precision, why should they not always be preferred to explanations in terms of thoughts and wants?

Well, they would not be preferable if there were animal movements that could not be explained chemically but could be explained in terms of thoughts and wants. But none of us thinks that that ever actually happens. Again, explanations in terms of cognitive teleology might be adopted because we didn't know what the mechanistic, efficient-cause explanations were; but I hope we can do better than that. The remaining possibility is the one yielded by the unity thesis, namely that an explanation in intentional terms might be justified because it brings out patterns, provides groupings and comparisons, that a chemical explanation would miss. What the animal did belongs to a class of behaviors in which it wants food and does what it thinks will provide food, and there is no unitary chemical explanation that covers just this range of data. This animal seeks food in many different ways, triggered by different sensory inputs, and it is not credible that a mechanistic, physiological view of the facts will reveal any unity in them that they don't share with behaviors that were not food-seeking at all. If this unifying view of the facts answers to our interests, gives us one kind of understanding of the animal, and facilitates predictions of a kind that are otherwise impossible (predictions like "It will go after that rabbit somehow"), we have reason for adopting it. These reasons leave us free still to acknowledge that each of the explained facts, taken separately, admits of an explanation that is deeper and more wide-ranging and – other things being equal – preferable.[16]

8. Morgan's Canon

What Is It?

It is often held by philosophers of mind that there are some senses of "higher" and "lower" that make true something that I shall, nearly following Dennett, call Morgan's Canon:

In no case may we interpret an action as the outcome of the exercise of a higher psychical faculty, if it can be interpreted as the outcome of the exercise of one which stands lower in the psychological scale.[17]

This and its ilk have been praised and obeyed by many of us, without attending closely enough to what it says or to why it is true. I shall try to get clearer about both.

To make any progress with this, we have to realize that the canon is useless when applied to the interpretation of particular behavioral episodes taken separately. Every individual bit of behavior – every simple or complex animal movement – can be interpreted as the outcome of chemical goings-on or (a little higher up the scale) of a virtually mindless stimulus–response mechanism. Whether such an interpretation is correct can be answered only by trying it on classes of behavioral episodes. So I take it that the canon should be understood to be saying:

> *In no case may we interpret a class of actions as the outcome of the exercise of a higher psychical faculty, if they can be interpreted as the outcome of the exercise of one that stands lower in the psychological scale.*

Furthermore, I take it that whatever "the psychological scale" is, any-thing that is on it is "higher" than anything that is off it. That makes the canon imply that a mentalistic explanation of a class of behaviors is wrong if the behaviors could be given a unitary mechanistic expla-nation, such as a chemical one. With the canon thus interpreted, it turns out to entail my unity thesis. What else does it imply? That is, of the items that *are* on the psychological scale, what is higher than what?

Well, presumably explanations in terms of stimulus–response pat-terns, whether hard-wired or learned, are as low as you can get on the scale, so that Morgan's Canon implies that a class of behaviors that can be given a single stimulus–response explanation ought not to be ex-plained in terms of beliefs and desires or anything like them.

As between two explanations that both attribute beliefs and desires, what could lead us to suppose that one is higher than another? Rela-tive logical strength isn't a help. "*P* entails *Q*" isn't necessary for "*P* is higher than *Q*," we must hope: Morgan's Canon wouldn't amount to much if it could never be applied between attributions that were logically unrelated, as in "The animal thinks there is a cat in the tree" and "The animal thinks that predators are less likely to be around when there has been rain within the past three days or snow within the past two." Nor is "*P* entails *Q*" sufficient for "*P* is higher than *Q*": It would be a funny psychological scale that put "It thinks that the cat is up the tree" higher than "It thinks that either the cat is up the tree or predators are less likely to be around when there has been rain within the past three days or snow within the past two."

Christopher Peacocke, who is one of the few philosophers to have attended much to this matter, offers what amounts to this criterion: Attribution S is lower (he says "tighter") than $S*$ if every concept involved in S is involved in $S*$, and not vice versa.[18] It follows, as Peacocke points out, that a tightness comparison is possible only if one "family of concepts has strictly greater expressive power than the other." But that does not mean that a comparison of tightness can be made only when one of the two attributions entails the other: The relation of entailment or inclusion is not between propositions but between sets of concepts involved in propositions.

The concept-inclusion criterion is relevant to issues like this: Should the animal's behavior be explained in terms of what it thinks about its present environment, or rather in terms of (i) what it thinks about some earlier state of affairs and (ii) what it thinks about how such states of affairs develop through time? Does it dig in that manner just because it thinks there is a bone under there, or does it do so because it thinks (i) that the bone was there yesterday and (ii) that buried bones generally stay put? The second diagnosis attributes to the animal a concept of the past, and a generalizing concept, and because of these it counts as higher than the other.

There are many cases where the concept-inclusion criterion needs help if it is to yield the answer we intuitively want. It seems right to suppose that "The animal wants the others to stop eating" is lower than "The animal wants the others to think that there is a predator in the vicinity"; but it is not clear that the former is "tighter" by Peacocke's criterion, because each statement attributes a concept not attributed by the other. It might be replied that the concept-inclusion criterion involves not only the concepts that are directly attributed but also ones that the animal would have to possess in order to have the ones that are directly attributed. That might seem to deal with the case in hand, if we suppose that no animal could have the concept of another animal's *thinking that P*, for any value of P unless it also had the concept of another animal's *doing A,* for various values of A. But what is needed is something stronger and less plausible, namely that no animal could have the concept of another animal's thinking that P for any value of P unless it also had the concept of another animal's *eating*.

Anyway, concept inclusion is clearly irrelevant to some clear cases of level difference. Consider the choice between "The animal wants the others to think there is a snake in the undergrowth" and "The animal wants the others to think that she thinks that there is a snake in the undergrowth." These use exactly the same conceptual repertoire, but intuitively one would want one of them to count as "lower" than the other: That is, one wants to understand Morgan's Canon in such a way that it condemns the explanation "When she sees a snake she gives that cry because she wants the others to think that she thinks that there is a snake in the undergrowth" if the behavior in question could as well be explained by "When she sees a snake she gives that cry because she wants the others to think that there is a snake in the undergrowth". But the difference here is not in what concepts are involved, but in the level of iterative complexity with which they are involved.

That is the best I can do to mark out the steps in the "psychological scale": from nonmentalistic and stimulus–response to belief-and-desire; and then from poorer to richer stocks of concepts, and from lesser to greater degrees of iterative complexity. The only way I can find of generalizing across the entire scale is to say that *P* is lower than *Q* just in case it attributes to the animal less complexity of structure than *Q* does, or that the attribution *Q* implicitly credits the animal with every capacity credited to it by *P* and some more as well. This is no triumph of hard-edged technical clarity; but it has some content, is not intolerably fuzzy, and draws the line in a plausible place.

Where and Why Is the Canon Binding?

It is obvious why we need some constraints on the attribution of mentality to animals. To put it mildly, the results of sloppy, easy, unconstrained attributions are boring because contentless. Conceptual analysis tells us that much; and I have contended that it also tells us that the unity condition should constrain our explanations of behavior, that is, that we shouldn't explain in terms of beliefs and desires a class of behaviors that could be given a unitary mechanistic explanation. But what about the rest of Morgan's Canon? Granted that within the domain of belief–desire explanations we need some constraints, what is the warrant for saying that the constraints must have the effect of always pushing explanations as far down the "psychological scale" as possible?

If there is one, it is presumably a warrant for saying that we should in general assume things to be homogeneous or unstructured except to the extent that the evidence points to structure or complexity. That seems to be what Peacocke has in mind in his brief statement of why the "tightness condition" is a valid constraint: "Without this requirement, the attribution of concepts is unconstrained by the presence of intentional actions responsive to the distinctions in the world drawn by these concepts" (p. 85). But so what? Neither Peacocke nor I has yet given a clear, convincing statement of what intellectual sin is being committed by someone who infringes the canon on this understanding of it. In considering this, we have to look at two different kinds of situation – two kinds of rivalry between competing explanations of a class of behaviors.

In one of them, each of the rival explanations accords with the facts so far observed, but they differ in their implications for behavior and are thus not empirically equivalent. In that case, the main advice to be given, having nothing to do with Morgan's Canon, is: Look for further data that fit one of them and not the other, perhaps by setting up situations designed to elicit behavior that will serve as an *experimentum crucis*.[19] For example, in trying to adjudicate between "When the animal screams like that, it is because it wants its companions to climb trees" and "When the animal screams like that, it is because it wants its companions to think there is a leopard in the vicinity," there is no theoretical need for Morgan's Canon. Each of these hypotheses, unless specially padded with supplementary hypotheses of a sort I'll discuss shortly, has behavioral implications that the other lacks, and the final arbiter should be the behavior of the animal in crucial situations.

If the canon has work to do here, it is only as advice about what we should believe provisionally while waiting for the issue to be settled empirically – advising us that in the meantime it would be wise to expect the decisive data to rule out the "higher" hypothesis and thus to favor the "lower" one. It could also be advising us about what we should believe tentatively if it's now too late ever to get the question settled (*e.g.*, because the animal is dead and its species extinct).

This is good advice on our planet, where most mentality is fairly low-level. But there could be planets where most of the known minds were high-level, sophisticated ones, and where most teleological patterns in animal behavior were not reducible to mechanistic ones. On such planets the provisional advice issued by Morgan's Canon would be bad. So this use of the canon reveals nothing about our mentalistic conceptual scheme.

The other kind of rivalry is that between two explanatory hypotheses which, though they differ in the "height" of the psychological capacities that they attribute, are empirically equivalent.[20] This can happen only if the "higher" one includes supplementary hypotheses to explain why the extra psychological capacity is not manifested in behavior. For example, the lower one might be:

> The animal has the concepts of one, two, and three, and the concept of
> equal numberedness, but not of the number four,

while its rival says that

> The animal has the concepts one, two, three, four, and equal numbered-
> ness, but it cannot be got to use its concept of four in any way except in
> doing number comparisons between quartets and other groups.

The second of these says not that the animal never has a reason to use *four* for anything except comparing quartets with other groups, but rather that even in situations where some other use of *four* would be to the animal's advantage, it reliably doesn't use its concept of four in that other manner.

How are we to choose between these? Well, one of them credits the animal with two more items than the other does – namely, an extra concept, and an impediment to its being implemented in most situations. So far as I can see, all we need here is a quite general principle that should regulate us in theory building, namely: Prefer what is simple to what is complex, unless there is independent justification for the complexity. What could justify the complexity? It would have to be something that I don't want to discuss in this paper, namely, a theory of the animal's internal cognitive dynamics – that is, that part of our psychological account of it that speaks of how changes in its beliefs cause not only behavior but other changes in its beliefs, and so on. Suppose we are constructing such a theory for an animal, and are faced with the rival stories about its grasp of the number four; one possibility is this: Our smoothest and generally most plausible explanation for the animal's grasp of one, two, and three implies that it does also have the concept of four; and we have good evidence for its having a natural class of cognitive obstacles that would include an inability to employ *four* except in number comparisons between quartets and other groups. In that (admittedly fanciful) case, we might justifiably prefer the more complex hypothesis and thus, incidentally, prefer the "higher" to the "lower" psychological attribution to the animal. Without something like that, the "lower" should be preferred, not because it is "lower" but because it is less complex and greater complexity is not justified. This result coincides with what Morgan's Canon would say, but the canon has nothing to do with it.

Considered as a rule of thumb to guide our provisional opinions about cognitive abilities, Morgan's Canon is fine. Considered as anything else, it is negligible. Having worshipped at its shrine for a quarter of a century, I say this with regret.

9. Intentionality as a Source of Explanations

The concepts of belief and desire are fundamentally explanatory. In the account I have been giving, explanatoriness is supposed to come in through the generalizations that define an animal's goals – that is, ones of the form "Whenever x registers that it could get G by doing F, it does F." But for all I have said to the contrary, such a generalization might be true merely by coincidence, which would unfit it to explain anything. That is, it might be a mere coincidence that this single system houses a lot of mechanisms whose overall effect is to make the system a G seeker; and if it is a coincidence, the system's intentionality cannot be used to explain its behavior. (By "mechanism" I mean: physical feature that makes it the case, for some value of I and some value of O, that if the animal receives input of sensory kind I it produces behavioral output of motor kind O.)

In plugging this gap in the account, I shall exploit the link between what *can explain* and what *could have predicted*. That is, I shall look for conditions under which a teleological generalization could be used to explain an animal's moving in a certain way at a particular time by looking for the conditions under which the generalization could be used to predict that the animal would move like that then. For this to serve my purpose, we have to be able to predict a link between one sensory kind of input and one motor kind of output on the basis of links between other pairs – ones in which the sensory kinds are different (and perhaps the motor kinds as well). That is, I want to know what can entitle us, when we know that an animal goes after rabbits in many different ways on the basis of many different sensory kinds of clue, to take that as *some* evidence that it will go after rabbits on the basis of kinds of clue that we haven't so far observed it to use.

There seem to be just two ways of supplying this need.

One of them uses evolutionary ideas. Simply and abstractly: Of all the potential mechanisms that got an initial genetic hold on the animal's ancestors through random mutations, relatively few survived; among the survivors were the bunch of mechanisms that make their owner a G getter, and *that is why they survived*. Why does this animal contain a lot of mechanisms that make it a G getter? It inherited those mechanisms from a gene pool that contained them *because they are mechanisms that make their owner a G getter*.

That makes it more than a coincidence that the animal has many mechanisms that are united in their G-getting tendency, and lays a clear basis for explanations that bring in cognition. That a species has evolved a G-getting tendency that is manifested in this, that, and the other links between sensory kinds of input and motor kinds of output creates some presumption that it has evolved other links that also have a *G*-getting tendency. So there is something predictive in this, and thus something explanatory as well.

(An analogous story could be told, without evolution, if animals were made by a creator who intended them to manifest the patterns of cognitive teleology. The animal does *G*-getting things on receipt of clues of various types; that is some evidence that its designer wanted it to be a *G* getter, which is some reason to think the animal will do *G*-getting things when it has clues of other kinds that we haven't yet seen it respond to. This would raise the question of how we are to understand statements about what the creator thinks and wants, and one might wonder whether *that* could be tackled along the functionalist lines that have informed this paper. I shall not pursue the matter.[21])

Notice that the evolutionary source of explanatoriness does not require that the animal be educable, flexible, capable of adapting as an individual to what it learns about its world.[22] The account would go through quite well for an animal like this: It picks up from its environments all kinds of information about ways to get *G*, and acts accordingly, but if one of these input–output pairs starts to let it down, leading not to *G* but to something unpleasant, that does not lead the animal to delete that input–output pair from its repertoire. Nor does it ever add anything to its repertoire in the light of chance discoveries about what works.

It is vastly improbable that any species should evolve the kind and degree of complexity that satisfies the unity thesis without also evolving a degree of individual adaptability to what experience teaches. But we know at what sort of world (or planet) such a thing might occur in the course of nature: It would be a world where behavioral complexity had great survival value whereas individual adaptability didn't. And the supposition itself clearly makes sense: It is the supposition of behaviorally frozen animals with a behavioral repertoire that falls into teleological patterns that don't map onto patterns of any other kind. Such animals would cope successfully and (it would seem) intelligently with their environments, but as soon as these altered a bit in some relevant way, the animals would be stuck.

To repeat what I said a moment ago, the behavior of such creatures could be explained and predicted through the generalizations of cognitive teleology. If an animal has a lot of (for short) *G*-seeking input–output patterns, that is evidence that they have been selected *because* they let the animal get *G;* and *that* is evidence that other input–output links that have the same upshot will also have been selected. By the

prediction test, therefore, we can use the premise that the animal is a
G seeker to explain a new bit of G seeking by it; the premise is at least
somewhat projectible, and is not a mere summation of observed behavioral episodes. In short: Evolution could make cognitive mentality
explanatory, even if the animal could not learn from its experience.

I emphasize this in order to introduce the point that individual
educability can make cognitive mentality explanatory even if the animal had not evolved.

Consider the case of educable parents that have an educable offspring with a goal that they didn't have: The offspring is the locus of a
large number of G-getting mechanisms, none of which were present
in the parents, their presence in the offspring being the result of a
very radical and sheerly coincidental set of genetic mutations. This
story, though utterly improbable, states a real conceptual possibility;
and if we knew that it was true of a given animal, we could explain
some of the animal's behavior in terms of its having G as a goal. For (i)
its having G as a goal and (ii) its being able to learn from experience
jointly give us reason to predict that it will pursue G in ways (and on
clues) that we have not previously seen it employ (assuming that the
animal may indeed have previously employed those ways and clues or
ones that were suitably related to them).

So our conceptual scheme does not insist that believers and wanters
must have evolution (or a personal creator) in their causal ancestry.
The scheme does demand that attributions of belief and desire be
capable of supporting explanations of behavior; this requires a context where the generalizations of cognitive teleology license predictions; and two such contexts suffice for this – evolution and individual
educability, or Mother Nature and soft wiring. Please note that I have
not invited you to consider intuitively whether you would be willing to
attribute beliefs and desires to an educable animal that didn't evolve
(and wasn't personally created), or to an evolved animal that wasn't
educable. I have tried to hush all that noise, and show what follows
from something that can be found at the humdrum, familiar, smoothly running core of our cognitive conceptual scheme.

NOTES

1. W. V. Quine, "Two Dogmas of Empiricism," in his *From a Logical Point of
   View* (Harvard University Press: Cambridge, Mass., 1953), pp. 20–46. For
   an account of how this contends that analytic/synthetic is a difference of
   degree, see the first three sections of Jonathan Bennett, "Analytic–
   Synthetic," *Proceedings of the Aristotelian Society*, new series Vol. 59 (1958–9),
   pp. 166–88. The fourth section is no good.

2. That is why it is right for Lewis to base an analysis on "platitudes . . . regarding the causal relations of mental states, sensory stimuli, and motor responses." He is interested only in "platitudes which are common knowledge among us – everyone knows them, everyone knows that everyone knows them, and so on," because "the meanings of our words are common knowledge, and I am going to claim that the names of mental states derive their meanings from these platitudes." David Lewis, "Psychophysical and Theoretical Identifications," *Australasian Journal of Philosophy* 50 (1972), pp. 249–58, at p. 256.

3. John R. Searle, "Minds, Brains, and Programs," *The Behavioral and Brain Sciences* 3 (1980), pp. 417–24; "Analytic Philosophy and Mental Phenomena," *Midwest Studies in Philosophy* 6 (1981), pp. 405–24.

4. Searle's thesis that only animals can think is supposed to be based (I don't understand how) on what we know about actual animal thinkers rather than on what we intuitively think about system *S* (Searle, "Analytic Philosophy and Mental Phenomena," *op. cit.*, at pp. 413*f*).

5. For a discussion of them, see Paul M. Churchland and Patricia Smith Churchland, "Functionalism, Qualia, and Intentionality," *Philosophical Topics* 12 (1981), pp. 121–45, at pp. 139–41.

6. Ned Block, "Troubles with Functionalism," in N. Block (ed.), *Readings in Philosophical Psychology*, Vol. 1 (Harvard University Press: Cambridge, Mass., 1980), pp. 268–305, at pp. 297*f*.

7. Evidence for this comes from the failure of attempts to explain the relevant concepts in ways that make them primarily descriptive and only secondarily and inessentially explanatory. See Jonathan Bennett, *Linguistic Behaviour* (Cambridge University Press: Cambridge, England, 1977; Hackett: Indianapolis, Ind., 1989), Section 13.

8. For a defense of the concept of fact causation, see Jonathan Bennett, *Events and Their Names* (Hackett: Indianapolis, Ind., 1988), Chapter 2.

9. R. B. Braithwaite, "The Nature of Believing," first published in 1932 and reprinted in A. P. Griffiths (ed.), *Knowledge and Belief* (Oxford University Press: Oxford, 1967). Alexander Bain, *The Emotions and the Will*, first published in 1859, and reissued by University Publications of America: Washington, D.C., 1977; the relevant part is the chapter entitled "Belief," especially pp. 568–73 in the reprint.

10. David Hume, *An Enquiry Concerning Human Understanding*, pp. 49*f* in the Selby–Bigge edition; *A Treatise of Human Nature* II.iii.3 (pp. 413–18 in the Selby–Bigge edition).

11. Ernest Nagel, "Teleology Revisited," in *Teleology and Other Essays* (New York, 1979), pp. 275–316.

12. William C. Wimsatt, "Teleology and the Logical Structure of Function Statements," *Studies in History and Philosophy of Science* 3 (1972).

13. William Lycan, "Form, Function, and Feel," *Journal of Philosophy* 78 (1981), pp. 24–50, at p. 32. In Lycan's more recent *Consciousness* (MIT Press: Cambridge, Mass., 1987), at p. 43, the deferential wave occurs again, still in the direction of "philosophers of biology," with special emphasis this time on unpublished work by Karen Neander.

14. What gives us our unlimited repertoire of possible beliefs and desires is, I think, our ability to articulate them in language. See Jonathan Bennett, *Rationality* (Routledge and Kegan Paul: London, 1964; Hackett: Indianapolis, Ind., 1989); "Thoughtful Brutes," *Proceedings of the American Philosophical Association* 62 (1988), pp. 197–210.

15. John R. Searle, *Intentionality* (Cambridge University Press: Cambridge, England, 1983), Chapter 1.

16. For more along this line, see Jonathan Bennett, *Linguistic Behaviour, op. cit.*, Sections 21–2; Daniel C. Dennett, *The Intentional Stance* (MIT Press: Cambridge, Mass., 1987), Chapter 2.

17. C. Lloyd Morgan, *Introduction to Comparative Psychology* (London, 1894), p. 53. Quoted from Christopher Peacocke, *Sense and Content* (Oxford University Press: Oxford, 1983), p. 86n. Dennett calls it "Lloyd Morgan's Canon," but so far as I can discover the author's surname was simply "Morgan."

18. Christopher Peacocke, *Sense and Content: Experience, Thought, and Their Relations* (Clarendon Press: Oxford, 1983), p. 84. Peacocke's discussion of Morgan's Canon (pp. 78–86) is in the spirit of my *Linguistic Behaviour, op. cit.*, Sections 36 and 37.

19. My unity thesis can be developed into some suggestions abut what sort of evidence would adjudicate between rival explanations. For details, see my "Folk Psychological Explanations," in John D. Greenwood (ed.), *The Future of Folk Psychology: Intentionality and Cognitive Science* (Oxford University Press: Oxford, 1989).

20. Rivalries between empirically equivalent hypotheses that differ in what they attribute, but not in the "height" of what they attribute, are beside my present point because they don't invite us to invoke Morgan's Canon.

21. For a determined assault on the problem of giving a functionalist analysis of attribution of cognitive states to a deity, see William P. Alston, "Functionalism and Theological Language," *American Philosophical Quarterly* 22 (1985), pp. 221–30; "Divine and Human Action," in T. V. Morris (ed.), *Divine and Human Action* (Cornell University Press: Ithaca, N.Y., 1988), pp. 257–80.

22. Nor does the explanation in terms of a personal creator. From now on I shall forget the personal creator option, and focus on the other. This is just for simplicity's sake. I justify it on the grounds that it is quite certain that actual animals did evolve. Perhaps a personal creator somehow made them do so; but as long as evolution by natural selection *did* occur, that is enough to give predictive and explanatory force to our attributions of beliefs and desires, whether or not the forces of evolution are themselves an expression of divine intent.

3

Folk Psychology and the Explanation of Human Behavior

PAUL M. CHURCHLAND

Folk psychology, insist some, is just like folk mechanics, folk thermodynamics, folk meteorology, folk chemistry, and folk biology. It is a framework of concepts, roughly adequate to the demands of everyday life, with which the humble adept comprehends, explains, predicts, and manipulates a certain domain of phenomena. It is, in short, a folk *theory*. As with any theory, it may be evaluated for its virtues or vices in all of the dimensions listed. And as with any theory, it may be rejected in its entirety if it fails the measure of such evaluation. Call this the *theoretical view* of our self-understanding.

Folk psychology, insist others, is radically unlike the examples cited. It does not consist of laws. It does not support causal explanations. It does not evolve over time. Its central purpose is normative rather than descriptive. And thus it is not the sort of framework that might be shown to be radically defective by sheerly empirical findings. Its assimilation to theories is just a mistake. It has nothing to fear, therefore, from advances in cognitive theory or the neurosciences. Call this the *antitheoretical view* of our self-understanding.

Somebody here is deeply mistaken. The first burden of this paper is to argue that it is the antitheoretical view that harbors most, though not all, of those mistakes. In the thirty years since the theoretical view was introduced (see, especially Sellars 1956; Feyerabend 1963; Rorty 1965; Churchland 1970, 1979, 1981), a variety of objections have been leveled against it. The more interesting of these will be addressed shortly. My current view is that these objections motivate no changes whatever in the theoretical view.

The second and more important burden of this paper, however, is to outline and repair a serious failing in the traditional expressions of the theoretical view, my own expressions included. The failing, as I

Acknowledgment: This chapter is a substantially expanded version of a short paper presented at the British Joint Session Meetings in 1988, and published in the *Proceedings of the Aristotelian Society,* supplementary Volume *LXII* (1988). My thanks to the editors for permission to use that material here.

see it, lies in representing one's commonsense understanding of human nature as consisting of *an internally stored set of general sentences,* and in representing one's predictive and explanatory activities as being a matter of *deductive inference* from those sentences plus occasional premises about the case at hand.

This certainly sounds like a major concession to the antitheoretical view, but in fact it is not. For what motivates this reappraisal of the character of our self-understanding is the gathering conviction that little or *none* of human understanding consists of stored sentences, not even the prototypically *scientific* understanding embodied in a practicing physicist, chemist, or astronomer. The familiar conception of knowledge as a set of "propositional attitudes" is itself a central aspect of the framework of folk psychology, according to the reappraisal at hand, and it is an aspect that badly needs to be replaced. Our self-understanding, I continue to maintain, is no different in character from our understanding of any other empirical domain. It is speculative, systematic, corrigible, and in principle replaceable. It is just not so specifically *linguistic* as we have chronically assumed.

The speculative and replaceable character of folk psychology is now somewhat easier to defend than it was in the 1960s and 1970s, because recent advances in connectionist artificial intelligence (AI) and computational neuroscience have provided us with a fertile new framework with which to understand the perception, cognition, and behavior of intelligent creatures. Whether it will eventually prove adequate to the task of replacing folk psychology remains to be seen, but the mere possibility of systematic alternative conceptions of cognitive activity and intelligent behavior should no longer be a matter of dispute. Alternatives are already abuilding. Later in this paper I shall outline the main features of this novel framework and explore its significance for the issues here at stake. For now, let me acquiesce in the folk-psychological conception of knowledge as a system of beliefs or similar propositional attitudes, and try to meet the objections to the theoretical view already outstanding.

1.   Objections to the Theoretical View

As I have illustrated (Churchland 1970, 1979, and 1984), a thorough perusal of the explanatory factors that typically appear in our commonsense explanations of our internal states and our overt behavior sustains the quick "reconstruction" of a large number of universally quantified conditional statements, conditionals with the conjunction of the relevant explanatory factors as the antecedent and the relevant explanandum as the consequent. It is these universal statements that are supposed to constitute the "laws" of folk psychology.

A perennial objection is that these generalizations do not have the character of genuine causal/explanatory laws: Rather, they have some other, less empirical, status (e.g., that of normative principles, or rules of language, or analytic truths). Without confronting each of the many alternatives in turn, I think we can make serious difficulties for any objection of this sort.

Note first that the concepts of folk psychology divide into two broad classes. On the one hand there are those fully intentional concepts expressing the various propositional attitudes, such as belief and desire. And on the other hand there are those nonintentional or quasi-intentional concepts expressing all of the other mental states, such as grief, fear, pain, hunger, and the full range of emotions and bodily sensations. Where states of the latter kind are concerned, I think it is hardly a matter for dispute that the common homilies in which they figure are causal/explanatory laws. Consider the following.

A person who suffers severe bodily damage will feel pain.
A person who suffers a sudden sharp pain will wince.
A person denied food for any length of time will feel hunger.
A hungry person's mouth will water at the smell of food.
A person who feels overall warmth will tend to relax.
A person who tastes a lemon will have a puckering sensation.
A person who is angry will tend to be impatient.

Clearly, these humble generalizations, and thousands more like them, are causal/explanatory in character. They will and regularly do support simple explanations, sustain subjunctive and counterfactual conditionals, and underwrite predictions in the standard fashion. Moreover, concepts of this simple sort carry perhaps the major part of the folk psychological burden. The comparatively complex explanations involving the propositional attitudes are of central importance, but they are surrounded by a quotidian whirl of simple explanations like these, all quite evidently of a causal/explanatory cast.

It won't do, then, to insist that the generalizations of folk psychology are on the whole nonempirical or noncausal in character. The bulk of them, and I mean thousands upon thousands of them, are transparently causal or nomological. The best one can hope to argue is that there is a central core of folk-psychological concepts whose explanatory role is somehow *discontinuous* with that of their fellows. The propositional attitudes, especially belief and desire, are the perennial candidates for such a nonempirical role, for explanations in their terms typically display the explanandum event as 'rational'. What shall we say of explanations in terms of beliefs and desires?

We should tell essentially the same causal/explanatory story, and for the following reason. Whatever else humans do with the concepts for the propositional attitudes, they do use them successfully to predict the future behavior of others. This means that, on the basis of presumed information about the current cognitive states of the relevant individuals, one can nonaccidentally predict at least some of their future behavior some of the time. But any principle that allows us to do this – that is, to predict one empirical state or event on the basis of another, logically distinct, empirical state or event – *has* to be empirical in character. And I assume it is clear that the event of my ducking my head is logically distinct both from the event of my perceiving an incoming snowball, and from the states of my desiring to avoid a collision and my belief that ducking is the best way to achieve this.

Indeed, one can do more than merely predict: One can control and manipulate the behavior of others by controlling the information available to them. Here one is bringing about certain behaviors by steering the cognitive states of the subject – by relating opportunities, dangers, or obligations relevant to that subject. How this is possible without an understanding of the objective empirical regularities that connect the internal states and the overt behaviors of normal people is something that the antitheoretical position needs to explain.

The confused temptation to find something special about the case of intentional action derives primarily from the fact that the central element in a full-blooded action explanation is a configuration of propositional attitudes in the light of which the explanandum behavior can be seen as sensible or rational, at least from the agent's narrow point of view. In this rational-in-the-light-of relation we seem to have some sort of supercausal *logical* relation between the explanans and the explanandum, which is an invitation to see a distinct and novel type of explanation at work.

Yet while the premise is true – there is indeed a logical relation between the explanandum and certain elements in the explanans – the conclusion does not begin to follow. Students of the subject are still regularly misled on this point, for they fail to appreciate that a circumstance of this general sort is *typical* of theoretical explanations. Far from being a sign of the nonempirical and hence nontheoretical character of the generalizations and explanations at issue, it is one of the surest signs available that we are here dealing with a high-grade theoretical framework. Let me explain.

The electric current I in a wire or any conductor is causally determined by two factors: It tends to increase with the electromotive force or voltage V that moves the electrons down the wire, and it tends to be reduced according to the resistance R the wire offers against their motion. Briefly, $I = V/R$. Less cryptically and more revealingly,

$$(x)(V)(R)[(x \text{ is subject to a voltage of } (V)) \, \& $$
$$(x \text{ offers a resistance of } (R)) \supset$$
$$(\exists I)((x \text{ has a current of } (I)) \text{ and } (I = V/R))].$$

The first point to notice here is that the crucial predicates – *has a resistance of (R), is subject to a voltage of (V)*, and *has a current of (I)* – are what might be called 'numerical attitudes': They are predicate-forming functors that take singular terms for numbers in the variable position. A complete predicate is formed only when a specific numeral appears in the relevant position. The second point to notice is that this electrodynamic law exploits a relation holding on the domain of numbers in order to express an important empirical regularity. The current I is the *quotient* of the voltage V and the resistance R, whose values will be cited in explanation of the current. And the third point to notice is that this law and the explanations it sustains are typical of laws and explanations throughout science. Most of our scientific predicates express 'numerical attitudes' of the sort displayed, and most of our laws exploit and display relations that hold primarily on the abstract domain of numbers. Nor are they limited to numbers. Other laws exploit the abstract relations holding on the abstract domain of vectors, or on the domain of sets, or groups, or matrices. But none of this means they are nonempirical, or noncausal, or nonnomic.

Action explanations, and intentional explanations in general, follow the same pattern. The only difference is that here the domain of abstract objects being exploited is the domain of propositions, and the relations displayed are logical relations. And like the numerical and vectorial attitudes typical of theories, the expressions for the propositional attitudes are predicate-forming functors. *Believes that P*, for example, forms a complete predicate only when a specific sentence appears in the variable position *P*. The principles that comprehend these predicates have the same abstract and highly sophisticated structure displayed by our most typical theories. They just exploit the relations holding on a different domain of abstract objects in order to express the important empirical regularities comprehending the states and activities of cognitive creatures. That makes folk psychology a very interesting theory, perhaps, but it is hardly a sign of its being *non*theoretical. Quite the reverse is true. (This matter is discussed at greater length in Churchland 1979, Section 14, and 1981, pp. 82–4.)

In summary, the simpler parts of folk psychology are transparently causal or nomic in character, and the more complex parts have the same sophisticated logical structure typical of our most powerful theories.

But we are not yet done with objections. A recurrent complaint is that in many cases the reconstructed conditionals that purport to be sample "laws" of folk psychology are either strictly speaking false or they border on the trivial by reason of being qualified by various *ceteris paribus* clauses. A first reply is to point out that my position does not claim that the laws of folk psychology are either true or complete. I agree that they are a motley lot. My hope is to see them replaced entirely, and their ontology of states with them. But this reply is not wholly responsive, for the point of the objection is that it is implausible to claim the status of an entrenched theoretical framework for a bunch of "laws" that are as vague, as loose, and as festooned with *ceteris paribus* clauses as are the examples typically given.

I will make no attempt here to defend the ultimate integrity of the laws of folk psychology, for I have little confidence in them myself. But this is not what is required to meet the objection. What needs pointing out is that the "laws" of folk theories are *in general* sloppy, vague, and festooned with qualifications and *ceteris paribus* clauses. What the objectors need to do, in order to remove the relevant system of generalizations from the class of empirical theories, is to show that folk psychology is significantly *worse* in all of these respects than are the principles of folk mechanics, or folk thermodynamics, or folk biology, and so forth. In this they are sure to be disappointed, for these other folk theories are even worse than folk psychology (see McCloskey 1983). In all, folk psychology may be a fairly ramshackle theory, but a theory it remains. Nor is it a point against this that folk psychology has changed little or none since ancient times. The same is true of other theories near and dear to us. The folk physics of the twentieth century, I regret to say, is essentially the same as the folk physics of the ancient Greeks (McCloskey 1983). Our conceptual inertia on such matters may be enormous, but a theory remains a theory, however many centuries it may possess us.

A quite different objection directs our attention to the great many things beyond explanation and prediction for which we use the vocabulary and concepts of folk psychology. Their primary function, runs the objection, is not the function served by explanatory theories, but rather the myriad social functions that constitute human culture and commerce. We use the resources of folk psychology to promise, to entreat, to congratulate, to tease, to joke, to intimate, to threaten, and so on (see Wilkes 1981, 1984).

The list of functions is clearly both long and genuine. But most of these functions surely come under the heading of control or manipulation, which is just as typical and central a function of theories as is either explanation or prediction, but which is not mentioned in the list of theoretical functions supplied by the objectors. Though the image may be popular, the idle musings of an impotent stargazer provide a poor example of what theories are and what theories do. More typically, theories are the conceptual vehicles with which we literally come to grips with the world. The fact that folk psychology serves a wealth of practical purposes is no evidence of its being nontheoretical. Quite the reverse.

Manipulation aside, we should not underestimate the importance for social commerce of the *explanations* and *predictions* that folk psychology makes possible. If one cannot predict or anticipate the behavior of one's fellows at all, then one can engage in no useful commerce with them whatever. And finding the right explanations for their past behavior is often the key to finding the appropriate premises from which to anticipate their future behavior. The objection's attempt to paint the functions of folk psychology in an exclusively nontheoretical light is simply a distortion born of tunnel vision.

In any case, it is irrelevant. For there is no inconsistency in saying that a theoretical framework should also serve a great many nontheoretical purposes. To use an example I have used before (1986), the theory of *witches, demonic possession, exorcism,* and *trial by ordeal* was also used for a variety of social purposes beyond strict explanation and prediction. For example, its vocabulary was used to warn, to censure, to abjure, to accuse, to badger, to sentence, and so forth. But none of this meant that demons and witches were anything other than theoretical entities, and none of this saved the ontology of demon theory from elimination when its empirical failings became acute and different conceptions of human pathology arose to replace it. Beliefs, desires, and the rest of the folk psychological ontology all are in the same position. Their integrity, to the extent that they have any, derives from the explanatory, predictive, and manipulative prowess they display.

It is on the topic of explanation and prediction that a further objection finds fault with the theoretical view. Precisely what, begins the objection, is the observable behavior that the ontology of folk psychology is postulated to explain? Is it bodily behavior as *kinematically* described? In some cases, perhaps, but not in general, certainly, because many quite different kinematical sequences could count as the same intentional action, and it is generally the *action* that is properly the object of folk psychological explanations of behavior. In general, the descriptions of human behavior that figure in folk-psychological explanations and predictions are descriptions that *already* imply perception, intelligence, and personhood on the part of the agent. Thus it must be wrong to see the relation between one's psychological states and one's behavior on the model of theoretical states postulated to explain the behavior of some conceptually independent domain of phenomena (Haldane 1988).

The premise of this objection is fairly clearly true: A large class of behavior descriptions are not conceptually independent of the concepts of folk psychology. But this affords no grounds for denying theoretical status to the ontology of folk psychology. The assumption that it does reflects a naive view of the relation between theories and the domains they explain and predict. The naive assumption is that the concepts used to describe the domain-to-be-explained must always be conceptually independent of the theory used to explain the phenomena within that domain. That assumption is known to be false, and we need look no farther than the special theory of relativity (STR) for a living counterexample.

The introduction of STR brought with it a systematic reconfiguration of all of the basic observational concepts of mechanics: spatial length, temporal duration, velocity, mass, momentum, and so on. These are all one-place predicates within classical mechanics, but they are all replaced by two-place predicates within STR. Each ostensible property has turned out to be a *relation*, and each has a definite value only relative to a chosen reference frame. If STR is true, and since the early years of this century it has seemed to be, then one cannot legitimately describe the observational facts of mechanics save in terms that are drawn from STR itself.

Modern chemistry provides a second example. It is a rare chemist who does not use the taxonomy of the periodic table and the combinatorial lexicon of chemical compounds to describe both the observable facts and their theoretical underpinnings alike. For starters, one can just smell hydrogen sulphide, taste sodium chloride, feel any base, and identify copper, aluminum, iron, and gold by sight.

These cases are not unusual. Our theoretical convictions typically reshape the way we describe the facts to be explained. Sometimes it happens immediately, as with STR, but more often it happens after long familiarity with the successful theory, as is displayed in the idioms casually employed in any working laboratory. The premise of the objection is true. But it is no point at all against the theoretical view.

Given the great age of folk psychology, such conceptual invasion of the explanandum domain is only to be expected.

A different critique of the theoretical view proposes an alternative account of our understanding of human behavior. According to this view, one's capacity for anticipating and understanding the behavior of others resides not in a system of nomically embedded concepts, but rather in the fact that one is a normal person oneself, and can draw on one's own reactions, to real or to imagined circumstances, in order to gain insight into the internal states and the overt behavior of others. The key idea is that of empathy. One uses oneself as a simulation (usually imagined) of the situation of another, and then extrapolates the results of that simulation to the person in question (cf. Gordon 1986; Goldman, 1989).

My first response to this line is simply to agree that an enormous amount of one's appreciation of the internal states and overt behavior of other humans derives from one's ability to examine and to extrapolate from the facts of one's own case. All of this is quite consistent with the theoretical view, and there is no reason that one should attempt to deny it. One learns from every example of humanity one encounters, and one encounters oneself on a systematic basis. What we must resist is the suggestion that extrapolating from the particulars of one's own case is the fundamental ground of one's understanding of others, a ground that renders possession of a nomic framework unnecessary. Problems for this stronger position begin to appear immediately.

For one thing, if *all* of one's understanding of others is closed under extrapolation from one's own case, then the modest contents of one's own case must form an absolute limit on what one can expect or explain in the inner life and external behavior of others. But in fact we are not so limited. People who are congenitally deaf, or blind, know quite well that normal people have perceptual capacities beyond what they themselves possess, and they know in some detail what those capacities entail in the way of knowledge and behavior. Moreover, people who have never felt profound grief, say, or love, or rejection, can nonetheless provide appropriate predictions and explanations of the behavior of people so afflicted; and so on. In general, one's immediately available understanding of human psychology and behavior goes substantially beyond what one has experienced in one's own case, either in real life or in pointed simulations. First-person experience or simulation is plainly not *necessary* for understanding the behavior of others.

Nor is it *sufficient*. The problem is that simulations, even if they motivate predictions about others, do not by themselves provide any explanatory understanding of the behavior of others. To see this, consider the following analogy. Suppose I were to possess a marvelous miniature of the physical universe, a miniature I could manipulate in order to simulate real situations and thus predict and retrodict the behavior of the real universe. Even if my miniature unfailingly provided accurate simulations of the outcomes of real physical processes, I would still be no further ahead on the business of *explaining* the behavior of the real world. In fact, I would then have two universes, both in need of explanation.

The lesson is the same for first-person and third-person situations. A simulation itself, even a successful one, provides no explanation. What explanatory understanding requires is an appreciation of the *general patterns* that comprehend the individual events in both cases. And that brings us back to the idea of a moderately general *theory.*

We should have come to that idea directly, since the empathetic account of our understanding of others depends crucially on one's having an initial understanding of oneself. To extrapolate one's own cognitive, affective, and behavioral intricacies to others requires that one be able to conceptualize and to recognize spontaneously those intricacies in oneself. But one's ability to do this is left an unaddressed mystery by the empathetic account. Self-understanding is not seen as a problem; it is other-understanding that is held up as the problem.

But the former is no less problematic than the latter. If one is to be able to apprehend even the *first*-person intricacies at issue, then one must possess a conceptual framework that draws all of the necessary distinctions, a framework that organizes the relevant categories into the appropriate structure, a framework whose taxonomy reflects at least the more obvious of the rough nomic regularities holding across its elements, even in the first-person case. Such a framework is already a theory.

The fact is, the categories into which any important domain gets divided by a learning creature emerge jointly with an appreciation of the rough nomic regularities that connect them. A nascent taxonomy that supports the expression of no useful regularities is a taxonomy that is soon replaced by a more insightful one. The divination of useful regularities is the single most dominant force shaping the taxonomies developed by any learning creature in any domain. And it is an essential force, even in perceptual domains, since our observational taxonomies are always radically underdetermined by our untrained perceptual mechanisms. To suppose that one's conception of one's *own* mental life is innocent of a network of systematic expectations is just naive. But such a network is already a theory, even before one addresses the question of others.

This is the cash value, I think, of P. F. Strawson's insightful claim, now thirty years old, that to be in a position to pose any question about other minds, and to be in a position to try to construct arguments from analogy with one's own case, is already to possess at least the rudiments of what is sought after, namely, a general conception of mental phenomena, of their general connections with each other and with behavior (Strawson 1958). What Strawson missed was the further insight that such a framework is nothing other than an empirical theory, one justified not by the quasi-logical character of its principles, as he attempted unsuccessfully to show, but by its impersonal success in explaining and predicting human behavior at large. There is no special justificational story to be told here. Folk psychology is justified by what standardly justifies *any* conceptual framework: namely, its explanatory, predictive, and manipulative success.

This concludes my survey of the outstanding objections to the theoretical view outlined in the opening paragraph of the present chapters. But in defending this view there is a major difference between my strategy in earlier writings and that of this paper. In my 1970 paper, for example, the question was framed as follows: Are action explanations *deductive–nomological* (D–N) explanations? I would now prefer to frame the question thus: Are action explanations of the same general type as the explanations typically found in the sciences? I continue to think that the answer to this second question is pretty clearly yes. The reasons are as covered above. But I am no longer confident that the D–N model itself is an adequate account of explanation in the sciences or anywhere else.

The difficulties with the D–N model are detailed elsewhere in the literature, so I shall not pause to summarize them here. My diagnosis of its failings, however, locates the basic problem in its attempt to represent knowledge and understanding by sets of sentences or propositional attitudes. In this, the framers of the D–N model were resting on the basic assumptions of folk psychology. Let me close this paper by briefly exploring how we might conceive of knowledge, and of explanatory understanding, in a systematically different way. This is an important undertaking relative to the concerns of this paper, for there is an objection to the theoretical view, as traditionally expressed, that seems to me to have some real bite. It is as follows.

If one's capacity for understanding and predicting the behavior of others derives from one's internal storage of thousands of laws or nomic generalizations, how is it that one is so poor at enunciating the laws on which one's explanatory and predictive prowess depends? It seems to take a trained philosopher to reconstruct them! How is it that children are so skilled at understanding and anticipating the behavior of humans in advance of ever acquiring the complex linguistic skills necessary to express them? How is it that social hunters such as wolves and lions can comprehend and anticipate each other's behavior in great detail, when they presumably store no internal sentences at all?

We must resist the temptation to see in these questions a renewed motivation for counting folk psychology as special, for the very same problems arise with respect to any other folk theory you might care to mention – folk physics, folk biology, whatever. It even arises for theories in the highly developed sciences, since, as Kuhn has pointed out, very little of a scientist's understanding of a theory consists in the ability to state a list of laws. It consists rather in the ability to apply the conceptual resources of the theory to new cases, and thus to anticipate and perhaps manipulate the behavior of the relevant empirical domain. This means that our problem here concerns the character of knowledge and understanding in general. Let us finally address that problem.

2. An Alternative Form of Knowledge Representation

One alternative to the notion of a universal generalization about F is the notion of a *prototype* of F, a central or typical example of F which all other examples of F resemble, more or less closely, in certain relevant respects. Prototypes have certain obvious advantages over universal generalizations. Just as a picture can be worth a thousand words, so a single complex prototype can embody the same breadth of information concerning the organization of co-occurrent features that would be contained in a long list of complex generalizations. Further, prototypes allow us a welcome degree of looseness that is precluded by the strict logic of a universal quantifier: Not *all* Fs need be Gs, but the standard or normal ones are, and the nonstandard ones must be related by a relevant similarity relation to those that properly are G. Various theorists have independently found motive to introduce such a notion in a number of cognitive fields: They have been called *paradigms* and *exemplars* in the philosophy of science (Kuhn 1962), *stereotypes* in semantics (Putnam 1970, 1975), *frames* (Minsky 1981) and *scripts* (Schank and Abelson 1977) in AI research, and finally, *prototypes* in psychology (Rosch 1981) and linguistics (Lakoff 1987).

Their advantages aside, prototypes also have certain familiar problems. The first problem is how to determine just what clutch of elements or properties should constitute a given prototype, and the second problem is how to determine the metric of similarity along which 'closeness' to the central prototype is to be measured. Though they pose a problem for notions at all levels, these problems are especially keen in the case of the so-called basic or simple properties, because common sense is there unable even to articulate any 'deeper' constituting elements (for example, what elements 'make up' a purple color, a sour taste, a floral smell, or the phoneme ā?). A final problem concerning prototypes is a familiar one: How might prototypes be represented effectively in a real cognitive creature?

This last question brings me to a possible answer, and to a path that leads to further answers. The relevant research concerns the operations of artificial neural networks, networks that mimic some of the more obvious organizational features of the brain. It concerns how they learn to recognize certain types of complex stimuli, and how they represent what they have learned. Upon repeated presentation of various real examples of the several features to be learned (*F, G, H,* etc.), and under the steady pressure of a learning algorithm that makes small adjustments in the network's synaptic connections, the network slowly but spontaneously generates a set of internal representations, one for each of the several features it is required to recognize. Collectively, these representations take the form of a set or system of similarity spaces, and the central point or volume of such a space constitutes the network's representation of a *prototypical F, G,* or *H.* After learning is completed, the system responds to any *F*-like stimulus with an internal pattern of neuronal activity that is *close to* the prototypical pattern in the relevant similarity space.

The network consists of an initial "sensory" layer of neurons, which is massively connected to a second layer of neurons. The sizes or "weights" of the many connections determine how the neurons at the second layer collectively respond to activity across the input layer. The neurons at the second layer are connected in turn to a third layer (and perhaps a fourth, etc., but we will here limit the discussion to three-layer networks). During learning, what the system is searching for is a configuration of weights that will turn the neurons at the second layer into a set of *complex-feature detectors.* We then want the neurons at the third or "output" layer to respond in turn to the second layer, given any *F*-like stimuli at the input layer, with a characteristic pattern of activity. All of this is achieved by presenting the network with diverse examples of *F*s, and slowly adjusting its connection weights in the light of its initially chaotic responses.

Such networks can indeed learn to recognize a wide variety of surprisingly subtle features: phonemes from voiced speech, the shapes of objects from gray-scale photos, the correct pronounciation of printed English text, the presence of metallic mines from sonar returns, and grammatical categories in novel sentences. Given a successfully trained network, if we examine the behavior of the neurons at the second or intermediate layer during the process of recognition, we discover that each neuron has come to represent, by its level of activity, some distinct aspect or dimension of the input stimulus. Taken together, their joint activity constitutes a multidimensional analysis of the stimuli at the input layer. The trained network has succeeded in finding a set of dimensions, an abstract *space,* such that all more-or-less typical *F*s produce a characteristic profile of neuronal activity across those particular dimensions, whereas deviant or degraded *F*s produce profiles that are variously *close* to that central prototype. The job of the third and final layer is then the relatively simple one of distinguishing that profile region from other regions in the larger space of possible activation patterns. In this way do artificial neural networks generate and exploit prototypes. It is now more than a suggestion that real neural networks do the same thing. (For a summary of these results and how they bear on the question of theoretical knowledge, see Churchland 1989a; for a parade case of successful learning, see Rosenberg and Sejnowski 1987; for the *locus classicus* concerning the general technique, see Rumelhart et al. 1986.)

Notice that this picture contains answers to all three of the problems about prototypes noted earlier. What dimensions go into a prototype of *F*? Those that allow the system to respond to diverse examples of *F* in a distinctive and uniform way, a way that reduces the error messages from the learning algorithm to a minimum. How is similarity to a prototype measured? By geometrical proximity in the relevant parameter space. How are prototypes represented in real cognitive creatures? By canonical activity patterns across an appropriate population of neurons.

Note also that the objective features recognized by the network can also have a temporal component: A network can just as well be trained to recognize typical *sequences* and *processes* as to recognize atemporal patterns, which brings me to my final suggestion. A normal human's understanding of the springs of human action may reside not in a set of stored generalizations about the hidden elements of mind and how they conspire to produce behavior, but rather in one or more prototypes of the deliberative or purposeful process. To understand or explain someone's behavior may be less a matter of deduction from implicit laws, and more a matter of recognitional subsumption of the case at issue under a relevant prototype. (For a more detailed treatment of this view of explanation – the *prototype-activation model* – see Churchland 1989b.)

Such prototypes are no doubt at least modestly complex, and presumably they depict typical configurations of desires, beliefs, preferences, and so forth, roughly the same configurations that I have earlier attempted to express in the form of universally quantified sentences. Beyond this, I am able to say little about them, at least on this occasion. But I hope I have succeeded in making intelligible to you a novel approach to the problem of explanatory understanding in humans. This is an approach that is grounded at last in what we know about the brain. And it is an approach that ascribes to us neither reams of universally quantified premises, nor deductive activity on a heroic scale. Explanatory understanding turns out to be not quite what we thought it was, because cognition in general gets characterized in a new way. And yet explanatory understanding remains the same *sort* of process in the case of human behavior as in the case of natural phenomena generally. And the question of the *adequacy* of our commonsense understanding remains as alive as ever.

REFERENCES

Churchland, P. M. (1970), "The Logical Character of Action Explanations," *Philosophical Review*, 79, no. 2.

(1979), *Scientific Realism and the Plasticity of Mind* (Cambridge: Cambridge University Press).

(1981), "Eliminative Materialism and the Propositional Attitudes," *Journal of Philosophy*, LXXVIII, no. 2.

(1984), *Matter and Consciousness* (Cambridge: The MIT Press).

(1986), "On the Continuity of Science and Philosophy," *Mind and Language*, 1, no. 1.

(1989a), "On the Nature of Theories, A Neurocomputational Perspective," in Savage, W., ed., *Scientific Theories: Minnesota Studies in the Philosophy of Science*, Vol. XIV (Minneapolis: University of Minnesota Press).

(1989b), "On the Nature of Explanation: A PDP Approach," *A Neurocomputational Perspective* (Cambridge, Mass., The MIT Press).

Feyerabend, P. K. (1963), "Materialism and the Mind–Body Problem," *Review of Metaphysics*, 17.

Goldman, A. (1989), "Interpretation Psychologized," *Mind and Language* 4.

Gordon, R. (1986), "Folk Psychology as Simulation," *Mind and Language* 1, no. 2.

Haldane, J. (1988), "Understanding Folk," *Proceedings of the Aristotelian Society,* Supplementary Vol. LXII.

Kuhn, T. S. (1962), *The Structure of Scientific Revolutions* (Chicago: University of Chicago Press).

Lakoff, G. (1987), *Women, Fire, and Dangerous Things* (Chicago: University of Chicago Press).

McCloskey, M. (1983), "Intuitive Physics," *Scientific American,* 248, no. 4: 122–30.

Minsky, M. (1981), "A Framework for Representing Knowledge," in Haugeland, J., ed., *Mind Design* (Cambridge: MIT Press).

Putnam, H. (1970), "Is Semantics Possible?," in Kiefer, H. and Munitz, M., eds., *Languages, Belief, and Metaphysics* (Albany: State University of New York Press). Reprinted in Putnam, H., *Mind, Language, and Reality* (Cambridge: Cambridge University Press).

(1975), "The Meaning of 'meaning'," in Gunderson, K., *Language, Mind, and Knowledge: Minnesota Studies in the Philosophy of Science,* Vol. 7. Reprinted in Putnam H., *Mind, Language, and Reality* (Cambridge: Cambridge University Press).

Rorty, R. (1965), "Mind–Body Identity, Privacy, and Categories," *Review of Metaphysics,* 1.

Rosch, E. (1981), "Prototype Classification and Logical Classification: The Two Systems," in Scholnick, E., ed., *New Trends in Cognitive Representation: Challenges to Piaget's Theory* (New Jersey: Lawrence Erlbaum).

Rosenberg, C. R., and Sejnowski, T. J. (1987), "Parallel Networks That Learn to Pronounce English Text," *Complex Systems,* 1.

Rumelhart, D. E., Hinton, G. E., and Williams, R. J. (1986), "Learning Internal Representations by Error Propagation," in Rumelhart, D. E., and McClelland, J. L., eds., *Parallel Distributed Processing: Explorations in the Microstructure of Cognition* (Cambridge: MIT Press, 1986).

Schank, R., and Abelson, R. (1977), *Scripts, Plans, Goals, and Understanding* (New Jersey: John Wiley & Sons).

Sellars, W. (1956), "Empiricism and the Philosophy of Mind," in Feigl, H., and Scriven, M., eds., *Minnesota Studies in the Philosophy of Science,* Vol. 1 (Minneapolis, University of Minnesota Press). Reprinted in Sellars, W., *Science, Perception, and Reality* (London: Routledge and Keegan Paul, 1963).

Strawson, P. F. (1958), "Persons," *Minnesota Studies in the Philosophy of Science,* Vol. 2, eds. Feigl, H., Scriven, M., and Maxwell, G. (Minneapolis: University of Minnesota Press).

Wilkes, K. (1981), "Functionalism, Psychology, and the Philosophy of Mind," *Philosophical Topics,* 12, no. 1.

(1984), "Pragmatics in Science and Theory in Common Sense," *Inquiry,* 27, no. 4.

4

Methodological Reflections
on Belief

ROBERT CUMMINS

1. Intentional Realism

Let's suppose there really are such things as propositional attitudes. And let's understand this claim as Putnam (1975) would have us understand claims about natural kinds so that it could turn out that most of what we believe about the propositional attitudes might be mistaken in one way or another. Or, if that is going too far, let's at least understand the claim in such a way that any particular thing we believe about the attitudes might turn out to be false. This, it seems to me, is the way we have to understand the claim that there are such things as propositional attitudes if we are to take the claim to be an empirical one on all fours with such claims as that there are elephants, genes, or crystals. Otherwise, we can legislate against surprising empirical discoveries about the attitudes by claiming that the discoverers have merely changed the subject. "Computationalists can't be talking about belief," we might say, "because beliefs are individuated, at least in part, by social factors, and computational states are not. At best, they are talking about 'shmaliefs', not beliefs."

The trouble with this sort of move is that the philosopher who makes it runs the risk that he or she is talking about nothing at all. If philosophers insist, for example, that beliefs are socially individuated, while good empirical theory insists that computational states are what there *are*, then it is open to the computationalist to say that the empirical evidence suggests that there are no beliefs as the philosopher chooses to define them.[1] Scientists who have no stomach for a fight over words will either cease talking to philosophers, or they will simply invent a new word. The philosophers will quite rightly be perceived as having won a petty squabble over semantic territory at the price of cutting themselves off from serious empirical research.

2. Methodology: Intentional Realism and the Philosophy
of Science

Lots of philosophers, I suspect, resist realism about the attitudes – in practice, if not explicitly – because it threatens to lead to unemployment. How, after all, can a philosopher who toes the realist line hope to discover anything about the propositional attitudes? Doesn't being a realist about the propositional attitudes amount to conceding them to the scientists?

The same thing might be said about space and time. If we are realists about these matters, shouldn't philosophers concede that the nature of space, time, and space–time is an empirical matter and stop poaching on the physicist's preserves? Yes, of course. But accepting that answer hasn't put philosophers out of the space and time business. Rather, it has led philosophers to treat the issues as issues in the philosophy of physics. Instead of asking what the nature of space and time is – a question philosophical methodology cannot properly address – the philosopher of physics asks, for example, how space must be conceived if some well-articulated physical theory or theoretical framework is to deliver the explanatory goods it advertises. How must we conceive of space if general relativity is to be true and explanatory? Should we be substantivalists? Is space a thing? Or is it a property of things? This kind of inquiry is especially pressing when the target is an explanatory primitive of the theory or theories that harbor it. Hence, a good deal of the philosophy of science is concerned with explicating the "foundations" of this or that theory or framework or research paradigm.

All this applies straightforwardly to the philosophy of psychology. Philosophers may, without concern for a misfit between their methodology and their conclusions, identify some theory (or theoretical framework or research paradigm) that invokes propositional attitudes and then ask how we should understand them if the invoking theory is to be true and explanatory. Thus, if our target is computationalist theories, and we determine that computational states are not individuated by social factors, then we may conclude that beliefs, at least as invoked by computationalists, had better be asocial too. We can then go on to attempt to construct an appropriate asocial conception of belief.[2]

3. Methodology and Belief Attribution

What I've been describing is not what philosophers have been doing. What they have been doing instead is trying to turn semantics into psychology. Here is a familiar example.[3]

3.1. Burge: Belief and Linguistic Affiliation

'Brisket' applies to cuts of breast meat generally. Tyler, however, believes that it applies only to breast of beef. Tyler* is just like Tyler except that he lives in a language community in which 'brisket' applies only to breast of beef. Tyler and Tyler*, we may suppose, are molecule-for-molecule identical, for, though their language communities differ slightly, Tyler has, in point of fact, never encountered the sort of situation that could distinguish him from Tyler*, for example, reading a dictionary entry for 'brisket'. In spite of their mereological identity, however, it seems we are prepared to attribute beliefs about brisket to Tyler but not to Tyler*. For when Tyler* says, for example: "Brisket is better than tenderloin," he is making a statement that has a different truth condition than the statement Tyler makes with the same words. Tyler's statement is about breast of beast; Tyler*, using the same words, makes a statement about breast of beef. But it seems obvious that what goes for the statements must go for the beliefs they express: The belief Tyler expresses when he says, "Brisket is better than tenderloin," is about breast of beast; the one Tyler* expresses is about breast of beef. It is concluded from all this that beliefs are not entirely "in the head." They are not, in fact, psychological states as psychologists normally conceive them, since they are individuated in part by such extrapsychological factors as the rules of one's language,[4] even in cases in which the relevant facts about the language have had no causal impact whatever on the believer.

How exactly is this sort of thought experiment supposed to lead to conclusions about the nature of belief? Can this sort of "intuition pump" (Dennett 1980) really show that beliefs are not psychological states,[5] that psychologists are mistaken to try to use 'believes' to characterize mental processes in a way that abstracts away from such things as the subject's linguistic affiliation?

I'm going to need a name for the methodology implicit in this sort of thought experiment. I'll call it the CRHS methodology, for *c*onsidered *r*esponse to a *h*ypothetical *s*ituation. It is difficult to see how CRHS can deliver the goods about belief. What we've got to go on is just whether we would say that Tyler but not Tyler* has beliefs about brisket. But how could this tell us anything about their beliefs? Isn't this like inferring that objects dropped from an airplane have a straight-line trajectory (relative to the earth) because that's the trajectory people tend to attribute in such cases?[6] Or isn't it like inferring that the rate of free-fall is a function of weight from the fact that people's attributions of rate are sensitive to the supposed weight of the falling object? Why assume that people are any better authorities about belief than about the trajectories or rate of free-fall of falling objects? Perhaps people can, within limits, tell you what they believe with fair reliability. But even if people were incorrigible about what beliefs they had, it wouldn't follow that they had any special knowledge about the nature of belief.

How could it even *seem* that investigating the conditions of belief attribution could yield conclusions about belief? The answer *seems* simple enough: If we know, for example, that

(A)   *Tyler and Tyler* are psychologically equivalent,*

and that

(B)   *Tyler and Tyler* have different beliefs,*

then it follows that

(C)   *individuation of belief is a function of extrapsychological factors.*[7]

The trouble, of course, is B: What entitles us to the claim that Tyler and Tyler* have different beliefs? CRHS serves up B for us: Reflecting on the story, we attribute different beliefs to Tyler and Tyler*. But why should we take our belief attributions seriously in a tough case like this, uninformed, as they are, by good empirical theory?

There are two reasons for caution. To see what they are, we need to look more closely at the underlying situation. Here's the plot outline:

(*i*)   *It is stipulated that Tyler and Tyler* are psychologically equivalent.*

(*ii*)   *We are moved, on reflection, to attribute different beliefs to Tyler and Tyler*.*

(*iii*) *It follows that our belief attributions are sensitive to extrapsychological factors – linguistic affiliation in this case.*

(*iv*)   *We conclude that the truth conditions of belief attributions contain extrapsychological factors, and hence that beliefs are individuated (in part) by extrapsychological factors.*

But (*iv*) doesn't follow from (*iii*). Extrapsychological considerations may be legitimate *evidence* for belief attributions, yet not be implicated in their truth conditions.[8] In this case, we are moved by the fact that what Tyler states when he says, "Brisket is better than tenderloin," is different than what Tyler* states in uttering the same words in the same circumstances. People generally believe what they sincerely state to be the case. What people sincerely state therefore provides a good bet concerning what they believe. But what someone states in uttering a sentence is a function of the meanings of the words in the sentence, and that in turn is a function of the language he or she is speaking. So here we have an uncontroversial case of an extrapsychological factor – word meaning in the language – counting as legitimate evidence for a belief attribution.

But it is only evidence. From the fact that attributions of belief are properly sensitive to extrapsychological factors, it doesn't follow that extrapsychological factors figure in the truth conditions of belief attributions. All we are entitled to conclude is that extrapsychological factors figure legitimately as evidence for belief attributions. In the particular case under discussion, it is easy to see why we shouldn't move to a conclusion about truth conditions. Why, after all, should we assume that Tyler means exactly what his words are conventionally suited to express?[9] Why, that is, should we assume that what Tyler says is an exact reflection of what he believes? Tyler *thinks* his words express what he believes, but, of course, he is wrong about this, for it is part of the story that he doesn't know what 'brisket' means in the language he is speaking. Corrected about this matter, it seems likely that Tyler would change his story: "Oh, I see. Well, then, it's breast of beef I like, not brisket! I really haven't given any thought to what you call brisket. Quite a mixed bag, after all." Or he might simply pull a Humpty-Dumpty: "That's not what *I* mean by 'brisket.' What I mean is breast of beef."

The point of the foregoing is not so much to argue that Tyler and Tyler* don't have different beliefs, but rather to emphasize that we cannot move from premises about our considered belief attributions to conclusions about the truth conditions of belief attributions. There is, of course, a kind of consistency argument available: *If* you agree that Tyler and Tyler* have different beliefs, then you must agree that beliefs are individuated by extrapsychological factors. But this won't carry much weight with thoughtful realists, for they will be rightly suspicious of their "intuitions" in cases like this. They will remember that plausible belief attributions may yet be false. They will remember that even justified belief attributions may yet be false.

More radically, they will remember what intelligent, well-informed people who happen to be innocent of mechanics say about things dropped from airplanes. People generally attribute incorrect trajectories to hypothetical objects dropped from hypothetical airplanes. They do this, presumably, because they have false beliefs about the trajectories of objects dropped from airplanes. Subjects with a knowledge of elementary physics don't make this sort of mistake. Similarly, people with false beliefs about belief can be expected to make mistaken attributions of belief in real and hypothetical situations. "Perhaps," the realist will think, "it is best to let well-motivated empirical theory inform our attributions of belief as it ought to inform our attributions of trajectories." Well-motivated empirical theory, of course, is just what CRHS cannot provide. If belief is to be a serious explanatory construct, then we had better put the *serious* explanations in the driver's seat and let our intuitions go along for the ride. If we are wrong about belief, we will make mistaken attributions. In the end, the only way to know about belief is to study belief. Studying belief attributions will, at best, tell you only what people believe about belief.[10]

It might seem that the problem with the Burgean argument is not with the methodology – not with CRHS – but with the mistaken assumption that sincerity is enough to guarantee a match between what someone states and the underlying belief. But this *is* a problem with the methodology: Our considered responses to hypothetical situations will depend on what we consider. It turns out that we should have considered the fact that sincerity isn't enough to match what is stated to what is believed. What else should we consider? This is just the sort of question that science is supposed to answer better than common sense.

The Burgean argument is instructive in part because we can *see* that we have been misled. Lacking a good empirical theory of belief, we normally have no really satisfactory way of knowing whether CRHS is yielding questionable attributions. But in this case, we are told that Tyler doesn't know what 'brisket' means in his language. Since we know that what one states is a function of the meanings of the words one uses, we can be pretty sure that Tyler doesn't succeed in stating what he intends to state, so we can be pretty sure that what he does succeed in stating isn't likely to be a perfect reflection of what he believes. Having come this far, it is tempting to say that, *on further reflection,* we can see that what Tyler believes is not that brisket is better than tenderloin, but that breast of beef is better than tenderloin. There's no harm in yielding to this temptation, provided that we don't suppose that *further reflection* has got around the need for empirical theory after all. CRHS isn't going to tell use how to individuate belief, unless the *further reflection* in question is adequately informed reflection. Only a good empirical theory of belief could seriously justify confidence that our reflections are adequately informed.

3.2.   Putnam: Belief and Environmental Affiliation

It is tempting, as I've just pointed out, to suppose that the difficulty we've uncovered is special to the sort of argument given by Tyler Burge for the relevance of linguistic affiliation to belief. The Burgean argument simply assumes that what is stated is what is believed:

(B-1) *If* S *sincerely states that* p, *then* S *believes that* p.

But B-1 is false. In the case lately imagined, it seems plausible to suppose that what Tyler states (viz., that breast of beast is better than tenderloin) is not what he intends to state (viz., that breast of beef is better than tenderloin). What he actually states is, of course, a function of the meanings of his words. But he is, by hypothesis, mistaken about the meaning of 'brisket' in his language. Hence he chooses the wrong words to express what he intends to state. The difficulty, one might suppose, is not with the methodology; the problem is just that it is an inadequately informed application of the methodology. Even if we accept the view that adequately informed reflection is reflection informed by good empirical theory, perhaps there is enough good empirical theory in hand to allow CRHS to yield the targeted result, namely *true* attributions of distinct beliefs to psychologically equivalent subjects. Consider Putnam's Twin Earth case (Putnam 1975). Twin Earth is an exact duplicate of earth except that where we have H_2O they have *XYZ*. When Hilary says, "Water is better than Pepsi," he makes a statement about H_2O. When Twhilary (Twin-Hilary) says, "Water is better than Pepsi," he makes a statement about *XYZ*. Once again, it is concluded that Hilary and Twhilary express different beliefs. But since, by hypothesis, the twins are molecule-by-molecule duplicates, it follows that beliefs are individuated by extrapsychological factors.

In this case, it seems we cannot object that one of the characters in the story fails to state what he intends to state on the grounds that one of them is mistaken about the meanings of the words he uses. It seems that neither character is mistaken about the meaning of 'water' in the language he uses. Both speak sincerely. It seems to follow that what each states is what each intends to state. Since what one sincerely intends to state is what one believes, both state what they believe. Since the statements are different, so are the beliefs. Q.E.D.

Should we concede that the CRHS *can* deliver the conclusion that beliefs are individuated by extrapsychological factors? How is this possible? Haven't we just reinstated armchair science? A realist about belief will surely want to give this argument very close scrutiny.

The argument makes use of a crucial assumption:

(P-1) *What the twins state is what they intend to state sincerely.*

P-1 is bolstered (though of course not entailed) by P-2:

(P-2) *Neither twin is mistaken about the meaning of 'water'.*

P-2 looks harmless enough. In the Burge case, it is an explicit assumption that Tyler is mistaken about the meaning of 'brisket', but there is no comparable assumption operative in the Twin Earth case. Still, P-2 is not as harmless as it appears.

Let's begin with the fact that the twins are, in a certain sense, ignorant of the reference of their words: Twhilary doesn't know that the referent of 'water' in Twinglish is *XYZ*. How, one might wonder, can Twhilary sincerely intend to state something about *XYZ* given that he doesn't know that what he calls water is *XYZ*? Aren't we simply assuming about intention what we are trying to prove about belief?

It seems that P-2 is wrong if it is understood to imply that the twins are fully informed about the reference of 'water' in their respective languages: While it is surely uncontroversial that, *in some sense*, Twhilary knows what 'water' refers to in Twinglish, it doesn't follow that he is fully informed about the nature of the stuff he refers to with his uses of 'water'. There is, therefore, a certain sense in which he doesn't know what he is talking about, namely, he doesn't know what proposition he is expressing when he says, "Water is better than Pepsi." It would seem to follow that he cannot sincerely intend to express that proposition in uttering those words. Hence, P-1 cannot be invoked to yield a conclusion about what he believes. Once again, it appears that the argument depends on a dubious psychological assumption linking what one believes to the reference of what one says. Here's how the trick is done:

(1)   *The meanings of one's words are determined by extrapsychological factors,*

hence,

(2)   *the truth conditions of one's statements are determined by extrapsychological factors.*

But,

(3)   *one's sincere statements express what one believes,*

hence,

(4)   *the truth conditions of one's sincere statements are the same as the truth conditions of one's beliefs.*

I have no quarrel with (1) and (2), but (3) is false, as we've seen, and so is (4). Something close to (3) is plausible, namely,

(3')   *one believes what one intends to state sincerely.*

But (3') merely shifts the burden from belief to intention. It may be true that the truth conditions of what one intends to state sincerely are the same as the truth conditions of what one believes. But this won't help you get a conclusion about the truth conditions of beliefs from premises about the truth conditions of statements, unless you already have a link between the truth conditions of intentions and the truth conditions of statements. Shifting the focus to intention is no help because there is no more reason to say that Twhilary intends to state that *XYZ* is wet than to say that he believes that *XYZ* is wet. On the contrary, the shift to intention makes the trick a little easier to spot.

That's not the end of the matter, of course. The Twin Earth case is different from Burgean cases in that we are still left wondering what Twhilary *does* believe, whereas we are pretty sure we know what Tyler believes. We will have to come back to this.

4. Semantics and Psychology

4.1. *The Psychological Reality of Semantic Values*

There is, of course, an intellectual tradition according to which you *can* discover the truth conditions for belief attributions without knowing anything about belief. Formal semantics in the Tarskian tradition espoused by Davidson (1967) is supposed to yield truth conditions for whatever it is that is truth-valuable in natural languages. But this kind of traffic in truth conditions isn't supposed to be the sort of thing that could supply fuel for the antiindividualist fire. For *that* you need to be able to discover such things as that the truth-value of a belief attribution can depend on an extrapsychological factor. If Tarskian semantics is serving up conclusions like that, then it is certainly doing more than telling us about the language, and is therefore overstepping the boundaries set by its original charter. No one in that tradition thought of semantics as the sort of thing that could overlap the psychology of belief.

Yet this crossing of boundaries – doing philosophy of mind, and even psychology, by doing philosophy of language – has become a small industry. What gives the trespassers such confidence?

I think a lot of the trespassing (or what I'm contentiously calling trespassing) began with the hypothesis that semantic values are psychologically real.

> (*Psychological reality of semantic values – PRSV): to understand (or know the meaning of) an expression requires knowing its semantic value.*

Examples of PRSV are (*a*) the claim that to understand a statement requires knowing its truth condition; (*b*) the claim that to understand a proper name requires knowing its sense; (*c*) the claim that to understand a proper name requires knowing its reference; (*d*) the claim that to understand a general term requires knowing what property it expresses; (*e*) the claim that to understand a statement requires knowing what proposition it expresses. Two clarifying remarks are essential.

First, *understanding* is to be construed psychologically in the PRSV: For example, (*b*) is to be construed as the idea that one must represent the sense of a name, and represent it as the sense of that name, in order to be a party to successful communicative episodes that employ that name. A corollary of PRSV is the assumption that learning a language involves learning the semantic values of its expressions.[11]

Second, *semantic values* are, in the first instance, to be understood in the model theoretic sort of way that is central to the Tarskian tradition: They are whatever one needs to assign to things in order to capture systematically the entailment relations that hold among things that are truth-valuable. The paradigm case is the assignment of satisfaction conditions to the primitive terms of a first-order language in such a way as not only to enable a truth definition, but to account for the entailment relations among statements. It is the fact that semantics aims for, and is constrained by, a proprietary goal independent of psychology that gives PRSV its bite: PRSV is the hypothesis that the stuff that tracks entailments is an essential part of the stuff a system needs to know in order to use and understand a language. This is how PRSV links semantics with psychology: Since the stuff that tracks entailments is the stuff that (in part) drives use and understanding, when we do the semantics we have done a good deal of the psychology as well.

Meaning and Semantic Values. I suspect that some have been seduced into accepting PRSV by the following line of thought: To understand an expression is just to know what it means. But to know what an expression means is to know its meaning (*i.e.,* to know its semantic value).

I suppose there is an innocent sense in which people who know English know the meaning of 'elevator' and 'rescue'. Perhaps they can even tell you what these words mean. I've asked a few people about 'elevator' just now. The best answer I got was this: "An elevator is like a closet. You go in, press one of several buttons with numbers on them, and the thing travels up a vertical shaft in the building, stopping at the floor corresponding to the number on the button you pushed. Faster and easier than stairs." This person certainly knows what 'elevator' means. But does this person know the semantic value of 'elevator'? Does she know which whatnot 'elevator' must be associated with in order to track the entailments of expressions in which 'elevator' occurs as a constituent? Maybe. But the fact that she knows, in this ordinary way, what 'elevator' means does not, on the face of it anyway, show that she does (or must) know, even tacitly, what semanticists want to know about 'elevator'.

Maybe the *psychology* works like this: When you encounter an 'elevator' you generate a pointer to a frame that allows you to access, more or less reliably, everything you know about elevators. On this rather plausible view, your ability to use and understand 'elevators' is closely related to your ability to use and understand elevators: It rests on what you know about elevators. You have the concept of an elevator, on this view, when you have a frame whose semantic value is (let's say) the property of being an elevator but whose psychological content is just whatever you know about elevators.[12] The crucial point is that there is a strong distinction between the psychological content of a concept and its semantic content. The psychological content is the *knowledge[13] in (or accessible via) the relevant data structure; the semantic content (what I've been calling the semantic value) is the sort of thing that enters into truth conditions. I'll call this view of concepts the encyclopedia view of concepts to emphasize the idea that the psychological content of a concept is like an encyclopedia entry rather than a dictionary entry (*i.e.*, an entry that specifies a meaning).

I think there is a good deal of empirical evidence for the encyclopedia theory of concepts. However that may be, the point I want to make is that it is incompatible with PRSV. Since the encyclopedia theory of concepts is plainly an empirical theory, so is PRSV. It doesn't follow, of course, that philosophers are not allowed to assume PRSV, but it does mean that they are required to acknowledge the empirical loan they are taking out when they do assume it. No argument that assumes PRSV, for example, can be used to criticize the encyclopedia theory of concepts.

Belief and the PRSV. Even if we know something about the semantic values of such things as beliefs or mental representations, nothing will follow about the psychological content of those representations or states unless we assume something like PRSV. If you have the semantics straight, you will be able to track the semantic relations among mental states. But it doesn't follow that you will be able to track their psychological relations. We should therefore be cautious of moves from premises about the truth conditions of belief attributions to substantive conclusions about belief. If the PRSV isn't true, then semantic values (*e.g.*, truth conditions) aren't in the head. The semanticist will be able, in one sense, to draw conclusions about mental states (viz., conclusions about their semantic values). But nothing will follow about the psychological contents of those states. Hence, even if, contrary to fact, philosophy were in a position to establish that Tyler and Tyler* have beliefs with different semantic contents, it wouldn't follow that they have beliefs with different psychological contents. Hence it wouldn't follow that they have, in any sense of interest to psychology, different beliefs. Empirical science must be left free to individuate its states in whatever way conduces to good theory. Philosophers can insist that states individuated by psychological content rather than semantic content are not beliefs, but this won't be worth taking seriously unless and until they catch psychologists using what they call beliefs in a way that assumes that they are semantically individuated.[14]

4.2.   The Old and the New Semantics

I have already emphasized that if philosophers are to be able to move from semantical theses to psychological theses, there has to be a sense in which semantics is independent from psychology. That is, it had better be the case that semantics has its own proprietary goals and constraints. Only thus will it be possible to establish some semantical thesis *and then* expose its implications for psychology. Semantics, I have supposed, is the theory of entailment. Semantic values are whatever one needs to assign to statements (or whatever is truth-valuable) to systematically track entailment relations.[15] So the idea behind what I have contentiously called philosophical trespassing on psychological turf can be put this way:

> (Easement) : Get the semantics of belief attribution right (i.e., find out what it takes to track their entailments) and this will put constraints on belief, and hence, on psychology.

From this perspective, it is possible to see how the Twin Earth argument depends on a rather recent conception of semantics. Twenty years ago, it would have been natural to respond to the argument along the following lines.

The Old Semantics. If the point is to track entailments, then the semanticist should not think of the reference of 'water' in English as H_2O, since "This is water," doesn't entail, "This is made up of hydrogen and oxygen." Semantics, like any other science, must choose its theoretical specifications carefully. In this case, specifying the reference of 'water' as H_2O is the wrong choice for semantics, though it is the right choice for chemistry. Of course, 'water' does refer to H_2O (in English), but that is the wrong way to specify its reference if you are interested in tracking entailments, though it is the right way if you are interested in tracking chemical interactions. Thus, although Hilary and Twhilary are referring to different things when they use the word 'water', this is not a difference that semantics will notice. And what goes for reference goes for truth conditions: Good semantic theory will not use the term 'H$_2$O' in specifying the truth conditions for statements containing 'water'. From the fact, then, that two beliefs or statements are about different things, it doesn't follow that good semantics will distinguish them. One shouldn't assume that a proper scientific specification of what a belief or statement is about is a proper semantic specification. Semantics, in short, is an autonomous discipline.

The New Semantics. Nowadays, most of us would object to the claim that Hilary's statement, that water is better than Pepsi, doesn't entail that H$_2$O is better than Pepsi. Of course, you cannot *formally derive* "H$_2$O is better than Pepsi," from "Water is better than Pepsi," without adding something like "Water is H$_2$O," but entailment is supposed to be a semantic notion, not a formal one. What we need to know, then, is whether "H$_2$O is better than Pepsi," is true in every possible world in which "Water is better than Pepsi," is true. Now, if "Water is H$_2$O," is true in every possible world if it is true at all, as Kripke and Putnam have made plausible, then the entailment is unproblematic.

Here, of course, the sentences in quotation marks are assumed to be bits of English. If they are assumed to be bits of Twinglish, we get quite different results. In Twinglish, "Water is *XYZ*," expresses something true in every possible world, so in Twinglish, "Water is better than Pepsi," entails "*XYZ* is better than Pepsi."

I have a lot of sympathy with this line of thought. But notice that if we understand entailment in this way, semantics is no longer an *autonomous* discipline: Our knowledge of what entails what must wait on such things as chemistry. Since we have enough chemistry in hand to know that water is H$_2$O, we know that beliefs about water are beliefs about H$_2$O. Twhilary certainly has no beliefs about H$_2$O, so his beliefs will be semantically distinct from Hilary's – Twhilary believes that *XYZ* is better than Pepsi – even though he is Hilary's computational (or neurophysiological) twin. From this perspective, the PRSV seems preposterous.[16] People don't need to know the chemistry of water to use and understand 'water'. And yet I think there are many who accept some form of the PRSV, at least tacitly, while embracing the new semantics. The problem is that we have updated our conception of semantics without noticing that it requires us to abandon PRSV, a view that made sense only against the background of a conception of semantics as an autonomous discipline. If you accept the conception of semantics that underlies the Twin Earth argument, you must abandon the PRSV. Hence Putnam's claim that meanings (semantic values, not psychological contents) aren't in the head.

The Individuation of Belief. If we accept the new semantics and reject the PRSV, what motivation could we have to *individuate* beliefs semantically? If we are realists about belief, we will want to individuate beliefs in whatever way conduces best to good psychological theory. Adherents of the new semantics should scoff at the idea that indexing beliefs to propositions will track their psychological relations. They will scoff precisely because it is so obvious that tracking entailments requires factors irrelevant to psychology. "Intentional realism" is therefore a potentially misleading name for contemporary realism about belief, for it suggests that we should take seriously the idea that psychology should individuate beliefs semantically. Of course, 'intentional individuation' doesn't *have* to mean semantic individuation, but it is an easy enough identification to make "intentional realism" a dangerous name for realism about belief. For the doctrine we are now considering is the doctrine that propositional attitudes should not be individuated in psychology by propositions. From the fact that p and q are distinct propositions, we cannot conclude that the belief that p is distinct from the belief that q.[17]

How *should* we individuate concepts (psychologically construed) and beliefs? You shouldn't ask me: I'm a philosopher. You wouldn't ask a philosopher what water is. Don't ask a philosopher what belief is either.

5. Folk Psychology

This paper has been mainly a complaint against armchair psychology disguised as the philosophy of mind or as the philosophy of language. The recent interest in so-called folk psychology is, I think, largely due to the fact that it provides philosophers an excuse to do psychology without having to bother about sound empirical method. If by "folk psychology" you mean the psychology of the folk – a theory on all fours with folk physics (and as likely to be true) – then I have no objection to *studying* it – that is, investigating it in the way psychologists study folk physics: empirically. There can be no serious talk of vindicating the psychology of the folk until we have some empirically justified account of what it *is*.

But, of course, this is not what philosophers typically mean by folk psychology. What they mean is some sort of psychological theory – the details are left unspecified because they are irrelevant – that makes central explanatory appeals to belief and desire. Folk psychology in this sense will be "vindicated" if it turns out that empirical psychology has some serious use for belief and desire. Now this *looks* to be a question for empirical psychology itself, or for the philosopher of science who asks whether any serious extant empirical theory in psychology makes use of something close to belief and desire – GOALS and KNOWLEDGE, say. And that is exactly the sort of question it is.

Yet that is not how philosophers have been treating the question, for what philosophers have been doing is (*i*) conceptual analyses of belief, and (*ii*) the semantics of belief attribution. But it is hard to see how (*i*) and (*ii*) could bear on psychology at all. For, first, there is no evident reason why a serious empirical psychologist should care what the ordinary concept of belief is any more than a serious physicist should care what the ordinary concept of force is.[18] And, second, the good semanticist will want to describe the way scientists use their concepts, not dictate to science how a certain concept must be used. If Putnam is right in his claim that the reference of 'water' waits on chemistry, then the reference of 'belief' must wait on psychology. But it isn't just reference that waits on science. Physicists created a sense for 'force'; they didn't just discover the reference of an ordinary concept or term. We can expect psychologists to do the same. When philosophers appreciate this point, they will be forced to concede that the semantics of ordinary belief attribution has essentially no relevance to psychology at all.

Still, philosophers will want to know what is involved in semantically characterizing mental states. This is fine, provided it isn't construed as a question about the "ordinary concept of belief" or the semantics of belief attribution, but as a question in the philosophy of science analogous to this: What is involved in the noncontinuous and nondeterministic characterization of the states of subatomic particles? And philosophers will want to know whether belief–desire explanations can be turned into good science. This question, I say, is analogous to this: Can alchemy be turned into good science? Chemists solved that question; let the psychologists solve the other one.

REFERENCES

Burge, Tyler (1979) "Individualism and the mental," in French, Euhling, and Wettstein (eds.) *Studies in the Philosophy of Mind*, Vol. 10, *Midwest Studies in Philosophy*, University of Minnesota Press, Minneapolis.

Davidson, Donald (1965) "Theories of meaning and learnable languages," *Proceedings of the 1964 International Congress for Logic, Mathematics, and Philosophy of Science*, North Holland, Amsterdam.

(1967) "Truth and meaning," *Synthese*, 42:3:304–23.

Dennett, Daniel (1980), comment on Searle, "Minds, brains and programs," *Behavioral and Brain Sciences*, 3:417–24.

Dretske, Fred (1981) *Knowledge and the Flow of Information*. MIT Press: A Bradford Book, Cambridge, MA.

Fodor, J. (1980) "Methodological solipsism considered as a research strategy cognitive science," *Behavioral and Brain Sciences*, 3:63–109.

Kaiser, M. K., J. Jonides, and J. Alexander (1986) "Intuitive physics: reasoning on abstract and commonsense problems." *Memory and Cognition.* 14(4)308–12.

McCloskey, M. (1983) "Intuitive physics," *Scientific American*, 24:122–30.

Putnam, Hilary (1975) "The meaning of 'meaning'," in Putnam, *Mind, Language, and Reality.* Cambridge University Press, New York.

NOTES

1. The situation is comparable to Dretske's (1981) insistence that mental states get their representational content during a learning period when they are perfect indicators of the properties they are said to represent. The theory runs the risk that no mental states have representational content as defined, or anyway no content worth bothering about, since it might turn out that no mental state is ever a perfect indicator of distal states of affairs.

2. In a similar vein, we might ask what belief must be if folk psychology is to be true and explanatory. To this I have no objection, but two comments are in order.

   First, to explicate the concepts of folk psychology one must begin by determining what folk psychology is. In practice, this is usually a matter of gesturing apologetically to some simple examples of alleged folk psychological explanation, examples that are generally conceded to be seriously flawed in some way. The assumption seems to be that we just know what folk psychology is. Psychologists who want to know what folk physics is (*e.g.*, what people would say about the trajectories of falling objects) do some controlled experiments to find out. Philosophers who make claims about folk psychology don't feel the need. Perhaps they are right: Perhaps folk psychology is rather more explicit in daily practice than folk physics. But I don't think this is what's really going on. Philosophers don't need to know what folk psychology is because they never appeal to it. It never matters to the philosophical arguments what the principles actually are – only that there are some. This is suspicious in itself: How can you know what the explanatory role of belief is in folk psychology if you don't know or care what folk psychology is?

   Second, it is worth knowing what belief must be if folk psychology is to turn out true and explanatory only if there is some reason to think folk psychology might turn out to be true and explanatory. It is amazing how certain philosophers are that folk psychology is true and explanatory given their avowed ignorance of its alleged principles.

3. The following example is taken from Burge (1979).

4. A psychologist will treat the rules of the language as a psychological factor only to the extent that they are represented in the speaker (or implicit in the speaker's functional architecture somehow).

5. Burge, of course, would not accept my description of these factors as "extrapsychological," nor would he condone my speaking of beliefs widely individuated as "not psychological states." I hope it is clear that, in the present context, this is merely a matter of terminology. I don't think I've begged any substantive questions.

In the context of a particular explanatory framework, we can get around this terminological issue by saying that if beliefs are individuated in part by linguistic affiliation, then they are not computational states, or neurophysiological states, or whatever the framework in question holds to be the relevant way to specify the "substrata" of mentality.

6. See, for example, McCloskey 1983; Kaiser, Jonides, and Alexander 1986.

7. Again, I don't mean to beg any questions by the use of "psychological" here. For a computationalist, the issue could be put this way: If we know that (A) Tyler and Tyler* are computationally equivalent, and that (B) Tyler and Tyler* have different beliefs, then it follows that (C) individuation of belief is a function of extrapsychological factors.

8. If you thought the CRHS methodology could lead to conclusions about the evidence conditions for belief attribution, and you assimilate truth conditions to evidence conditions, then you would have a route to conclusions about belief. This route, however, is bound to be unattractive to those who have learned Quine's lesson: If anything can be evidence for anything else (via intervening theory), then reflection on what might justify a belief attribution is not likely to tell you much about the truth conditions for belief attribution.

9. If there is such a thing: Actually, it is just *stipulated* that Tyler's words mean that breast of beast is better than tenderloin.

10. "At best" means empirically, under controlled conditions. CRHS is bound to yield biased conclusions, for your *considered* responses will depend on what you consider, including your philosophical theories.

11. Since you can't learn an infinite list, the corollary amounts to the claim that learnable languages must be *finite-based:* There must be a finite number of primitive terms, and a finite number of rules, such that learning the semantic value of each of the primitives, and learning the rules, allows one to generate the semantic value of any expression of the language. (See Davidson 1965.)

12. Or perhaps, whatever knowledge or misinformation in fact drives your use and understanding of 'elevators' and elevators. If it is mostly or all misinformation, perhaps we say you don't have the concept of an elevator. Or perhaps we say that everything you believe about elevators is wrong. In that case, we credit you with a frame whose semantic value is appropriate to 'elevator'. A consequence will be that whether you have the concept of an elevator will not depend on the psychological content of

the frame in question at all (or only minimally – perhaps it must be the frame accessed in response to encounters with 'elevators' if not to elevators).

13. By *knowledge I mean something that functions like knowledge, but needn't be true or justified or conscious.

14. This is harder than it sounds. Psychologists *seem* to acquiesce in the semantic individuation of beliefs, but they don't mean by *semantics* what philosophers (and some linguists) mean by *semantics*. When psychologists talk about semantics, they typically have in mind *how something is understood, what it means to the subject;* they don't have model–theoretic considerations in mind at all.

15. Perhaps there is a better way to characterize the proprietary goal of semantics, though I rather doubt it. What matters here, in any case, is just that semantics *has* a proprietary goal that is independent of psychology.

16. This is Fodor's point (in Fodor 1980).

17. Everyone has known for a long time that it doesn't work the other way: From the fact that p and q are the same proposition, it doesn't follow that the belief that p is the same as the belief that q.

18. A serious psychologist might, of course, be interested in how people conceive of belief. But (*i*) no serious psychologist would employ the method of reflective equilibrium in such an investigation (I hope), and (*ii*) no one in his right mind would suppose that the way to construct an important explanatory concept in science is to discover what the "ordinary concept" is.

5

Consciousness and Content

COLIN McGINN

Naturalism in the philosophy of mind is the thesis that every property of mind can be explained in broadly physical terms.[1] Nothing mental is physically mysterious. There are two main problems confronting a naturalistically inclined philosopher of mind. There is, first, the problem of explaining consciousness in broadly physical terms: In virtue of what does a physical organism come to have conscious states? And, second, there is the problem of explaining representational content – intentionality – in broadly physical terms: In virtue of what does a physical organism come to be intentionally directed towards the world? We want to know how consciousness depends upon the physical world; and we want to know, in natural physical terms, how it is that thoughts and experiences get to be *about* states of affairs. We want a naturalistic account of subjectivity and mental representation.[2] Only then will the naturalist happily accept that there are such things as consciousness and content.

Recent years have witnessed a curious asymmetry of attitude with respect to these two problems. Although there has been much optimism about the prospects of success in accounting for intentionality, pessimism about explaining consciousness has deepened progressively. We can, it is felt, explain what makes a mental state have the content it has; at least there is no huge barrier of principle in the way of our doing so. But, it is commonly conceded, we have no remotely plausible account of what makes a mental state have the phenomenological character it has; we don't even know where to start. Books and articles appear apace offering to tell us exactly what mental aboutness consists in, while heads continue to be shaken over the nature of consciousness. Indeed, standard approaches to content simply tend to ignore the problem of consciousness, defeatedly postponing it till the next century. True, there are those rugged souls who purport to see no difficulty of principle about consciousness; but among those who do appreciate the difficulty there coexists much optimism about content. This is curious because of the apparently intimate connexion

between consciousness and content: Intentionality is a property precisely of conscious states, and arguably only of conscious states (at
least originally). Moreover, the content of an experience (say) and its
subjective features are, on the face of it, inseparable from each other.
How then can we pretend that the two problems can be pursued quite
independently? In particular, how can we prevent justified pessimism
about consciousness spreading to the problem of content? If we cannot say, in physical terms, what makes it the case that an experience is
like something for its possessor, then how can we hope to say, in such
terms, what makes it the case that the experience is *of* something in
the world – since what the experience is like and what it is of are not,
prima facie, independent properties of the experience? That is the
question I shall be addressing in this paper.

I mean to be considering a broad family of naturalistic theories of
intentionality here; the tension just mentioned does not arise from
one sort of theory alone. There are currently a number of theories to
choose from: causal theories, functionalist theories, computational
theories, teleological theories.[3] Take any of these and ask yourself
whether that theory accounts satisfactorily for consciousness: Does it,
specifically, provide sufficient conditions for being in a conscious
state? If it does not, then the question must be faced how it can be an
adequate explanation of content *for* conscious states. Consider, for
instance, teleological theories (my own favourite). This type of theory
identifies the content of a mental state with (roughly) its world-
directed biological function. A desire state has a content involving
water, say, just if that state has the function of getting the organism to
obtain water. A perceptual experience represents squareness, say, just
if its function is to indicate (covary with) the presence of square things
in the environment. But now these contents serve to fix the phenomenological aspects of the states in question, what it is like subjectively to be in them; yet the theory itself seems neutral on the question
of consciousness. Certainly the teleological descriptions of the states
seem insufficient to confer conscious subjective features on them. *Any*
naturalistic theory of the kinds currently available looks to be inadequate as an account of what makes a mental state have a particular
conscious content, a specific phenomenology. Yet phenomenology
seems configured by content.[4]

This question is especially pressing for me, since I have come to
hold that it is literally impossible for us to explain how consciousness
depends upon the brain, even though it does so depend.[5] Yet I also
believe (or would like to believe) that it is possible for us to give
illuminating accounts of content.[6] Let me explain briefly my reasons

for holding that consciousness systematically eludes our understanding. Noam Chomsky distinguishes between what he calls 'problems' and 'mysteries' that confront the student of mind.[7] Call that hopeful student *S*, and suppose *S* to be a normal intelligent human being. Chomsky argues that *S*'s cognitive faculties may be apt for the solution of some kinds of problem but radically inadequate when it comes to others. The world need not in all of its aspects be susceptible of understanding by *S*, though another sort of mind might succeed where *S* constitutionally fails. *S* may exhibit, as I like to say, *cognitive closure* with respect to certain kinds of phenomena: Her intellectual powers do not extend to comprehending these phenomena, and this as a matter of principle.[8] When that is so, Chomsky says that the phenomena in question will be a perpetual mystery for *S*. He suspects that the nature of free choice is just such a mystery for us, given the way our intellects operate. That problem need not, however, be intrinsically harder or more complex than other problems we can solve; it is just that our cognitive faculties are skewed away from solving it. The structure of a knowing mind determines the scope *and limits* of its cognitive powers. Being adept at solving one kind of problem does not guarantee explanatory omniscience. Human beings seem remarkably good (surprisingly so) at understanding the workings of the physical world – matter in motion, causal agents in space – but they do far less well when it comes to fathoming their own minds. And why, in evolutionary terms, should they be intellectually equipped to grasp how their minds ultimately operate?

Now I have come to the view that the nature of the dependence of consciousness on the physical world, specifically on the brain, falls into the category of mysteries for us human beings, and possibly for all minds that form their concepts in ways constrained by perception and introspection. Let me just summarise why I think this; a longer treatment would be needed to make the position plausible. Our concepts of the empirical world are fundamentally controlled by the character of our perceptual experience and by the introspective access we enjoy to our own minds. We can, it is true, extend our concepts some distance beyond these starting points, but we cannot prescind from them entirely (this is the germ of truth Kant recognised in classical empiricism). Thus, our concepts of consciousness are constrained by the specific form of our own consciousness, so that we cannot form concepts for quite alien forms of consciousness possessed by other actual and possible creatures.[9] Similarly, our concepts of the body, including the brain, are constrained by the way we perceive these physical objects; we have, in particular, to conceive of them as spatial entities essentially similar to other physical objects in space, however inappropriate this manner of conception may be for understanding how consciousness arises from the brain.[10] But now these two forms of conceptual closure operate to prevent us from arriving at concepts for the property or relation that intelligibly links consciousness to the brain. For, first, we cannot grasp other forms of consciousness, and so we cannot grasp the theory that explains these other forms: That theory must be general, but *we* must always be parochial in our conception of consciousness. It is as if we were trying for a general theory of light but could only grasp the visible part of the spectrum. And, second, it is precisely the perceptually controlled conception of the brain that we have which is so hopeless in making consciousness an intelligible result of brain activity. No property we can ascribe to the brain on the basis of how it strikes us perceptually, however inferential the ascription, seems capable of rendering perspicuous how it is that damp grey tissue can be the crucible from which subjective consciousness emerges fully formed. That is why the feeling is so strong in us that there has to be something *magical* about the mind–brain relation. There must *be* some property of the brain that accounts nonmagically for consciousness, since nothing in nature happens by magic, but no form of inference from what we perceive of the brain seems capable of leading us to the property in question. We must therefore be getting a partial view of things. It is as if we were trying to extract psychological properties themselves from our awareness of mere physical objects; or again, trying to get normative concepts from descriptive ones. The problem is not that the brain lacks the right explanatory property; the problem is that this property does not lie along any road we can travel in forming our concepts of the brain. Perception takes us in the wrong direction here. We feel the tug of the occult because our methods of empirical concept formation are geared towards properties of kinds that cannot in principle solve the problem of how consciousness depends upon the brain. The situation is analogous to the following possibility: that the ultimate nature of matter is so different from anything we can encounter by observing the material world that we simply cannot ever come to grasp it. Human sense organs are tuned to certain kinds of properties the world may instantiate, but it may be that the theoretically basic properties are not ones that can be reached by starting from perception and workings outwards; the starting point may point us in exactly the wrong direction. Human reason is not able to travel unaided in just any theoretical direction, irrespective of its basic input. I think that honest reflection strongly suggests that nothing *we* could ever empirically discover about the brain *could* provide a fully satisfying account of consciousness. We will either find that the properties we encounter are altogether on the wrong track or we shall illicitly project traits of mind into the physical basis.[11] In particular, the essentially spatial conception we have, so suitable for making sense of the nonmental properties of the brain, is inherently incapable of removing the sense of magic we have about the fact that consciousness depends upon the brain. We need something radically different from this but, given the way we form our concepts, we cannot free ourselves of the conceptions that make the problem look insoluble. Not only, then, is it *possible* that the question of how consciousness arises from the physical world cannot be answered by minds constructed as ours are, but there is also strong positive reason for supposing that this is actually the case. The centuries of failure and bafflement have a deep source: the very nature of our concept-forming capacities. The mind–body problem is a 'mystery' and not merely a 'problem'.

The foregoing is only intended to provide a flavour of the reasons I would give for abject pessimism over the problem of consciousness. My question in this essay concerns the consequences of such pessimism for the problem of content. Must we suppose likewise that intentionality is closed to our theoretical understanding, that the correct naturalistic theory treats of properties that lie outside the area of reality we can comprehend? Or is there some way to stop the mystery of consciousness spreading to content? Before considering some possible suggestions on how to contain the mystery, let me focus the tension a bit more sharply.

Consider conscious perceptual experiences, such as my now seeing a scarlet sphere against a blue background. We can say, following Thomas Nagel and others, that there is something it is like to have such experiences; they have a subjective aspect.[12] That is to say, there is something it is like *for the subject* of such experiences: Subjective aspects of experience involve a reference to the subject undergoing the experience – this is what their *subject*ivity consists in. But we can also say that perceptual experiences have a world-directed aspect: They present the world in a certain way, say as containing a scarlet sphere against a blue background. This is their representational content, what states of affairs they are *as of*. Thus perceptual experiences are Janus-faced: They point outward to the external world but they also present a subjective face to their subject; they are of something other than the subject and they are like something for the subject. But these two faces do not wear different expressions: for what the experience is like is a function of what it is of, and what it is of is a function of what it is like. Told that an experience is as of a scarlet sphere you know what it is like to have it; and if you know what it is like to have it, then you know how it represents things. The two faces are, as it were, locked together. The subjective and the semantic are chained to each other. But then it seems that any conditions necessary and sufficient for the one aspect will have to be necessary and sufficient for the other. If we discover what gives an experience the (full) content it has, then we will have discovered what gives it its distinctive phenomenology; and the other way about.

But now we are threatened with the following contraposition: Since we cannot give a theory of consciousness, we cannot give a theory of content, since to give the latter would *be* to give the former (at least in the case of conscious experiences). Accordingly, theories of content are cognitively closed to us: We cannot say in virtue of what an experience has the content it has. Suppose, for example, that we favoured some sort of causal theory of perceptual content: Content is fixed by regular causal connexions between experiences and properties instantiated in the surrounding world, say being scarlet or spherical.[13] Such causal facts would be deemed sufficient for having the kind of content in question. But if this content fixes the subjective side of the experience – what it is like for the subject – then we are committed, it seems, to holding that such causal facts are sufficient for this subjective side also. For what fixes content fixes qualia. But these causal conditions seem manifestly *in*sufficient for subjectivity, intuitively, and the claim contradicts the closure I said I concede. Intentionality has a first-person aspect, and this seems impossible to capture in the naturalistic terms favoured by causal theories and their ilk.[14] If consciousness is a mystery, then so must its content be. So the challenge runs.

How, if at all, can we escape this argument? One response would be not to try: Accept that intentionality is inexplicable by us but insist that it is not inherently mysterious or inconsistent with what we know of the physical world. This would be to extend to content the treatment I would propose for consciousness. About consciousness I would say that there is no objective miracle in how it arises from the brain; it only seems to us that there is because of the veil imposed by cognitive closure. We project our own limitations onto nature, thus making nature appear to contain supernatural facts. In reality, there is no metaphysical mind–body problem; there is no *ontological* anomaly, only an epistemic hiatus. The psychophysical nexus is no more intrinsically mysterious than any other causal nexus in the body, though it will always strike *us* as mysterious. This is what we can call a 'nonconstructive' solution to the problem of how consciousness is possible. But if that solution removes the basic philosophical problem, as I think it does, then we can say the same about intentionality. We do not need to be able to produce a constructive solution to Brentano's Problem in order to convince ourselves that there is no inherent mystery in the phenomenon of intentionality; we can rest secure in the knowledge that *some* property of the physical world explains that phenomenon in an entirely natural way – though we cannot ever discover what that property is.[15] To the omniscient intellect of God intentionality in a physical organism is no more remarkable than digestion is. Thus there is no pressure towards eliminativism about content arising from the fact that *we* can never make content (physically) comprehensible to ourselves; any more than a minded creature who is constitutionally unable to grasp the correct theory of digestion has to deny that anything ever gets digested. So we can, according to this response, solve the philosophical problem of intentionality without actually *specifying* the correct theory.

I do not think this nonconstructive response can be rejected on general grounds, since I believe it applies to the case of consciousness. But I think it is implausibly extreme in the case of content; for we can, I believe, produce naturalistic theories of content that provide substantial illumination as to its workings. It is not as if the theories now available strike us as just hopelessly misguided, as telling us nothing whatever about the nature of intentionality, whereas I do think that the usual theories of consciousness (*e.g.,* functionalism) do not even begin to make a dent in our incomprehension. Thus it seems to me that teleological theories, in particular, promise to shed a good deal of light on the roots of intentionality; they provide real insight. Who can deny that the vast amount of work devoted to the nature of reference and belief in the last twenty or so years has added significantly to our understanding of their nature? Something, I venture to suggest, has been learned. So it cannot be that the whole nature of intentionality is hidden from us, that we simply cannot form the kinds of concepts that would shed light on it. The question is how to square this apparent illumination with extreme pessimism about consciousness. How is such illumination *possible,* given that we are completely in the dark about consciousness?

At this point it is natural to pin one's hopes on what I shall call the 'insulation strategy'. The insulation strategy proposes radically to separate the two theories: In particular, it proposes to do the theory of content in complete isolation from the theory of consciousness. How might this insulation of theories be made plausible? The obvious first move is to switch theoretical attention to (so-called) subpersonal content, the kind that exists without benefit of consciousness. We attribute content of a sort to machines and to subconscious processes in the nervous system; and this kind of content might be thought to be explicable without bringing in consciousness. It is true that content is also possessed by conscious states, but this is only a contingent truth about content, a dispensable accretion. Then, once we have a theory for subpersonal content, we can extend it to conscious content, simply by adding in the fact that the content is conscious. In principle, this strategy insists, the conditions necessary and sufficient for content are *neutral* on the question whether the bearer of the content happens to be a conscious state. Indeed, the very same range of contents that are possessed by conscious creatures could be possessed by creatures without a trace of consciousness. Consciousness is simply a further fact, superadded; it is not itself in any way constitutive of content. This contingency claim might then be bolstered by the consideration that the outstanding problem in the naturalistic theory of content – namely, accounting for the possibility of error or misrepresentation – does not seem to require invoking consciousness: It is not the fact that a state is conscious that makes it susceptible to error and hence semantic evaluation. We do not ascend from mere natural indication or nomic dependence to full-blown truth and falsity by ensuring that there is something it is like to be in the state in question. Subjectivity is not what creates the possibility of error. Hence subjective features lie quite outside the proper domain of the theory of content.

There are two problems with this suggestion. The first is tactical: We do not want the possibility of a theory of content to depend upon the particular conception of the relation between content and consciousness that the suggestion assumes. One view, by no means absurd, is that *all* content is originally of conscious states. There is no (underivative) intentionality without consciousness. (Brentano's thesis was that all consciousness is intentional; this 'converse Brentano thesis' is that all intentionality is conscious – or somehow derivative from consciousness.) Our attributions of content to machines and cerebral processes is, on this view, dependent or metaphorical or instrumental; there would be no content in a world without consciousness. Accordingly, we labour under an illusion if we think we can *complete* the theory of content without even mentioning that contentful states are associated with consciousness. There is no ofness without likeness. When we think we are conceiving of content in the absence of consciousness we are really treating a system *as if* it were conscious, while simultaneously denying that this is what we are up to.

Now, it is not that I myself agree with this extreme thesis of dependence; I have yet to see a convincing argument for the claim that any kind of representation worthy of the name requires consciousness. But I would agree that the possibility of subpersonal content of *some* kind does not serve to insulate the two theories when it comes to the kind of content distinctively possessed by conscious states. And this brings us to the second point. There may indeed be two species of content, personal and subpersonal, but this does not show that the personal kind lacks distinctive properties that tie it essentially to consciousness. I doubt that the selfsame *kind* of content possessed by a conscious perceptual experience, say, could be possessed independently of consciousness; such content seems essentially conscious, shot through with subjectivity. This is because of the Janus-faced character of conscious content: It involves presence to the subject, and hence a subjective point of view. Remove the inward-looking face and you remove something integral – what the world *seems* like to the subject. Just as there are two types of 'meaning', natural and nonnatural, so there seem to be two types of content, conscious and nonconscious; the subjective perspective creates, as it were, a new and special kind of content. This is why what an experience is as of already contains a phenomenological fact – how the subject is struck in having the experience. So we cannot hope to devise an exhaustive theory of the nature of conscious content while remaining neutral on whether such content is conscious. Content distinctions confer subjective distinctions. Experiential content is essentially phenomenological.

I suspect that the insulation strategy is fueled by a conception of consciousness that we can call the 'medium conception': Consciousness is to its content what a medium of representation is to the message it conveys. Compare sentences, spoken or written. On the one hand, there is their sound or shape (the medium); on the other, their meaning, the proposition they express. We can readily envisage separate studies of these two properties of a sentence, neither presupposing the other. In particular, we could have a theory of the content of sentences that was neutral as to their sound or shape. The meaning could vary while the sound or shape stayed constant, and there could be variations in sound or shape unaccompanied by variations in meaning. Message and medium can vary along independent dimensions. Suppose, then, that we try to think of perceptual experience in this way: Subjective features are analogous to the sound or shape of the sentence, content to its meaning. The content is *expressed* in a particular conscious medium but we can in principle separate the properties of the medium from the message it carries. What it is like to have the experience is thus fixed by intrinsic features of the medium, whereas what the experience is about is fixed by certain extrinsic relations to the world. According to this conception, then, the absolute intractability of consciousness need not infect the theory of content in the slightest. Consciousness is to be conceived, in effect, as a mysterious medium in which something relatively mundane is (contingently) embedded.

I think the medium conception is the kind of view which, once clearly articulated, sheds whatever attractions it may have initially possessed. In effect, it tries to treat perceptual experience as if its phenomenology were analogous to that of (nonrepresentational) bodily sensations: Content comes from subtending this intrinsic phenomenology with causal or other relations to the world, these relations being strictly orthogonal to that intrinsic phenomenology. Or, again, it tries to conceive of experiential content as if it operated like truth or veridicality: Whether a belief is true or an experience veridical is not a phenomenological property of the state in question, so that any theory of what confers these properties need not encroach on consciousness itself. A causal account of veridicality, for example, is not, and is not intended as, an account of what gives an experience the representational *content* it has (what it is as of). *If* we could think of content itself as lying in this way 'outside' of phenomenology, then we could indeed insulate the two theories. But, as I have insisted, this attempted extrusion of the subjective from the semantic just does not work. The content of an experience simply does contribute to what it is like to have it, and indeed it is not at all clear that anything else does.

A visual experience, for example, presents the world to the subject in specific ways, as containing spatially disposed objects of various shapes and colours, and this kind of 'presentation-to' is constitutive of what it is like to have visual experience. It is true, of course, that different sense modalities may present the same kinds of environmental feature (*e.g.*, shape or texture – as with sight and touch), but the subjectively distinct experiences that present these features also present *other* features. It is not that sight and touch present precisely the *same* range of features yet differ phenomenologically, so that we need something like a medium conception to capture the difference; it is rather that they overlap in the features they present at certain points but are disjoint at others – notably, in the secondary qualities they present. These differences in the range of contents available to different types of experience seem enough to capture the *obvious* phenomenological differences in the experiences associated with different senses. Bats perceive different secondary qualities from us when they employ their echolocation sense; it is not that they perceive precisely the same qualities and embed them in a different (nonrepresentational) medium. But even if there were subjective distinctions that could not be captured in terms of distinctions of content, this would not help the insulation strategy, since there are too many subjective distinctions that *are* generated by distinctions of content. The difference between a visual experience of red and a visual experience of green just is a difference in what it is like to have these two types of experience. The case is quite unlike the difference between a veridical and an hallucinatory experience, or a true belief and a false one. Content, we might say, is *internal* to phenomenology; the link here is anything but contingent.

If this is right, then we cannot suppose that the theory of content has nothing to do with the nature or constitution of consciousness. Since distinctions of content can constitute (or contribute towards) distinctions of phenomenology, we cannot totally insulate the theory of the former from the theory of the latter; we must admit that a correct theory of content will deliver resources sufficient to capture subjective features of conscious states. But if we are convinced that no naturalistic theory of the kinds available to us can explain conscious features, then we are again in a state of tension. Either we can explain features of consciousness ('qualia') naturalistically or we can't explain content naturalistically. The fate of the one theory seems yoked to the fate of the other. Yet I, for one, would like to believe that we can make progress with content, while accepting that consciousness is beyond us. Where then can I turn to have this tension relieved?

Instead of attempting to insulate the two theories entirely, I want to suggest that we limit the scope of the theory of content. We should accept that there is a part or aspect of intentionality that our theories do not and probably cannot capture, but we should also hold that there is a part or aspect that they do have some prospect of illuminating. There is *partial* cognitive closure with respect to content: We can naturalise certain properties of the total phenomenon but we cannot naturalise all of its properties (though, as I said earlier, all properties are in themselves entirely natural). And this will imply that there are *some* features of consciousness – subjective features – that we can treat naturalistically. There is a feasible branch of the theory of content that delivers an account of certain phenomenological facts: but this falls short of a full explanation of conscious intentionality.

Let me distinguish two questions. The first is the question of what *individuates* contents: What accounts for identity and difference between contents, what makes a content of this rather than that. We classify experiences according to what they represent, and the question is what principles underlie these classifications. The second question concerns the *nature* of content: What it consists in for a creature to have intentional states at all, what makes a creature enjoy 'directedness' onto the world in the first place. Thus, we can ask what natural facts make a creature an intentional being, and then we can ask what natural facts *target* this intentionality in specific ways. The question of nature is the more fundamental question: It asks what this directedness, grasping, apprehension, encompassing, reaching out ultimately consists in. It wants to know by virtue of what natural facts the mind is endowed with the power to 'point' beyond itself. The question of individuation takes this for granted and enquires how the intentional capacity picks up the particular objects and properties it does. *Given* that consciousness has the power to 'lasso' things in the world, what determines the direction of its throw? Putting it in terms of linguistic intentionality or reference: We can ask what makes a physical organism capable of referring (the act itself), and we can ask how it is that this act is tied down to particular objects and properties. "What is reference?" is one question; "How does reference get targeted this way rather than that?" is another question.

Now, assuming this distinction is sufficiently clear, I can state my proposal: The *nature* of intentionality is cognitively closed to us but the *individuation* of intentional contents is in principle open. We can say what makes a content of this rather than that but we cannot say what the relation of intentionality itself consists in. We cannot specify, in naturalistic (*i.e.*, broadly physical) terms, the essential nature of the conscious mental act of apprehending states of affairs, but we can say in such terms what distinguishes one such act from another. Let me now try to defend this proposal. First I will explain why the proposal is consistent. Then I will defend the pessimistic part of the proposal. Finally I will urge a qualified optimism about the question of content individuation.

The proposal is consistent because we do not need to fathom the nature of the intentional *act* in order to provide constraints on the identity conditions of instances of the act. I can tell you what distinguishes referring to redness from referring to greenness without being able to tell you what referring is *au fond*. The direction of reference may be constrained by relations with which reference itself cannot literally be *identified*. An analogy from action theory may help here. We can ask what distinguishes different kinds of world-directed bodily action without asking what the nature of intentional action in general is. Thus I can tell you what distinguishes intentionally kicking a brick from intentionally kicking a cat – there are different objects on the end of my toe – without having to explain what intentional action is in general. Consider, then, causal theories of mental aboutness. I can tell you, in terms of causal history, what distinguishes thinking about London from thinking about New York – there are different cities at the causal origin of these thoughts – without having to venture on the question of what, to start with, mental aboutness is.

The causal relations in question make these thoughts home in on certain objects, but we do not need to infer that mental aboutness is reducible to these relations. I don't have to be able to explain or analyse the act of grasping itself in order to be able to lay down laws that fix *what* is grasped. I don't have to be able to provide a naturalistic account of the intentional *structure* of consciousness in order to be in a position to pin down what gives that structure the specific content it has. Specific content is, as it were, the 'logical product' of the intentional capacity and the natural relations that target that capacity in particular ways; the capacity is not reducible to the relations. In view of this distinction of questions, we have to be very careful when we offer what we are pleased to call a 'theory of intentionality/reference'. Suppose we favour causal theories of perceptual content: Content is individuated by regular causal links between experiences and properties instantiated in the subject's environment. It is tempting to suggest that such links give us the very nature of perceptual representation, that the conscious act of enjoying an experience, as of a scarlet sphere against a blue background, is analysable as a special kind of causal relation. But, if I am right, this is not what we should say. Rather, we should say that causal relations tie the intentional structure of perceptual experience down to specific states of affairs but that such relations do not constitute the very nature of that structure. Intentional directedness is not exhaustively analysable as a causal relation, however complex; and similarly for teleological theories. Neither do we need to suppose this in order to find a point for naturalistic theories of content; we need rather to locate their legitimate area of application some way short of a full account of what it is to stand in intentional relations to things.

The pessimism about the essential nature of intentionality can be motivated in two ways. First we can simply deduce it from pessimism about consciousness: If consciousness cannot be explained (by us) naturalistically, in broadly physical terms, then neither can the constitutive structures of consciousness. The intentionality of experiences and thoughts belongs with the subjective 'feel' of sensations: Neither admits of objective physical explanation. But, second, we can also generate a mood of pessimism more directly: We can ask ourselves whether it really seems plausible that any of the standard theories capture the complete nature of conscious intentionality. In the case of sensations, we have a strong sense that standard naturalistic theories (*e.g.,* reductive functionalism) omit something essential – the 'feel' of the sensation. And I think our intuitions about intentionality parallel our intuitions about sensations: It really does seem that causal or teleological theories omit something essential in the intentional relation as it occurs in consciousness. They do not capture that phenomenological feature we describe (somewhat metaphorically) as grasping, apprehending, reaching out, taking in, and so forth.

There is an *internality* about the relation between an experience and its object that seems hard to replicate in terms of 'external' causal or teleological relations. Presence *to* the subject of the object of his experience seems not exhaustively explicable in terms of such natural relations. These kinds of relations hold, after all, between all sorts of things, not just brains and items in their environment, and it seems unsatisfactory to try to assimilate conscious intentional directedness to these ordinary relations. Conscious intentionality is more special than this sort of account suggests. (This is, of course, why Brentano claimed that intentionality is what distinguishes minds from mere physical objects.) Naturalistic theories fail to do justice to the *uniqueness* of conscious intentionality. Nothing we know about the brain, including its relations to the world, seems capable of rendering unmysterious the capacity of conscious states to 'encompass' external states of affairs.[16] I think this is a very primitive intuition, by which I suspect many of us have been struck at some point in our philosophical lives. How *can* our minds reach out to the objects of experience? What is it about our brains, and their location in the world, that could possibly explain the way consciousness *arcs out* into the world? Consciousness seems to extend an invisible hand into the world it represents (if I may put it so): How on earth could my *brain* make that possible? No ethereal prehensile organ protrudes from my skull! Phenomenologically, we feel that the mind 'lays hold' of things out there, mentally 'grasps' them, but we have no physical model of what this might consist in. We flounder in similes. It is precisely our perplexity about this question that makes it seem to us that there could be a creature whose brain had all the same natural properties and relations as ours and yet enjoyed no such conscious arcing out. For none of the natural properties and relations we come across seems to add up to what we know from the first-person point of view of conscious aboutness. It is thus reasonable to suspect that cognitive closure is operative here. Somehow we are not keyed in to the kinds of natural fact that actually underlie intentionality – as we are not to consciousness in general. Something about our makeup explains how consciousness can reach out into the world in the way it does, but we seem constitutionally blind to what that something is.

Cautious optimism is possible, however, since we do not need to explain everything about intentionality in order to be able to say something illuminating about it. And I think it is undeniable that illuminating things have been said about content in recent years; all is not darkness. Teleological theories, in particular, seem to me to contain valuable insights. The question is *what*, precisely, has been illuminated. And my suggestion is that these naturalistic theories should be seen as contributions to the individuation conditions of mental states: They tell us what differentiates one kind of intentional state from another; they tell us how intentional states collect their specific content.

They may also tell us something about the natural antecedents of conscious intentionality – what basic natural relations got transformed by consciousness into genuine content. First there were preconscious states with certain functions relating them to things in the world; then consciousness built upon this natural foundation to produce the intentional relation. The 'intentional arc' is not reducible to this foundation but it takes its rise from it. So there is room for naturalistic speculation about where intentionality came from, if not what it ultimately consists in. We can pursue these more modest questions without having to take on the full explanatory task of reducing intentionality to something we can understand, something broadly physical. In fact, something like this perspective is already implicit in much work on reference and content. It is not invariably assumed that causal theories (say) give us the real nature of the reference relation, that they successfully analyse the capacity to refer; rather, they tell us how that capacity gets targeted, what constrains the direction of acts of reference.[17] So we can be grateful for this kind of illumination without insisting that it be spread across the whole phenomenon.

Yet there is a residual puzzle. We have resisted the insulation strategy, arguing that content colours consciousness. Differences of content do determine differences of subjectivity, ofness fixes likeness. But this staining of subjectivity by reference does imply that we can provide a naturalistic theory of subjective distinctions, since we can say in naturalistic terms what individuates the content of experience. Here we have an objective handle onto the constitution of the subjective. An experience as of a red square thing is subjectively distinct from an experience as of a green triangular thing, in virtue of the fact that different kinds of objects are represented; and this distinction can be captured, we have agreed, in terms of natural relations that these experiences stand in to the properties represented – say, teleological relations. So it looks as though we are committed to accounting for *some* features of consciousness naturalistically; not *all* phenomenological facts are closed to us. I think this does indeed follow: There are some features of consciousness whose natural explanation, in broadly physical terms, is in principle available to us.

Our concept-forming capacities afford us partial access to the natural basis of these subjective features of consciousness. But this is puzzling because one would expect the closure to be total: How can it be impossible for us to explain how consciousness arises from the physical world and yet not so very difficult to account naturalistically for distinctions *within* consciousness? Why should the general phenomenon of consciousness be so recalcitrant to natural explanation while specific determinations of consciousness yield to naturalistic account? It's puzzling. Even where consciousness is not mysterious it is mysterious why it is not mysterious!

This puzzle should be set beside another. A moderate externalist about content will hold that objective properties (*e.g.*, being square) enter into the identity of contentful states; they occur as 'constituents' of content.[18] Thus objective properties penetrate experiences in ways that fix their phenomenology. Again, the subjective is invaded by the objective. Combining this act of colonisation with the previous one we get a double dependence of the subjective on the objective: Objective items figure as 'constituents' of subjective states, so shaping their phenomenology, *and* these states collect those objective 'constituents' by way of objective natural relations – say, biological function. What now begins to look mysterious is the way consciousness is so resistant to objective physical reduction and yet is so permeated by the objective and physical. Consciousness, as it were, appropriates the objective while holding itself aloft from it; it takes the physical in but it refuses to be ruled by it. And, oddly enough, it is just this capacity to 'incorporate' the physically objective, to bring it within consciousness, that the physical brain seems so inadequate to do.[19] The puzzles multiply. But then the more you think about consciousness the more puzzling it comes to seem. It is comforting to reflect that from God's point of view (*i.e.*, the point of view of Nature), there is no inherent mystery about consciousness at all. The impression of mystery derives from our own incurable cognitive poverty, not from the objective world in which consciousness exists. There is no real magic in the link between mind and matter, however incapable we are of seeing how the trick is performed. Cold comfort, perhaps, but whoever said that the nature of the mind should be fully accessible to those with a mind?

Some may be inclined to draw a different lesson from the foregoing reflections. They may point out that the notions of consciousness and content come from our commonsense psychology, the kind of psychology we employ before we start to get scientifically serious about the mind and behaviour. The right conclusion, accordingly, is that this prescientific psychology deserves repudiation, since it carries with it notions that resist explanation – notions that cannot be accounted for within any science we can grasp. The case is like primitive animism, it may be said. Certainly it will prove forever impossible for us to explain how spirits can inhabit rocks and lightning and earthquakes, but that is simply because the whole idea of such inspirited matter is a huge illusion, crying out for elimination. It would be silly to claim that animism should be persisted in, despite this problem of explanation, on the ground that there exists some unknowable science that makes sense of what *we* cannot make sense of. Or, closer to home, consciousness and content may be compared to the folk-psychological notion of free will, which arguably harbours incoherencies: Just as the idea of free will deserves elimination on account of its inexplicability, so those other two notions should also be sent packing. If we stick to talk of neural states and behaviour in our theorising, then we will not be presented with these insolubilities. Why saddle ourselves with commonsense notions, inherited from the dark ages, which refuse to fit into our scientific worldview? Thus the argument of the present paper should be seen as a *reductio* of the commitments of folk psychology, a reason to cancel those commitments and start afresh.

This radical eliminativist response to the kinds of cognitive closure I have urged raises large questions, which it would be out of place to consider fully here. Let me just make a few brief remarks. First, it seems to me quite wrong, on metaphysical grounds, to jump from cognitive closure to eliminativism: That is just antirealism in another guise. We must not infer unreality from inexplicability by us (which is to be distinguished from demonstrable incoherence by us). Indeed, a properly naturalistic theory of our knowledge-forming capacities requires precisely that we not make that jump. Second, the phenomena of consciousness and content have the status, I would say, of *data;* they are not mere posits we are at liberty to replace with more useful posits. To reject them would be like rejecting our perceptual data with respect to the physical world: not perhaps utterly inconceivable but certainly not to be undertaken lightly. Rejecting the data is a sure sign of avoiding the problem. Third, it is a mistake to think that cognitive closure is an affliction only of common sense, as if it could not arise from notions employed in accredited scientific theories. So we cannot rule out the possibility of such closure simply by banning common sense. Closure is not what demarcates nonscience (or nonsense) from science (or sense). On the contrary, one of the areas in which the possibility of cognitive closure looks most real is theoretical physics – quantum theory and the origin of the universe being the standard examples. The more advanced a theory becomes the more likely it is to approach the limits of what we can know. In general, there is no good reason to assume that every scientific theory we can grasp treats only of facts and properties we can explain. We have sophisticated theories that postulate the existence of certain kinds of particle, but it is not thereby guaranteed that we can explain how these particles came into being in the first place. (Compare the origin of consciousness.) Fourth, it is inadvisable to eliminate that which performs a useful explanatory role, even if it in turn raises problems of explanation. I think the notions of content and consciousness do figure usefully in psychological explanations of behaviour, so that rejecting them would be giving up something valuable. Something can explain without itself being explicable (by us). The right conclusion, then, is that commonsense psychology is indeed not fully naturalisable by us, but that this is no reason to condemn it as just so much murky mythology.[20]

NOTES

1. This is the standard contemporary view of naturalism. (See, *e.g.*, Jerry Fodor, *Psychosemantics:* The MIT Press, Cambridge, Mass., 1987, Chapter 4.) I do not say that it is my view of what it takes to be a good naturalist. As will become clear, I think we can view the mind naturalistically without being able to offer broadly physical explanations of its powers. (I say "broadly physical" in order to include biological properties and higher-order causal properties, as well as the properties directly treated in physics.) An alternative way of putting the naturalistic demand is this: Explain *why* it is that the mental is supervenient on the physical, given that it is. The general motive behind such naturalism is the avoidance of some sort of radical 'emergence' of the mental with respect to the physical. See

Thomas Nagel, "Panpsychism," *Mortal Questions:* Cambridge University Press, 1979, on why emergence is to be avoided.

2. A third, and connected, problem is explaining how a physical organism can be subject to the norms of rationality. How, for example, does *modus ponens* get its grip on the causal transitions between mental states? This question is clearly connected with the question about intentionality, since rationality (as we ordinarily understand it) requires intentionality (the converse thesis is less obvious). But it is not so clear how closely connected are the problems of rationality and consciousness: Can the former exist without the latter? If we find consciousness theoretically daunting (as I argue we should), then we should hope that rationality can be separated from it. There is a general question here: How much of the mind can be explained without being able to explain consciousness? This, as I suggest later, is the same as the question of how much of the mind can be explained.

3. For discussions of these approaches see: Jerry Fodor, *Psychosemantics:* The MIT Press, Cambridge, Mass., 1987; Fred Dretske, *Knowledge and the Flow of Information:* The MIT Press, Cambridge, Mass., 1981; Hilary Putnam, *Representation and Reality:* The MIT Press, Cambridge, Mass., 1988; Ruth Millikan, *Language, Thought, and Other Biological Categories:* The MIT Press, Cambridge, Mass., 1984; Colin McGinn, *Mental Content:* Basil Blackwell, Oxford, 1989.

4. My focus in this chapter is on the content of perceptual experiences, mental states for which the notion of a subjective phenomenology is best suited. But essentially the same questions arise for thoughts, mental states for which the notion of what it is like to have them seems strained at best (thoughts are not inherently 'qualia-laden'). Thoughts are conscious, of course, and the question of what confers this consciousness is equally pressing for them as it is for experiences. Moreover, the content of thoughts looks even more closely tied to their conscious features than in the case of experiences; so it is even harder to see how we could pull apart the theory of content for thoughts and the theory of what gives thoughts their conscious aspect. What more is there to the specific way a thought is present in the stream of consciousness than its having the particular content it has?

5. See my "Can We Solve the Mind–Body Problem?" *Mind,* April 1989.

6. See my *Mental Content:* Basil Blackwell, Oxford, 1989. The present chapter is an attempt to reconcile the optimism of that book with the pessimism of the paper cited in Note 5.

7. See his *Reflections on Language:* Pantheon Books, New York 1975, Chapter 4.

8. Cf. Fodor's notion of 'epistemic boundedness' in *The Modularity of Mind:* The MIT Press, Cambridge, Mass., 1983, Part 5.

9. Nagel discusses this in *The View from Nowhere:* Oxford University Press, 1986, Chapter 2.

10. That is, our natural perception-based sense of similarity underestimates the objective difference there must be between brains and other physical objects, if brains are to be (as they are) the basis of consciousness. To God, brains seem *sui generis*, startlingly different from other physical objects. God's sense of similarity, unlike ours, does justice to the uniqueness we know the brain must possess. (Compare the fallibility of our natural sense of similarity with respect to natural kinds.)

11. This latter tendency gives rise to illusions of understanding. We think we are seeing how consciousness depends upon the brain when all we are doing is reading consciousness into the physical basis. This tendency is particularly compelling when the brain is conceived as a computer: Thinking of neurons as performing computations, we are tempted to credit them with conscious states (or protoconscious states). Then it seems easy enough to see how neurons could generate consciousness. But, of course, this just pushes the question back (as well as being false): for how do these conscious properties of neurons arise from their physical nature? (Panpsychism now threatens.) If we are to describe physical processes computationally, then we must be clear that this does not involve consciousness — and then it will also be clear that we can't get consciousness out of such descriptions. Either we presuppose what we should be explaining or we find ourselves as far away as ever from our explanandum.

12. Thomas Nagel, "What Is It Like To Be a Bat?" in *Mortal Questions:* Cambridge University Press, New York, 1979; Brian Farrell, "Experience," *Mind,* 1950.

13. This kind of theory is defended by (among others) Tyler Burge, "Individualism and Psychology" in *Philosophical Review,* January 1986. I criticise such views in *Mental Content:* Basil Blackwell, Oxford, 1989.

14. Such theories stress the third-person perspective: how we determine what someone else is referring to or thinking about. But we must not forget the perspective of the subject: how she experiences the intentional directedness of her mental states. It is the same stress on the third-person perspective that makes the likes of functionalism about sensations seem more adequate than it ought to seem.

15. Here, then, is a possible response to Hartry Field's demand that truth and reference be reducible if they are to be respectable: see his "Mental Representation" in *Readings in Philosophy of Psychology,* Ned Block (ed.): Harvard University Press, Cambridge, Mass., 1981. We need to distinguish being able to *give* a reduction from knowing that a reduction *exists* — in order not to rule out the possibility that the reduction can be specified only in a science that is cognitively inaccessible to us. We cannot infer elimination from irreducibility *by us.* Nor can we simply *assume* that the correct naturalistic account of intentionality employs "broadly physical" notions, if this means that these notions do not extend our present physical concepts beyond what is intelligible to us. In a word, we must not be dogmatic conceptual conservatives. The correct reduction (if that is the

right word) might not be recognisable by us as correct. (I take this to be an expression of realism.)

16. Two thinkers who have recognised the mysterious-seeming nature of meaning and reference are Thomas Nagel and Ludwig Wittgenstein. Nagel draws attention to the way meaning seems to be able to 'take in' much more of the world than its basis in the particular doings and undergoings of speakers could permit: It can reach across vast stretches of space and time; it has a universality or generality that transcends the particular actions and experiences of speakers; it determines indefinitely many uses of language, past and future, as correct or incorrect. See his *What Does It All Mean?:* Oxford University Press, 1987, Chapter 5. Wittgenstein, for his part, speaks of "the mysterious relation of the object and its name," and he says of the "mental activities" of wishing and believing that "for the same reason [they] have something mysterious and inexplicable about them," in *The Blue and Brown Books:* Basil Blackwell, Oxford, 1958, pp. 172–3. Wittgenstein's idea, though, is that this sense of mystery arises from a (correctable) mistake: "A primitive philosophy condenses the whole usage of the name into the idea of a relation, which thereby becomes a mysterious relation" (p. 173). I am inclined to agree with him about the aura of mystery, but I doubt that it can be dispelled in the way he suggests, namely by reminding ourselves of how we actually use names or ascribe propositional attitudes. I don't think a deflationary response of this kind is adequate to the problem.

17. This seems the right way to interpret Saul Kripke's remarks about naming and reference in *Naming and Necessity:* Basil Blackwell, Oxford, 1980. Kripke disavows any intention of analysing or reducing the relation of reference, offering us only a 'picture' of how reference operates; but he does give us substantive constraints on *which* object is being referred to by the use of a name – the object which lies at the origin of the 'causal chain' of uses that historically lead up to the use in question. And there is nothing in the kind of closure I acknowledge to preclude descriptive work in the theory of reference: distinguishing the different kinds of referential device, articulating the modes of identification that underlie uses of these different devices, showing how sense and reference are related in different cases, and so forth. Nothing I say undermines the viability and usefulness of, say, Gareth Evans's work in *The Varieties of Reference:* Oxford University Press, 1982. What I am doubting is the possibility of a certain kind of explanatory enterprise: giving a broadly physical account of the very nature of the reference relation. We can prune the pretensions of causal theories (say) without declaring them completely out of a job.

18. For a discussion of this see my *Mental Content:* Basil Blackwell, Oxford, 1989. I set aside here the question of how secondary qualities enter into the content of experience. If these are subjectively constituted, then there is a sense in which the subjective gets turned back on itself when colours

(say) penetrate the content of colour experience. Still, colours are properties of external objects, so colour experience – like shape experience – does reach out to the world beyond the subject. (We may wonder whether the ultimate explanation of why we perceive secondary qualities at all is one of those questions about consciousness whose answer is forever closed to us. That would certainly account for my struggles to explain it in *The Subjective View:* Oxford University Press, 1983.)

19. Genuine externalism therefore requires us to reject the more obvious kinds of physicalism, since the brain cannot incorporate the external in the way the mind can. We have no physical model of how consciousness can lay hold of the physical world in the peculiar way it does.

20. I am grateful, for comments, to Thomas Nagel, Simon Blackburn, and various members of an Oxford discussion group.

6

The Inevitability of Folk
Psychology

ADAM MORTON

There are many things one can mean by folk psychology, and most of them exist. One can mean the characteristic commonsense *vocabulary* of mind: 'belief', 'desire', 'memory', 'fear', and so indefinitely on. One can mean explanatory *theories* of different degrees of generality, current in different cultures. One can mean the *beliefs* one forms about particular people at particular times. One can mean the *strategies* for forming beliefs, expressed in commonsense terms, which can be used in explaining people's actions. All of these have their place. I am particularly interested in the last of them, strategies. (Perhaps it is the only one whose existence could be seriously questioned!)

The important questions about all of these can be classified as semantical and syntactical. Semantical questions concern relations to nonconceptual things: Do vernacular psychological terms refer to real features of people? Are any of the theories true? Syntactical questions concern form and mental representation: Do we learn the theories one by one as part of our general wordly lore? Are the meanings of the terms represented by definitions in a language of thought or by some connectionist schema?

Semantical and syntactical questions interact. In particular the answers one gives to semantical questions about folk psychology partly determine which syntactical questions it makes sense to ask. Someone might, for example, deny that folk psychology involves any beliefs at all. (She might think it consists just of attitudes such as affection and fear.) Such a person would then also deny the intelligibility of questions about how much of folk psychology is true. That would be an extreme position. The position I shall be explaining in this chapter does take our commonsense understanding of mind to involve claims which can be true or false. I shall, however, discuss rather more subtle semantical questions than whether folk psychology "is" true or false. (In fact it seems to me just obvious that that is the wrong sort of question to ask.) The grand claim lying behind this chapter can be stated crudely as: Folk psychology is a very natural, perhaps an inevitable, device for understanding nervous systems like ours. In fact, it is a special case of a very sophisticated explanation-finding strategy, which is also used in recent attempts in physics to come to terms with chaos and other forms of inherent complexity. If one were designing a species like ours and at the same time were designing a mode of understanding for members of the species to use with respect to one another, one would choose something like the strategy underlying the vernacular psychologies of human cultures.

I will first argue for a semantical claim. It is, roughly, that we do not need to satisfy the assertions of any folk-psychological theory to be minds. Commonsense principles of mind can be false about us and yet we – and other creatures – can still fall under the concepts 'mind', 'sentient', and so on, which we grasp in part because we understand these commonsense principles. Then I shall argue for a syntactical claim. It is, roughly, that principles of practical reasoning or laws of the interaction of beliefs and desires are not central to folk psychology. In fact, the representation of states of mind as propositional attitudes is not really essential, though it is a very natural development from the core of folk psychology. Only at the end of the chapter, in explaining how these two claims support each other, will I relate them to the grand claim about the inevitability of folk psychology.

This chapter is divided into four parts. Part 1 gives a semantical theory. Part 2 describes an explanatory strategy, the Q strategy. It illustrates a possible relation between the semantics and the syntax of systems of concepts and is a model for the kind of strategy, the P strategy, I find in folk psychology. Part 3 describes the P strategy by giving a core syntax for folk psychology, in which practical reasoning and the interaction of beliefs and desires occupy at most a peripheral place. And Part 4 argues that the Q and P strategies are good ways of explaining the outputs of human nervous systems. The arguments in Parts 1, 2, and 3 are independent. Don't look for many connections with earlier parts while reading 2 and 3. Part 4 is meant to bring things together.

1.   Picking Out

Cause versus Function. Consider a family or network of concepts which are understood in part because we apply them to familiar standard examples and in part because of our grasp of a body of explanatory principles. The intended example is of course the concept network of belief, desire, memory, perception, and so on. But there is nothing atypical about it in this respect. Most concepts are understood in terms of a mixture of paradigm cases and explanatory theories.

If you concentrate just on the standard examples you are naturally led to a naively simple causal account of reference for the terms concerned. This is especially true when there is a class of standard examples specific to each concept (like the class of human beings for the concept of mind). Then one is tempted to say: Predicate P refers to things objectively like the standard examples. ('Objectively like' is the central unclear idea here. More about it below.) If, on the other hand, you concentrate just on the explanatory theory you naturally see the importance of the relations between the concepts in the theory, and are led to some sort of a functionalist account. This is especially true when the standard examples satisfy many concepts of the network simultaneously (as people's satisfaction of belief, desire, and memory are inseparable from one another). Then one is tempted to say: P refers to any property $P0$ for which there are other properties $P1, P2, \ldots, Pn$ such that $\text{Th}(P0, P1, P2, \ldots, Pn)$ is satisfied in the intended domain.

Naive causal semantics interprets each concept or predicate in isolation, and thus allows the extension of the predicate not to satisfy the associated theory. Functionalist semantics interprets each concept or predicate as a part of a network of concepts and thus insists that the associated theory be satisfied if the concept is to have an extension. Functionalist semantics are now standard for psychological concepts. The reason for their popularity is the recognition of the inevitable role of the connections between psychological concepts: You cannot attribute beliefs without attributing desires and memories, and vice versa. This organic feature seems obviously right to me. On the other hand the inviolability of the associated theory seems to me far from obvious. And so my first job is to show how you can have the organicity without the inviolability.

Referring versus Picking Out. Functionalist semantics are a special case of the Ramsey–Lewis technique.[1] In the general case we have a theory T involving predicates $P1, \ldots, Pn$, and a set S such that T is true when the predicates P_i are given particular subsets $S1, \ldots, Sn$ of S as extensions. Then each P_i *Ramsey-denotes* the corresponding S_i (with respect to S and T). Note that there may in general be more than one way of choosing subsets of S so as to satisfy T. The larger an S we choose, the more likely multiple possible instantiations of T are. Ramsey-denotation is a natural device to use because it enforces the interdependence of the P_i: Each Pi Ramsey-denotes the corresponding S_i only if all the remaining P_j can be given denotata which together with that for P_i enable T to be satisfied.

In looking for something more flexible let us stick to the raw materials of this account, a set of predicates P_i and a theory T directed at a set of sets of objects (or complex objects) S. I shall refer to members of

S as *systems*, as most of the relevant examples will be of physical or
dynamical or biological systems. (Think of the solar system or the
circulatory system.) Suppose also that there are (*a*) items of 'behavior'
of the systems, for example observable qualities of a class of dynamical systems or behavior of a species of living organism, (*b*) a predicate
Q expressing the sense 'system to which *T* applies', and (*c*) a class *C* of
systems among which the extension of *Q* is to be determined. If *T* is a
commonsense psychological theory and the P_i are its psychological
predicates then *Q* is 'is sentient' (or 'is/has a mind') and *C* is the class of
creatures, terrestrial and extraterrestrial, biological and artifactual
(that should cover it!), whose behavior invites psychological explanation.

The first task is to constrain the interpretation of *Q*. *Q* applies to
systems whose behavior *T* is trying to explain. *T* may present a mistaken explanation of this behavior, but the intention of *T* is to discuss
the processes which are responsible for the behavior of the given
systems. *Q* should therefore apply to most of the given systems – most
members of *S* – because they are taken to be explained by *T*. It should
also apply to other systems which are 'like' the standard examples in
S. Depending on the construal of 'like' this can result in various causal
construals of reference or, indeed, in the limit to a functionalist account. Let us introduce a relation of similarity, $\simeq$, to allow a first
semantical definition.

Q picks out a class of systems *D* if *D* is a subset of *C* and each system in
D bears $\simeq$ to some system in *S*.

There are many possibilities for $\simeq$. At one extreme $\simeq$ is total physical similarity (if that makes sense). Then *D* is a very tight natural kind
around *S*. $\simeq$ could more plausibly be a relation of biological or mechanical similarity. At the other extreme, $S \simeq S'$ when either *S* and *S'*
both satisfy *T* or both do not. Then *D* is either the set of models for *T*
or the null set. That sets the scene for functionalism.

The interesting cases are those between the extremes of total physical similarity and mutual satisfaction of *T*. Between these extremes
the relation $\simeq$ can depend on the theory *T* – and thus so can the
extension of *Q* – although not all members of *Q* satisfy *T*. In fact, this
possibility is already apparent in the case when $\simeq$ is biological similarity, since this is most naturally explained in terms which involve
some class of biological theories, which are probably false in detail.

Finding the right similarity relation is a large part of a semantical
characterization of a concept. Different relations are required for
proper names, species terms, substance words, artefact words, and so
on. And in all of these something playing the role of the theory *T*

appears. It is not the only factor, though. At least as important is the true nature of the set of standard examples. If, for example, they do not in fact form a biological kind then biological similarity is not the right relation. (Unless the list changes. Whales are exiled from fishery.) The standard examples must fit the similarity relation in two ways. *Homogeneity:* The standard examples must have common properties which make them fall into the same similarity class. *Appropriateness:* Some such common properties must be involved in a range of explanations of properties or behavior of the examples. (In effect, a similarity relation projects the examples to a larger class, that of all things picked out by the word in question. This larger class must have some explanatory usefulness.)

If homogeneity and appropriateness are not satisfied the predicate does not pick out any objective extension. (There may be a stable 'nonobjective extension' of things that people thinking that the conditions were satisfied would take the predicate to pick out.) Even given the restrictions of homogeneity and appropriateness there is a very great variety of similarity relations which can be used to project from any given set of examples, in particular the set of human beings. One way in which similarity relations vary is in their tightness: how much larger a class they project to. The functionalist intuition is that physical or biological similarity is too tight a relation. It forces possessors of mental attributes to be too similar to human beings. I share that intuition. Extreme functionalism construes similarity just in terms of satisfaction of a theory; just for want of a better idea, I suspect, since there are many workable nonextreme ways of projecting from S to D.

Predicates can be said to pick out extensions inasmuch as they sum up the general import of a network of concepts united by a theory. Concepts within the network are expressed by predicates which have rather less semantical individuality. Let us say that a predicate P_i is *dominated by* a predicate Q to the extent that P_i is understood as one of a number of predicates $P1, \ldots, Pn$ figuring in a theory whose intended application is expressed by Q. Then the *reference* of the whole sequence $P1, \ldots, Pn$ is that sequence of properties or sets which when taken as extensions for the P_j makes T most nearly true of the system picked out by the dominating predicate P.

Note the two evasions: "to the extent that" a predicate is understood as part of a network, and the reference which makes T "most nearly true." The second of these is inevitable when any account along anything like the Ramsey–Lewis lines is applied to a real theory and a real subject matter. I shall say nothing about it here, important though it is. But the first of them is central to my aims here. Most predicates are both embedded in theory-linked networks and have a semantical life of their own dominating other predicates. They are both P_i and Q. One reason is that there are hierarchies of theories, so that a predicate can be associated with two theories, as one among the predicates occurring in one theory and as defining the intended domain of another more general theory. An example might be 'massive object' in Newtonian mechanics, which is to be interpreted as required by its relation to other concepts of mechanics, but also as a particular term in a wider and vaguer implicit theory of physical objects. Another, not completely different, reason is that most real predicates both function as terms within theories and have independent ostensive or other connections with observed phenomena. For example perceptual terms in folk and scientific psychologies – 'see', 'pain' – are understood both as links in motivational and cognitive chains and also through our experience of seeing and hurting.

The result is that a predicate can be pulled in (at least) two semantical directions, which I have called picking out and reference. A predicate has a reference as one of the terms of a theory (or some other network of concepts) relative to the extension picked out by that theory. And it can itself pick out a class of instantiations relative to a set of standard examples and a similarity relation. (Usually a theory is involved here, too.) Since most of our theories are false the result is that very many of our predicates can be taken both as empty myths and as picking out wide and varied classes of objects. This is certainly true both of 'mind' and of the concepts it dominates, 'belief', 'desire', 'remembers' and the rest. Both the particular explanatory claims we make using these concepts, and the elusive deep network of concepts underlying them, are no doubt riddled with falsehoods. But that should not prevent them from picking out us and other actual and possible creatures as possessors of minds.

2.   The *Q* Strategy

Explanatory Strategies. The projection from S to D – from the set of standard examples to the set of systems picked out by a theory – depends on the similarity relation. In this part I want to say more about this relation. It is central to questions of what can be picked out as a mind and how the concepts of folk psychology can be said to apply to systems of which folk psychology is not literally true.

I shall discuss similarity relations (associated with predicates) in a rather more general context than that of particular explanatory theories (involving the predicates). I shall relate similarity relations to families of theories, in fact to what it is natural to call explanatory strategies. I shall discuss a particular explanatory strategy, found in a part of physics called qualitative mechanics, because it is a good example of an explanatory strategy, and one which defines a similarity relation between physically very different systems. Moreover I will argue in Part 3 that this explanatory strategy is not unlike that of folk psychology, so that we can take the right similarity relation to be, to a first approximation, the one given by qualitative mechanics. That will give some substance to the quasi-functionalist position I was sketching in Part 1.

Qualitative Mechanics. The physicists' strategy that I find exemplary began a century or so ago with some remarks of Maxwell's and with Poincaré's work on the mind–body problem. It has now developed into the study of chaotic systems and catastrophe theory, sometimes referred to jointly as qualitative mechanics.[2] Qualitative mechanics is founded on the realisation that even when one has a set of deterministic laws governing the development of a system its use for direct prediction and explanation is usually pretty limited. For the prediction of future states given earlier states, forces, and boundary conditions is usually beyond our capacities, even when the equations of motion can be solved. And very often the equations cannot be solved. There are two general ways of dealing with the situation. One, statistical mechanics, applies when the source of the difficulty is just the number of component subsystems and the complexity of their interactions. I shall not be concerned with it. The other strategy, that of qualitative mechanics, can apply to quite simple systems when the calculation of their later states from their initial states is practically impossible. (Sometimes, in fact, the calculation is more than just practically impossible, but beyond anything that a finite agent could perform.) Then, although exact later states cannot be deduced from earlier ones, useful properties of them can be determined. One can get a 'qualitative solution'.

There is now a standard strategy for getting such a qualitative solution. I shall call it the *Q strategy*. There are two parts to the *Q* strategy – I shall call them "dimension splitting" and "transition analogy" – linked by a very important and still somewhat mysterious fact. The first part, dimension splitting, consists in separating the relevant variables of the system into two classes, called *control parameters* and *state variables*. Heuristically, the control parameters change more slowly and predictably and influence the less-easily grasped evolution of the state variables. Then one looks for *attractors*. These are sets of values of the state variables to which the system will eventually gravitate: If the system begins in a given range of the state parameter, for suitable values of the control parameters, then it will eventually assume a value within one of the corresponding attractors. The route between initial state and attractor may be unpredictable, however, and the time to get there may vary unpredictably. Different control parameters may mean different attractors, and this fact leads to the central explanation-finding strategy. One tries to discover the range of attractors for each combination of values of the control parameters, and thus to discover the pattern of transitions between attractors as the control parameters are varied.

Some extremely simply physical systems cannot be understood simply by deducing their states at later times from their states at earlier times by deterministic laws, even though such laws exist. For example, a pendulum suspended from a point that is oscillated even very slightly follows a path which is in effect unpredictable. Arbitrarily small differences in initial conditions lead to great differences in the pendulum's state in a very short time. But the pendulum's behavior is quite nicely handled by the strategy of state variables, control parameters, and attractors. Given each range of frequencies of the point of suspension there is a set of stable patterns traced out by the pendulum bob (ellipses, figures of eight, and so on) into which the pendulum eventually settles. If the frequency is changed while the pendulum is in one stable pattern it will shift to a stable pattern appropriate to the new frequency. So by taking the frequency of the point of suspension as control parameter, the location of the bob as state parameter, and the regions of space occupied by the bob in finite periods of time as attractors we find that we have a manageable and useful account of the pendulum's behavior. But note that this account does not tell what course the pendulum will take between its starting point and its settling into the attractor, nor how long it will take to get there, nor which among the permissible attractors it will settle into.

It is rarely very easy to find a suitable way to split the dimensions of the state space or to discover the corresponding pattern of attractors. So here the other part of the Q strategy, transition analogy, enters. There is a rather surprising fact behind this. Take simple and easily understood systems – including imaginary systems – and work out the pattern of dependence of their attractors on their control parameters. Then look for these patterns in more complex systems. Very often they fit: The attractors and the relations between changes in the control parameters and changes in the set of attractors that hold for simple systems fit the data for complex systems. Very often there are deep mathematical reasons for this. And in the special case of catastrophe theory these are well-understood: The topology of projections from spaces of higher to spaces of lower dimensions ensures that there are only so many forms that catastrophes can take. Elsewhere in qualitative mechanics it is often not clear why transition analogy works, though topological foundations for some cases are emerging. But the general phenomenon is now well-established: By working with simple systems one can develop a zoo of attractors, transitions, and routes to chaos, into the cages of which the behavior of complex systems fits.

The Q strategy – dimension splitting and transition analogy – is an explanatory strategy rather than a theory, for two reasons. The first is that it requires a set of underlying dynamical laws to be given in advance. (It can be applied, with whatever set of laws you are working.) The second is that there is no mechanical way of coming up with a suitable division of the relevant variables into control parameters and state variables and of finding attractors and a helpful pattern of transitions. But with patience and ingenuity very often the strategy pays off. Ideally, what one gets is a splitting of the dimensions such that variation of the control parameters leads the system to move from a (relatively fast) evolution to a small set of attractors, to a (relatively fast) evolution to a more complex set of attractors, and eventually to complete chaos. Physicists like to set things up so that increasing values of the control parameters lead from smaller to larger numbers of attractors. In the limiting case, a kind of chaos, there is a continuous set of attractors.

Chaological Taxonomy. Physically very different systems may show the same pattern of transitions between attractors. The pattern of equilibria exhibited by, say, a pendulum bob, given a range of frequencies of oscillation for the point of suspension, may be the same as that of, say, a complex electronic system, given a range of input signals. As a result we may classify physical systems by the way they fit into the explanatory strategy of qualitative mechanics. Two systems may be said to be *chaologically similar* when they can be described by the same number of variables, taking the same values, when the same division into control and system variables leads in each system to the same set of attractors related in the same way. ('Chaological' because the characteristic path a system takes to chaos will play a large role in this taxonomy. One could put this more formally in terms of a homeomorphism of the two phase spaces, which preserves initial and final

points of paths but not metric properties of the paths themselves.)
Note that this does not require that the systems follow the same paths
between attractors, or even that the underlying mechanical laws be
the same.

The result is a dual taxonomy. We can describe systems in terms of
the basic vocabulary of their physical structure and the physical properties of their parts. And we can also describe them in terms of their
chaological similarities to other systems. There is no simple relation
between these two descriptions. *But both are physically real: Neither simply reflects the attitude or stance we take to a system, and both provide real
explanations of aspects of a system's behavior.*[3] So – returning to the semantical ideas of the last section – we have a similarity relation which
while coming straight out of physics is rather unphysical. Similar systems can be made of completely different materials, physically structured in completely different ways, and subject to somewhat different
laws. Still, systems which are chaologically similar can naturally be said
to work in the same way, or to produce similar behavior by similar
means. They are similar machines, taken at a level of abstraction
above the physical – physical construction and physical law – but
below that of the semantical – satisfaction of a theory. This may in fact
express the original intentions behind functionalism better than the
Ramsey–Lewis semantical approach does.

3.   The *P* Strategy

Differential Explanation. Some crude similarities between psychological
concepts and those of qualitative mechanics should be evident. In
both cases we have a double taxonomy: Systems which are very similar
in their basic physical constitution can be very dissimilar in their
chaological and their psychological characteristics, and physically very
different systems can be chaologically or psychologically very similar.
The reason for this is that folk psychology is based on an explanatory
strategy not that different from qualitative mechanics. Or so I believe.
(I conjecture something more precise, that folk psychology and qualitative mechanics are both instances of a general strategy for classifying complex systems, which the evolution of the species and its culture
stumbled upon millenia before another version of it resurfaced in
physics.) I shall defend a slightly more cautious formulation: If you
suppose folk psychology to embody an explanatory strategy rather
like qualitative mechanics you are led to ascribe a particular form, a
'syntax', to it. And this form is one that it does seem to have.

The argument focuses on one central characteristic of our commonsense understanding of mind, which Christopher Peacocke has

called "differential explanation."[4] Differential explanation is naturally construed as an application of an explanatory strategy much like that of qualitative mechanics. In fact, there are two intuitively natural applications of differential explanation, to perception and to action, and combining them with the aid of what I shall call the "parallel-tracks principle" we get a very plausible articulation of what is central and what peripheral or optional to folk psychologies. The strategy of looking for differential explanations focusing on perception and intentional action, combined by the parallel-tracks principle, is what I call the *P strategy*.

Differential explanation is the mode of explanation appropriate to states or processes which 'track' situations in an organism's environment. The easiest examples concern perception and action. An example: Someone is looking towards the West while the sun slowly sinks between many-coloured clouds towards the horizon and a tiger slowly crawls towards her. The person may be perceptually tracking the sun or the tiger. If it is the sun then she will notice its position and trajectory, and anticipate its reappearances beneath layers of clouds. If it is the tiger then she will keep track of its motion until it is clear that it is her that the tiger is approaching, and then take flight. And the tiger is of course tracking the person, and with any luck will not loose track of her as she runs away, so that she can feed her starving cubs. The perceptual states and the actions performed by the person and the tiger are determined by the states of features of their environments as if they were linked to these features by some continuous connection. Tracking states are a kind of counterfactual disposition: If the environment were different in respect X then the state of mind or action would be different in respect $f(X)$. Peacocke, in *Holistic Explanation*, tries to specify suitable conditions for the function f.

Note the delicate mixture of cause and indeterminacy here. The person may track the tiger or may track the sun, but we cannot predict which. But if she is tracking the sun then a certain parallelism between the sun and her perceptions is predicted. (And though she is tracking the sun she may suddenly notice the tiger, *i.e.*, begin to track it.) Moreover, the connection between the environment and her perceptions is far from 'mechanical'. If she is to track the tiger she must notice it at some point, but no commonsensical principle predicts this point, and we could expect it to vary somewhat even for identical agents in identical situations. It is equally underdetermined – from the standpoint of commonsense psychology – exactly how changes in the tiger's position and motion will translate into changes in the agent's perceptual state. There may be delays, and some details will inevitably be missed.

But to describe the relation between agent and environment in this quasi-causal way is to see it in much the manner of qualitative mechanics. It resembles the dimension-splitting part of the Q strategy. The control parameters are set (in part) by the states of the environment, for example by the location of a perceived object. The attractors of the system are stable perceptual states, for example those registering the locations of perceived objects. Given a specific value of the control parameters and a nervous system in a wide but far from universal set of initial states (*e.g.*, an object perceived by an observer under normal conditions) the system will settle down to a state within the corresponding attractor (*e.g.*, the appropriate perceptual state will result). And given control parameters, initial conditions, and attractors it is *not* determined which paths, taking what lengths of time, will lead from the initial conditions to the attractors. Nor are the boundaries of the initial conditions or of the attractors usually knowable in enough detail to allow an exact prediction of toward which attractor the system will gravitate.

We have here the root of a whole explanatory strategy. To explain human actions we try to find internal states of two kinds, perceptual and volitional. Each is characterized by a type of differential explanation correlating it with situations in the environment. The differential explanations are then filled out with particular explanatory principles, which are derived by something much like transition analogy: One assumes that the types of process found in simple or easily imagined human situations will also crop up – though not necessarily in easily predicted ways – in more complex situations. Thus we find both parts of the Q strategy. Call this the P strategy.

Perceptual states simply track perceived things. Given an object causally related to a person it is possible that some range of properties which the object can assume corresponds to a range of perceptual states, and that in the given instance changes in the object's properties, within this range, will lead to corresponding changes in the perceptual states. (As the tiger or the sun moves through a range of positions the person's perception changes correspondingly.) We don't expect that given a person's situation we can automatically predict which things in it will be tracked, or which of their properties will be registered (though we have pretty firm ideas about what is likely and unlikely). Note that the basic relation is three-termed: Person n perceptually tracks object o through range of properties R. In all commonsense vocabularies this can be expressed with an apparently two-termed relation between the agent and the object (*e.g.*, n sees o, n hears o). The choice of two-termed relation – of perceptual verb in a language like English – implicitly indicates the appropriate range of properties.

Volitional states, on the other hand, are subject to a rather different kind of differential explanation. You might say they track their own satisfaction. If a person wants something, then, all going well, he ends up having it. The "something" here is a general characteristic of the environment, like the person's having an apple or mating with a particular other person. And if the agent had wanted a different something then he would have ended up getting something else. Note that to say this is perfectly compatible with saying that people often do not get what they want: When they do not get what they want this kind of principle does not explain their behavior. (But see the basic scheme, next paragraph.) Again the basic relation is three-termed, though the terms are different: Person n volitionally tracks property P with respect to range of properties R. For example, n tracks apples with respect to apples being eaten by n. Again this is idiomatically expressed as a two-termed relation: n hungers after As, n wants-harm-to Os, n lusts for o. (The English 'wants', without a complement verb – 'n wants x' – represents many of these, with the appropriate range of properties being indicated contextually.) Then the element of differential explanation enters, but in the opposite direction. Given a change in the volitional state, the corresponding change in the object follows. Again it is not assumed that we can predict which things will be objects of which volitional states or which volitional trackings will succeed.

Basic Schemes. This gives the outline of a rock-bottom scheme of vernacular psychological explanation.

Simplest scheme

Vocabulary:	perceptual relations $P(n, o)$
	volitional relations $W(n, P)$
	perceptual situations $S(n, o)$
	achievement situations $G(n, P)$
Explanatory principles:	$M(n, o) [S(n, o) \rightarrow P(n, o)]$
	$M(n, o) [W(n, o) \rightarrow G(n, P)]$
	$M(n, o) \{[S(n, o) \text{ and } P(n, o)] \rightarrow W(n, o)\}$

Note: – $M(n, o)$ is a modal quantifier, "it can happen for a person n and an object o that."

– Not all explanatory principles satisfying these general patterns need be found. And even those that are found may not apply to a given case. So two vernaculars instantiating the pattern could differ not only in their choice of vocabulary – which percep-

---

tual relations and so on they appeal to – but also in their choice of
explanatory principles using this vocabulary.

   – The concept of belief is not used; and desire appears not
as a propositional attitude but as a relation between a person and
something desired.

   Typical applications: explanation of bodily movements in terms of
people's desires about the position of their limbs; explanation of a
person's accomplishments in terms of her social position.

   The explanatory range of this scheme is extremely limited. Principles of the form $M(n, o)$ $[W(n, o) \rightarrow G(n, o)]$ only apply when the
person gets what he wants. These principles are of limited use not
only because people as often as not don't get what they want, but also
because there is a lot more to explain about most human actions than
why agents achieved what they did. One also wants to know why they
went about it in the way that they did, and whether or not they
succeeded. There is a very natural way of filling this gap, which I
believe is used by common sense. I call it the parallel-tracks principle.

   The parallel-tracks principle states in effect that action is based on
perception. Or, more precisely, when a person is tracking an object
perceptually, then the information gained – that is, the perceptual
state which tracks the property of the object – is used to guide the
agent's attempts to get the object. There is thus a third class of differential explanations, this time correlating changes in the properties of
an object of desire with changes in the actions an agent performs.
Thus the person running from the tiger wants to be in her village and
not to be in the jaws of the tiger, and therefore as she is running she
changes her direction in accordance with her changing relative location to these two objects. One crude way to build this into a vernacular
explanatory scheme is to add a category of 'attempts', for example,
running in a particular direction or searching along a particular path.
Then we get a just slightly less fundamental explanatory scheme:

The basic scheme

Vocabulary:	as in the simplest scheme, plus attempt situations $A(n, o)$
Explanatory principles:	as in the simplest scheme, plus $M(n, o)$ $\{[P(a, o)$ and $W(a, o)] \rightarrow A(a, o)\}$

> or more formally, $M(n, o) \{[Qo \ \& \ P(a, o)$
> and $W(a, Q)] \to A(a, o)\}$
>
> *Note:* This explanation schema is filled in by replacing P, W, and A with predicates which complement each other. For example, $P(a, o)$ might be "n sees o," while $W(n, o)$ is "n wants to eat o," and $A(n, o)$ is "n moves in the direction in which n sees o." Understanding the principles for selecting complementary P, W, A amounts to tacit knowledge of the range of properties involved in the full relation of perceptual tracking.
>
> *Typical applications:* explanation of search and avoidance behavior in terms of perceptual situation.

The Core of Folk Psychology. The basic strategy of folk psychology is that of looking for differential explanations in accordance with the basic scheme. This will usually involve using familiar instances of its explanatory principles, involving vocabulary drawn from one's culture. The meanings of this vocabulary are partially given by subsidiary folk theories, such as the theory that seeing involves light and the use of the eyes. Sometimes an explanation will involve inventing new explanatory principles and even new vocabulary to fit the case at hand.

I think that just about any commonsense concept of mind will be based on this strategy. This is in part an empirical claim. But direct empirical evidence, for example from anthropology, about what is basic and universal in folk psychology is hard to get and hard to interpret.[5] I have four kinds of reason for believing in the centrality of the P strategy. Each of them really needs an extended exposition, so here I shall just give a quick intuitive sketch of each.

The first reasons come from studies of children's acquisition of the concept of mind. As summarized by Paul Harris[6] these data show clearly that even young babies respond in distinctive ways to expressions of distinct states of mind in those around them. Moreover, these responses are particularly sensitive to the object of the other person's attention. To quote Harris

For instance in one study mothers were asked to express delight, disgust, or neutrality (*i.e.*, silence) towards a particular toy when it was introduced. . . . Their children aged 12 months responded appropriately but selectively: they stayed further away from the designated toy and played less with it if the mother expressed disgust, but behaviour towards the other toys and overall mood was unaffected.

The implication is that babies ascribe to their mothers attention to particular objects around them. (Or rather that they do something which is a precurser of psychological ascription and which refers to mothers' attention to things.) The ascription of relational perception, tracking, thus seems pretty basic and universal.

It also emerges from the studies cited by Harris that children's behavior toward others seems to show a recognition of others' wants at an age – three years and younger – when they do not yet show a recognition of others' beliefs. (It seems that between three and four children typically come to grips with the fact that a person's information about a situation can be mistaken.) This is consonant – one shouldn't put it too strongly – with my inclusion of relational desire but not nonperceptual belief in the basic scheme.

The second set of reasons amounts to an inference to the best explanation of a rather scattered set of data from what little I know of languages and literatures. The most easily stated part of this evidence consists in the syntax of perceptual and volitional expressions. These tend to be relational, relating just the terms involved in the corresponding differential explanation. Thus, when unsophisticated English describes perception, it says that 'n sees (hears, smells, notices, scrutinizes) o'. (And unsophisticated Chinese says 'n kan o'.) With a little more effort or sophistication one can say 'n sees that o is P'. And with a little more yet one can say 'n sees a P', in which the indefinite article represents a quantifier with wide scope: '(For some x) (Px and n sees x)'. Only with a great deal more linguistic sophistication and filling in of background assumptions can one say 'n sees that something is P', where the quantifier has a narrow scope: 'n sees that (for some x) (x is P)'. (So that 'n sees that something is P but n sees nothing that is P' is not contradictory.) The simple 'n sees a P' can almost never take this interpretation. Moreover other perceptual verbs (e.g., 'touch') can only support a wide-scope reading: 'n touches a P' can only mean '(for some x) (Px and n touches x)', and 'n touches that there is a P' is not grammatical. (Similarly, in Chinese either 'n kan mao' [n sees cat] or 'n kan you mao' [n sees there is cat] means that n sees a particular cat.) This would be very curious if the underlying concept were that of a propositional operator 'n sees that P'. Then 'n sees that (for some x) (x is P)' would be easier to understand than the two relational idioms. But if we see the underlying concept as relational, the true order of intelligibility is exactly what we would expect.

And similarly when we naively speak of volition the simplest and least context-dependent idiom is to say just 'n wants o' or 'n wants P' ('she wants her mother' or 'she wants food'). But 'n wants a P', unlike '*n* sees a *P*', normally bears a narrow-scope reading: '*n* wants that there is something which is *P* and which *n* has'. With volition it is the wide-scope reading which takes more grammar and context: '*n* wants a *particular P*' (and even that tends to be heard as '*n* wants a particular kind of *P*'). (Chinese is similar: Both '*n yao mao*' [*n* wants cat] and '*n xiang you mao*' [*n* wants there is cat] mean that *n* wants to-have-a-cat.) Both this basically relational form and this contrast with perception are what you would expect if the explanatory function of volition were as described in the *P* strategy.

The third set of reasons concerns imaginability. It is pretty clear that we tie our everyday explanations of people's actions to our capacity to imagine their situations.[7] That is not to say that it is clear what this capacity for psychological imagination consists in. But it is clear both that there is an absolutely routine, everyday imagination of others' minds which consists in being able to imagine most of the states we attribute to others, and, going somewhat beyond it, there are ways in which we can expand our explanatory and predictive powers by imagining states and connections between states for which our vernacular does not provide us with names. And then there is virtuoso or beyond-the-call-of-duty empathy, in which one imagines what it is like to be the other person.

The important fact is that the first of these is independent of the others: One can imagine the state of another in a perfectly routine way without any heroic empathic grasp of what it is like to be the other. And in terms of the *P* strategy this is very easy to explain. What one does in basic imagining of a perceptual or motor state is not to focus on that state. Instead, one focuses on the object perceived or the action performed, and imagines it. One simulates tracking the object from the other's physical position or performing the action in the other's physical situation. One does not simulate the other's perceptual or motor state. At any rate, that is not what one aims at. One aims at the act or object of the state, and as long as one can imagine the environment and mentally rehearse actions the result will be a crude simulation of the state itself. It is crude because the individual subjective detail of the other's state is inevitably missed. The subjective feel is not what is imagined: What is imagined is the directedness at an object or an act. But this can easily be imagined, and so an explanatory strategy which makes directedness central isolates states which are a suitable first achorage point for psychological imagination.

The fourth class of reasons for believing that folk psychology has the form I suggest lies in the partial congruence of these ideas with one, at any rate, of the current traditions in the philosophy of mind. I mean the tradition that runs from Charles Taylor through Jonathan Bennett to Fred Dretske.[8] I take the ambition of this tradition to be to understand the concept of mind as a development out of a very natural strategy of explanation-by-purpose which it is reasonable to use to explain things like animal behavior. The similarity to the line I am developing here can be seen in Dretske's latest work. There the central idea is that of a state which represents a situation and causes behavior, and causes behavior because it represents what it does (and, moreover, where the connection between the representing and the causing must lie within the organism). In working out this idea, Dretske finds that his central examples are those of (a) perceptual tracking states where the tracking is mediated by a learned process and (b) volitional states directed at a particular object but where a variety of means can be taken to getting what is wanted.

One similarity is fairly obvious. The states which are central on Dretske's account are also central on mine. And as a result a minimal Dretskean folk-psychological scheme would look much like mine. Another is more indirect. Dretske's representational states are connected to behavior by mechanisms which can be as varied as the ways in which different individuals can learn to make the connection between the representation and the behavior. This is why the reference of the representation is needed in order to explain the behavior: There may be no common factor to all the neural connections between representation and behavior except that they all are results of the fact that the state represents what it does. The volitional consequences of the representational state can thus be seen as attractors: They are states to which other states lead by routes which vary unpredictably from one occasion to another. This is the kind of formulation one would expect on the Q strategy, cousin to the P strategy.

(I am in fact skeptical about Dretske's insistence that learning always must lie behind intrinsic representation. I think it is just one way in which a more general condition can be satisfied, which is more easily expressed in my terms than his. The connection between representation and behavior can depend essentially on the representational function of the representing state as long as there are no available general explanations of the connection in terms just of bare descriptions of the states involved. This can happen if the connections are chaotic: Token state A may lead deterministically to token state B, but there may be no neurological types which A and B belong to which allow the explanation of B in terms of A. Yet the fact that A is within an attractor correlating it with a particular class of environmental conditions may explain why it itself lies in the basin of attraction for an attractor containing B. In effect: In a chaotic system, occasion-to-occasion unpredictability may do the work that the individual-to-individual variability produced by learning does for Dretske.)

The Gap. The two foci of differential explanation in the simplest scheme do not meet: Perceptual situations explain perceptual states and volitional states explain accomplishments, but perceptual states do not explain volitional states. We can explain the input and we can explain the output, but there is a gap in the middle. And the third focus of differential explanation added in the basic scheme links perception to action but not to volition, so the gap remains. I do not think this is a defect in my description of the basic scheme. I think rather that it is a very basic fact about our understanding of ourselves. There just is a gap between the two most easily conceptualized and imagined aspects of our psychology. One of the ways in which human cultures vary and distinguish themselves is in the ways in which they fill this gap.

In our culture we fill it in part with a conception of practical reasoning, of the interaction of beliefs and desires. This conception can be described very vaguely as the insistence that there is a single relation between what someone wants and how they think the world is, which determines what, if they are rational, they will do. There are many virtues to this conception. It allows us to describe processes of deliberation, and harmonizes well with a culture in which problems are thought out and talked out in a step-by-step manner. And it helps introduce the idea that many states of mind have propositional content, so that they are capable of truth or falsity. Think of this as the Greek stage of vernacular psychology. (Classical Greek: The Homeric vernacular is more inclined to fill the gap with the Gods' interventions than with practical reasoning.) Then we can add a 'Cartesian' strand by allowing that people very often know what beliefs and desires they are entertaining. The result is a way of getting from perception to nonperceptual beliefs to desires (with the help of other, preexisting, desires) to intentions to actions.

For all that, it is a decidedly parochial gap filler, and not to be taken as the intrinsic center of folk psychology. I doubt that it is particularly central even in the folk psychology of here and now. The most basic disqualification of an account of practical reasoning for this role is just that very few intuitively obvious, platitudinous principles of rationality exist. There is no uncontroversial account of how people should act when their desires conflict, or their beliefs are inconsistent with their desires, or when they face risky situations. Common sense evidently does not embody any answers to these questions. What we do have are sophisticated and controversial theories of these matters. They are valuable, but they do not come from the folk. Moreover, most such theories label as irrational the behavior of very many people in very many situations, particularly in situations involving risk. (Perhaps most people in most risk-taking situations are irrational according to most theories.) Whatever their origins, then, these theories do not straightforwardly predict people's actions. They can be used as parts of the explanations of actions, to be sure, but they must be embedded in very particular explanatory contexts involving other theories and other explanatory ideas.

The uncommonsensical nature of theories of rationality is linked to their nonschematic quality, their need for a very specific construal of their terms. Philosophical accounts of practical rationality are usually expressed in terms of belief and desire. That is, they use 'philosophers' belief' and 'philosophers' desire'. Philosophers' belief includes many things that people normally don't count as belief, like the belief that if I drink this cup of coffee I will not turn into a dinosaur, and it excludes a few things that people normally do count as belief, like the state of the conventionally religious person who would be horrified at denials of holy dogma but who doesn't actually think it true. And 'philosophers' desire' lumps together my interest in living another day, my inclination to have another cup of coffee, and my hope that my rich uncle will die and leave me his fortune (which leads to no action because I love him more than I love his money). If we try to express an account of practical rationality in more colloquial terms we find that the rules are different, in particular that belieflike states and desirelike states influence belieflike states more than is allowed with philosophers' desire and philosophers' belief. The point is that the way theories of rationality deal with such things as conflicts of beliefs and desires makes it impossible to express them in terms of general categories of states (*e.g.,* states defined by their tracking role or by their representational content). They need much more specific concepts. But this makes it very unlikely that they will be found at the heart of something general and schematic like folk psychology, which unites many varying vocabularies taking their content from many different applications and generalizations.

The virtues of philosophical accounts of practical reasoning are therefore not those of an accurate representation of a core part of common sense. Practical reasoning is too sensitive to the vocabulary used and too dependent on other explanatory principles to be an autonomous core. Accounts of rational action are, rather, parts of two distinct projects. On the one hand they are first steps toward cognitive psychological theories of various processes, involving reasoning, memory, decision, perceptual processing, and much more. As such they are steps toward a range of differing theories of a variety of essentially different phenomena, not toward a single core conception out of which different parts of psychology would magically drop. And on the other hand accounts of rational action (usually under the label 'rational choice' rather than 'practical reasoning') are theories of which actions will, in the long run, give us the most of what we want. They are explanations of the idea of expected utility, and of its connections to the situations we find ourselves in. But there is a great deal of evidence by now that human behavior cannot very often be seen as maximizing expected utility. Probabilistic rationality and actual human choice are entirely different things.

One thing theories of rationality definitely cannot do, then, is give identity conditions for a class of abstract objects, propositions, which are the theoretical terms of folk psychology.[9] For folk psychology is not based on propositional attitudes. And, inasmuch as our culture is equipped with a rich variety of propositional attitudes, as it undeniably is, when we come to describing their contents we can find no stable middle point between specifying the *de re* object of a state and the potentially infinite task of describing the full individual content of a particular person's state at a particular time.[10]

4. The Appropriateness of Folk Psychology

P-similarity. This is where the pieces have to come together. I have argued for a semantical theory which reconciles holistic considerations with the possibility of misdescription. I have described a kind of mathematical modeling in physics, the Q strategy, which illustrates some of the possibilities of the semantical theory. (It shows how the projection from cases to general extension can be based on an explanatory strategy as well as on a theory.) And I have presented an articulation of folk psychology, the P strategy, which makes it resemble this kind of mathematical modeling.

The ideal way to glue all these together would be to argue for some very grandiose claims. One might be that there exists, potentially, an ultimate synthesis of folk psychology and neuroscience, a deep and elaborate theory which conforms to both the P and Q strategies and fits the true workings of the nervous system in an accurate and explanatory way. (It would not be the vernacular psychology of our culture, evidently.) I do not think we have any reasons to think this is true (or false, for that matter).

A grandiose claim that I do think true is that folk psychology is an instance of a very general, and generally profitable, strategy for classifying and predicting qualitative aspects of the behavior of complex systems. The closest I could come to stating such a strategy was the Q strategy, but that was clearly not general enough. In fact, all anyone can do at the moment is to point to the signs that there are very deep and important results waiting to be found. The primary sign is the trickle of results from topology giving foundations for the double taxonomies empirically worked out in the study of chaos. (The topological foundations of catastrophe theory, the other big branch of qualitative mechanics, are now pretty clear.[11]) These results generally show a priori connections between the fundamental laws entailing the infinitely varied behavior of a class of dynamical systems and a finite classification of qualitative aspects of its behavior. In effect, a certain strategy or stance toward classification of the behavior of a class of systems becomes not a mere heuristic but a source of real explanations referring to the physical sources of their behavior. What we need – and what I prophesy – is a digesting of these results together with some statistical insight to give a description of strategies which will reasonably often give the right taxonomy of unknown complex systems. (The possibility is of immense epistemological insight. It would be sad if philosophers yet again missed the boat on something so close to their central concerns.) How much of the intentional stance will thus be vindicated as more than heuristic? We will have to wait and see.

But we are still in the desert, waiting for revelation to strike. The main philosophical task for someone like me, a materialist with a highly noninstrumental view of our ordinary conception of ourselves, must be to find some weaker and more intellectually manageable versions of this claim.

The claim I shall defend depends on the semantical theory of Part 1. The class of systems picked out by a predicate, according to that theory, depends essentially on a relation of similarity between systems. The relation determines the projection from the standard examples or objects of baptism which give the initial grasp of the intended class to that whole intended extension. In Part 2 I argued that the appropriate similarity relation for a predicate can often be taken as given by the explanatory strategy underlying the theory that gives the predicate its immediate home. For vernacular psychological predicates, linked to the P strategy, the appropriate similarity relation must be something along these lines: Systems S and T are P-similar if they track the same features of the environment – or more carefully, are equipped to track the same features of possible environments – and track the same range of actions with parallel sets of volitional states, and have the same pattern of stable states linking the perceptual and volitional states.

Is this the *right* similarity relation? The manageable part of the question is: Does P-similarity fit us? Does the class of human nervous systems satisfy the conditions I laid down in Part 3 for a similarity relation to fit a class of exemplars: homogeneity and appropriateness? The P-strategy as employed in actual folk psychologies has to pick out some real and characteristic features of us, and there has to be some reason to believe that some basic principles of our psychological workings can be captured in terms of it.

Homogeneity: The Reality of Tracking. The position of primitive humans trying to understand others of their own and similar kinds has resemblances to that of the physicist confronting a system whose equations of motion cannot be squeezed to yield predictions of its behavior. (Sellars's Jones is cousin to Poincaré.) So the explanatory strategy they adopt is natural and reasonable. And, within definite limits, it works. But that does not mean that the states of mind it leads us to postulate are real states of the human organism. The strategy might be natural, appealing, and wrong.

This seems a real possibility if you focus on the details of a particular, developed vernacular psychology such as ours, with its particular lists of emotions and categories of propositional attitudes, shaped in detail by social contingency and by moral and religious traditions. It becomes much less probable if you focus instead on the basic skeleton of folk psychology: perceptual and volitional tracking with a gap between them to be filled by improvisation and imagination. Consider perception and volition, in turn.

First, *perception:* It is clear that we do track objects in the environment, and that there are determinate states to which the nervous system gravitates under normal conditions corresponding to the situations of the objects tracked. And in some cases the Q- and P-theoretical characterization of the tracking state leaps out as the right way to catch it. One example of this is given by categorial perception. In many perceptual situations, particularly with hearing, there are two quite distinct possible perceptual states a stimulus within a given range of physical characteristics can produce. As the stimulus is varied through the range the perceptual state changes suddenly from one to the other. There is no ambiguous or half-way state, and little uniformity between subjects in the point at which the transition occurs. Indeed, the point of transition can vary from one occasion to another for a single subject. The contrast between unvoiced and voiced consonants, such as p and b, is a good example. As the point at which the vocal cords are engaged is moved further toward the beginning of the sound the perceived phoneme suddenly changes from the unvoiced to the voiced member of the pair. There is no half-way perception. But the point of transition varies from subject to subject and – to a lesser extent – from occasion to occasion.[12] The natural way to describe this is to say that the speech-perception system has two attractors. For suitable values of the control parameters – the stimuli – the system may evolve to either attractor.

This style of analysis could be applied to all forms of perception. For example, Skarda and Freeman,[13] discussing olfactory processes in the rabbit, conclude that

During late inhalation and early exhalation a surge of receptor input reaches the [olfactory] bulb . . . and induces an oscillatory burst. This is a bifurcation from a low-energy chaotic state to a high-energy state with a narrow temporal spectral distribution of its energy, suggesting that it is governed by a limit cycle attractor. . . . [The] local amplitudes of oscillation take on values that are reproducibly related to particular odorants serving as CSs [conditioned stimuli]. The values differ for different odors, indicating that multiple limit cycle attractors exist, one for each odorant an animal has learned to discriminate behaviorally . . .

Here the vocabulary of quantitative mechanics is being used to get a grasp on the mechanisms behind a comparatively small set of perceptual states. And it is the 'shape' of the attractors that is of interest. I know of no such study of visual perception. In its absence, the point to make is the unpredictability of visual state given visual input. For example, much of the neural processing of visual information about the shape of objects proceeds independently of that of information about their color, and vice versa. And the perception of motion is similarly quite independent of the perception of both form and color. Many stages in processing which one might naively think would be shared by form, color, and movement are in fact duplicated, carried out in parallel for the different submodalities.[14] Moreover all of these channels can be influenced by top-down cognitive feedback. So in many cases it may be quite unpredictable exactly what a person will report herself as seeing, although the range of possible states is predetermined and limited. There is a developmental aspect to this, too. The nervous systems of higher mammals develop after birth in ways that depend on quite fine details of the experience of the animal. For example, in cats the relative importance of the pathways from each eye within the visual areas of the cortex depends on the stimulation available to each eye between the second and the fourth month after birth.[15] Thus even if the workings of each individual's visual system were somehow predictable in detail there would be no completely detailed generalization across individuals.

As a result the patterns of activity between stimulus and perception will vary wildly from individual to individual and occasion to occasion. But the end states are not wild: One perceives fixed shapes, colors, and locations. These are the attractors of the system. The important point is that research into the neurology of vision implicitly shapes itself around the search for the nature, configuration, and relations between these attractors.

Now, *volition:* It is less obvious that differential explanation gives an accurate account of the way volitional states are translated into action. But the evidence, such as it is, can be taken my way. Consider the simplest species of volition-to-action, motor control.

Assume that the following, from Patricia Churchland,[16] is an accurate description of the way in which some actions are controlled.

. . . the input from the cerebral cortex specifies in a *general* way what bit of behavior is called for. For example, suppose the incoming "intention" to my cerebellum is "touch *that* (apple) with my right hand." The incoming "intention" vector specifies this position . . . but it does not specify a curve in the motor space that says exactly how the goal position is to be achieved. . . . [The cerebellum] will have to coordinate all the muscles relevant to the behavior, based on an updated representation of the body's current configuration.

In effect, motor control involves the coordination of rather different functions. An aim to be accomplished is first specified, together with a general way of accomplishing it (*e.g.*, which limb to use). (The manner of accomplishment could be specified very loosely indeed. I would guess that it often is, in sporting and artistic activities, where the agent has a large number of ways of accomplishing a result, *e.g.*, making the pitch of a note drop, and that the choice of limb used, *e.g.*, lip, throat, or breathing muscles, may depend on sensory feedback during the course of the action.) Then an action has to be put together and carried out. It is put together out of fixed, probably innate and 'hard-wired' component subroutines for performing small subactions in accordance with sensory information before the initiation of the action and with sensory–motor feedback during the action.

In these circumstances, it is inevitable that, given the initiation of an act, which we can think of neurologically as an input from the cerebral cortex to the cerebellum or psychologically as an intention or a

desire for something immediately available, we cannot predict the
exact form in which the act will be implemented. But, for all that,
some final configurations have a privileged position. Consider a person setting out to touch an apple with his right hand. He has cataracts
and Parkinson's disease, so that the path his hand follows is unsteady
and erratic. He may or may not succeed in touching the apple, and
the paths his hand follows will be affected by subtle biochemical factors and incidental features of the environment. (What materials for
his diminished dopamine synthesis have been provided by his meals
in the past day? What intensity and color of light is coming through
the window?) But one class of results is special: Those in which his
hand finally touches the apple. They are special in that they are the
normal output of the system. From a wide class of initial configurations, given the initiation of the act, the system will evolve to a state in
this class. It is an attractor, and, in the familiar way, the routes to it are
incalculably varied and unpredictable.

Appropriateness. The *P* strategy captures real perceptual and volitional
processes. And the general strategy is right, to the extent that the
'laws of motion', the detailed neural mechanisms which govern the
transitions between attractors, are not available to us. But, if we knew
enough, could we perhaps dispense with this attitude, and explain
and predict Laplace-like, from a perfect knowledge of the state of the
nervous system and its operating rules?

No, if the nervous system is at all the way we now, still speculatively,
think of it, with massive parallelism built into almost every aspect:
numerous parallel pathways branching and combining, with the relative dominance and timing of different pathways depending on subtle
biochemical balances affected by the person's whole nervous activity,
and what she had for breakfast. Then the output of a perceptual
stimulus or of the initiated motion may be completely unpredictable.
We still will usually be able to find a later stage of processing where
the result of the joint output of the parallel processes can be predicted
to be one of a determinate number of attractor states. But we won't
know which one it will be.

I take it that it is really a pretty safe thing to say, that the detailed
workings of complex neural networks are not to be explained and
predicted like the motions of ideal billiard balls. A deeper and more
interesting question is whether something general and useful can be
said about the particular way in which our nervous systems depart
from Newtonian predictability (our *Q*-theoretical type). There is a
curious confluence of suggestions from several directions, though,
that one characteristic of nervous systems, at any rate, has a charac-

teristic *Q*-theoretical form. That characteristic is learning. I cannot do any more than cite what others say.

Hinton and Sejnowski, describing a parallel distributed processing (PDP) model of learning,[17] list three virtues of their model: resistance to damage, rapid relearning, and spontaneous recovery of unrehearsed items. In other words, if the system is disturbed it can often get back into an equilibrium, and in fact sometimes will get into an equilibrium that was not available to it before. The reason both for the stability of the system's equilibria and for the availability of new equilibria is the characteristic 'landscape' of attractors (equilibria, minima). Minima are just local minima: If the system is in equilibrium it will stay there given sufficiently small variations of the control parameters, but given a greater jolt from the outside it will move on and sometimes find a yet more stable equilibrium.

The idea is really fairly crude. Brains like ours must be fluid, changeable, in order that they can learn; but they also need to retain what they have learned, so they need to be immune to many changes. They need stable states and they need them not to be too stable. So there must be a particular kind of hierarchy of attractors, with the right kind of trajectories between them. The hierarchy of attractors must allow what Skarda and Freeman call 'destabilization'. To quote them again:

In an alert, motivated animal, input destabilizes the system, leading to further destabilization and a bifurcation to a new form of patterned activity. We hypothesize that convergence to an attractor in one system (*e.g.*, the olfactory bulb) in turn destabilizes other systems (*e.g.*, the motor system) leading to further state changes and ultimately to manipulation of and action with the environment. . . . Input to the system continually destabilizes the present stable state and necessitates convergence to a new form of behavior.

(Destabilization resembles what Smolensky calls 'symmetry breaking' in PDP models of learning.[18]) Skarda and Freeman go on to conjecture that the pattern of chaos and stability found in nervous systems is fundamentally different from that in many other natural self-organizing systems. Their conjecture is the same as mine: There is a characteristic way we work, a characteristic landscape of attractors and connecting trajectories. The effects of this landscape are the characteristic attributes – perception, action, learning – of sentient creatures. But as to its actual shape, in any useful form at all, they, as with me and everyone else at this stage of things, can say nothing.

Real Commonsense States. What can we conclude about the status of vernacular psychological explanations? If they are based on a single folk-psychological theory whose central claims turn on propositional belief, desire, and rationality, then we can conclude nothing. If they result from an explanatory strategy something like what I have called the *P* strategy, then there is more to say. I have given reasons to believe that the core foci of the *P* strategy are in fact real and causally efficacious properties of people, and I have begun to articulate a conjecture, which is at any rate shared by other intelligent people, that the more general *Q* strategy may be the best way to uncover some fundamental and characteristic qualities of us. So our instincts and our culture are on the right track.

Belief, memory, and propositional desire might be useful illusions. Rationality certainly has very limited explanatory usefulness. That does not prevent us from giving intuitively graspable vernacular explanations of our actions, which moreover appeal to the real sources of our action. For common sense is a body of strategies as much as a body of assertions, and the particular strategy of commonsense psychology is well-equipped with sites at which different new concepts and different explanatory ideas can be grafted on. This is the main source, I suspect, of the richness of human culture. And, like human culture, vernacular psychology is only beginning. Its most interesting developments may be yet to come.[19]

NOTES

1. David Lewis, "An Argument for the Identity Theory" in D. Rosenthal (ed.), *Materialism and the Mind—Body Problem* (Englewood Cliffs, N.J.: Prentice Hall, 1971), and "How to define theoretical terms," *Journal of Philosophy* 67, 1970, 427–46. F. P. Ramsey, "Theories" in R. Braithwaite (ed.), *The Foundations of Mathematics* (London: Routledge, 1931).

2. For the physics see Heinz George Schuster, *Deterministic Chaos* (Weinheim, Physik-Verlag, 1984); Tim Poston and Ian Stewart, *Catastrophe Theory and Its Applications* (London: Pittman, 1978); and J. P. Crutchfield, J. D. Farmer, N. H. Packard, and R. S. Shaw, "Chaos," *Scientific American* 255, 1986, 46–57. For philosophical reactions see G. M. K. Hunt "Determinism, probability, and chaos," *Analysis* 47, 1987, 129–33; and A. Morton, "The chaology of mind," *Analysis* 48, 1988, 135–42. And, for a very readable popular account, James Gleick, *Chaos,* (Penguin, 1987).

3. See my "Mathematical modeling and contrastive explanation," *Canadian Journal of Philosophy,* sup. vol. 16, 1990, 251–70. Christopher Zeeman, "Catastrophe theory," *Scientific American* 234 no. 4, 1976, 65–83, is very suggestive about the conditions under which qualitative mechanics will really explain the phenomena which fit its patterns.

4. Christopher Peacocke, *Holistic Explanation* (Oxford: Oxford University Press, 1979).
5. For some empirical work relevant to these questions see Paul Heelas and Andrew Lock (eds.), *Indigenous Psychologies* (New York: Academic Press, 1981); and for some ideas about how changes in vernacular psychology can be charted see my "Freudian Common Sense" in R. Wollheim and J. Hopkins (eds.), *Philosophical Essays on Freud* (New York: Cambridge University Press, 1982, pp. 60–74). Also very helpful and suggestive is Amelie Oksenberg Rorty, *Mind in Action* (Boston: Beacon Press 1988), especially Chapters 4, 15, 16.
6. Paul Harris, *Children and Emotion* (Oxford: Blackwell, 1989).
7. See my *Frames of Mind* (Oxford: Oxford University Press, 1980), Chapter 3; Robert Gordon, *The Structure of the Emotions* (New York: Cambridge University Press, 1988); and Paul Harris, *Children and Emotion*, Chapters 3 and 9.
8. Charles Taylor, *The Explanation of Behaviour* (London: Routledge 1964); Jonathan Bennett, *Linguistic Behaviour* (Cambridge, England: Cambridge University Press, 1976); Fred Dretske, *Explaining Behavior* (Cambridge, Mass.: MIT Press, 1988), especially Chapters 4 and 5.
9. See Paul Churchland, *Scientific Realism and the Plasticity of Mind* (Cambridge, England: Cambridge University Press, 1979), implicitly accepted in the very useful discussion in D. C. Dennett's "Midterm Examination" in his *The Intentional Stance* (Cambridge, Mass.: MIT Press 1987).
10. See Andrew Woodfield, "On Specifying the Content of Thought," in A. Woodfield (ed.), *Thought and Object* (Oxford: Oxford University Press, 1982), and "Two categories of content," *Mind and Language* 1, 1986, 319–54.
11. See Ian Stewart, *The Problems of Mathematics* (Oxford: Oxford University Press, 1987), Chapters 13 and 14; and Gleick, *Chaos*, "Strange Attractors" and "Universality." See the footnotes and references to each of these.
12. See J. Fodor, T. Bever, and M. Garrett, *The Psychology of Language* (New York: McGraw-Hill, 1977), Chapter 6.
13. Christine Skarda and Walter Freeman, "How brains make chaos in order to make sense of the world," *Behavioral and Brain Sciences* 1987, 10, 161–95.
14. Margaret Livingstone and David H. Hubel, "Psychophysical evidence for separate channels for the perception of form, color, movement, and depth," *Journal of Neuroscience* 1987, 7, 3416–68.
15. Chiye Aoki and Philip Siekevitz, "Plasticity in brain development," *Scientific American* 1988, 259, 34–43.
16. Patricia Churchland, *Neurophilosophy* (Cambridge, Mass.: MIT Press, 1986), p. 430.
17. G. E. Hinton and T. J. Sejnowski, "Learning and Relearning in Bolzmann Machines," in J. McClelland and D. Rumelhart (eds.), *Parallel Distributed Processing*, Vol. 1 (Cambridge, Mass.: MIT Press 1986), pp. 282–317.
18. P. Smolensky, "Information Processing in Dynamic Systems: Foundations

of Harmony Theory," in J. McClelland and D. Rumelhart (eds.), *Parallel Distributed Processing*, Vol. 1 (Cambridge, Mass.: MIT Press 1986).

19. I have had useful encouragement and discouragement from Hugh Mellor, Jim Russell, and Andrew Woodfield, and invaluable discussions with David Hirschmann, who pointed out many mistakes in an earlier draft.

7

How Is Eliminative Materialism Possible?

ALEXANDER ROSENBERG

Eliminative materialism is the thesis that our common-sense conception of psychological phenomena constitutes a radically false theory, a theory so fundamentally defective that both the principles and the ontology of that theory will eventually be displaced, rather than smoothly reduced, by completed neuroscience.[1]

The trouble with this bald claim is that it threatens eliminative materialism (EM) with unbelievability, unassertability, evidential groundlessness, self-stultification, self-referential falsehood, and other defects. The allegation is widely known: A sentence expressing the thesis of eliminative materialism would be just a concatenation of ink marks or a bare acoustical disturbance unless it meant something. But for inscriptions or vocalizations to mean anything they must have the right causal provenance, one that involves intentional states of various kinds in myriad possible ways. Moreover, assertions are actions, but actions are caused by desires and beliefs. Additionally, nothing could be evidence for a thesis unless there are agents who recognize it as evidence. Since eliminative materialism expressly denies the existence of beliefs and desires, and thereby precludes assertions and all other actions, as well as evidence for or against anything, it follows that its truth cannot be asserted, believed, hoped for, substantiated to any degree by any evidence, or rationally defended.[2] Call this the incoherence problem.

The incoherence problem has rarely been a serious issue between defenders of EM (hereafter EMists) and their opponents.[3] Perhaps this is because, in Lynne Rudder Baker's words, "[a]rguments about the allegedly self-defeating character are . . . frustrating to people on both sides of the issue. People on each side think that those on the other side miss the point" (p. 137).

There is, however, a related objection to EM that does not issue in the conclusion that EM is incoherent. Rather, according to this argument EM has a consequence so incredible that no one can seriously entertain the theory. According to this objection, EM implies the falsity of all the causal claims we make in the vocabulary of folk psychology (hereafter FP). So, for instance, when we explain our own or others' behavior by describing it as action and citing our beliefs and/or desires, in every case these claims are false, if EM is true. After all, if there are no desires and beliefs, there are no actions, and neither the causes nor the effects we enumerate actually obtain. Thus, it is false that I wrote this paper because I wanted to discuss these arguments. It is false that I read the paper to an audience because I wanted to hear their reactions. It is false that members of the audience raised their hands in the discussion period because they wanted to say something. It is false that you are now reading it because, at least a few minutes ago, you wanted to do so. No matter how strongly these claims impress themselves upon us by introspection and by observation of human affairs, they must all be false, if EM is right, because there are no desires, beliefs, or actions like writing, sending papers, accepting them, reading, and so on. But this is incredible, it makes false not just everyday explanations and predictions, but turns all history and biography into fiction, and not just into historical novels. It turns them into fantasy fiction, the realm of mystical powers and occult forces that have no basis in fact. EM is thus a view at variance with the most well-established human practices, and with what we seem to know on the basis of introspection alone.

If EM isn't self-refuting, it's the next worst thing to it: patently false. Call this the incredibility problem.

In this paper, I examine how eliminative materialism can circumvent these charges. My reason for doing so is simple. I *believe* that eliminative materialism is true, that the failure of commonsense or folk psychology provides *evidence* for the thesis. I have *asserted* this thesis elsewhere, and examined its consequences for social science.[4] I am therefore committed to *defending* the thesis. My beliefs about EM and my desire to communicate them have jointly *caused* me to write this paper. All these facts about me require a defense of EM. The first step in any defense is to show that it is even a coherent possibility. This is my present task.

1. Churchland's Gambit

Paul Churchland responds to the charge that EM is self-refuting by claiming that the argument against it is question begging. The argument that EM is self-refuting works as a *reductio ad absurdum* that starts with two premises: EM and a certain theory of meaning. But, writes

Churchland, the theory of meaning is one that EM explicitly denies. EM denies this theory because it is part and parcel of the "common-sense conception of psychology" that EM rejects. It is thus no surprise that a *reductio* follows from the conjunction of EM and the theory of meaning in question. As Churchland notes, ". . . formally speaking, one can as well infer, from the incoherent result, that this theory of meaning is what must be rejected."

Churchland does not identify the theory of meaning in question, but he seems to have in mind a Gricean one, which presupposes intentions to communicate.[5] In fact the *reductio* probably follows from any of a large number of theories of meaning. All the argument really requires is that inscriptions or noises have meaning only if there are at least some mental state types. This necessary condition on a theory of meaning, that it imply the existence of some mental state types, is a pretty weak one, and is common to a vast array of theories of meaning. Every one of them is "off-limits" to the defender of EM. But "all" EM needs is some theory of meaning or other that does not entail the existence of intentional states like beliefs and desires.

What would such a theory look like? The most obvious candidate for an intention-free theory of meaning is a highly Platonic one: Inscriptions and noises have meaning because they *express* propositions – abstract entities whose existence, whether as sets of worlds or otherwise, is entirely independent of anyone's thought. The relation of 'expressing' that stands between inscriptions/noises and propositions cannot obtain in virtue of the mediation of intentional states, but must somehow be *intrinsic* to the concatenation of marks and the acoustical vibrations that constitute inscriptions and noises.

This sort of a theory would be remarkably unnaturalistic. Philosophers, like EMists, who reject the suggestion that neural configurations can express propositions intrinsically, will hardly be comfortable with a commitment to ink marks and acoustical disturbances having such content. Nevertheless, we will be committed to such a theory, by the conjuncts of the claim that EM is true and that expressions of it are meaningful. Still, such a intentionless account of meaning is not obviously self-refuting, so its mere possibility may suffice for purposes of defending the mere intelligibility of EM.

But the mere possibility of such a theory is not enough to undercut the associated charges that, even if meaningful, the thesis of EM cannot be entertained, asserted, argued for, defended, confirmed by piling up evidence, and so on. For all these activities are clearly *actions*. And even if meanings are some how free of intentions, actions are not. They are undeniably the effects of intentional states. If EM denies the coherence of notions like 'belief', and 'desire', then it denies the coherence of the concept of 'action'.

The solution here can't be sought in some intention-free theory of what actions are, paralleling the hoped-for intention-free theory of meaning. For no such theory is possible. Without desires and beliefs there are no actions. There may well be complex behaviors that look for all the world like actions, but in the absence of desires and beliefs, they will turn out to be just that, *mere behavior,* different only in degree from yawns, blinks, and twitches.

So, no intentional states, no action; no action, no assertions. But, if no assertions, then one is forced to ask, exactly what are EMists doing, when we offers EM as a theory? Are we asserting it, trying to convince us of it, defending it, giving reasons why one should believe it? If we are doing any of these things, EMists condemn our thesis with every syllable we utter, even if we have an intention-free theory of meaning up some sleeve or other.

2. Watering Down EM and Changing the Subject of FP

EM is a metaphysical thesis, based on an epistemological argument, with a methodological moral. The thesis is that there are no intentional states, the argument is that the theory that quantifies over them is a scientific dead end, and the moral is that psychology should pursue a neuroscientific research program, not an intentional one. One way to circumvent the problem of self-refutation is to water down EM into a purely methodological prescription: For purposes of scientific psychology, avoid commitment to intentional states, pursue neuroscientific explanations for behavior!

This imperative is silent on the existence of intentional states, and, on the cognitive status of FP, it merely recommends avoiding appeal to them. But a methodological prescription requires an argument to recommend it.[6] If EMists can't argue from the sterility of FP taken as a theory, what can they offer to sustain their admonition? They could withdraw their claim that FP is a dead-end scientific theory, and instead argue that it is not a scientific theory at all, so that on the one hand, it need not be taken seriously by psychology, and on the other, neuroscience will not displace it, even as it ignores FP for scientific (though not perhaps philosophical and other) purposes.

Such a stratagem, however, threatens to recapitulate a generation of blind alleys and repudiated arguments in the philosophy of mind. If FP is not a theory, what is it? Is it a set of definitions and their consequences, a set of hypothetical imperatives that characterize rationality and provide noncausal explanations that illuminate human affairs? These views, associated with followers of the later Wittgenstein,[7] were decisively undermined as long ago as 1963.[8]

Briefly, to see the problems involved in this tactic, take, for example, a proposition that Churchland identifies as a generalization of FP:

(1) $(x)(p)(q)$ [(x desires that p) and (x believes that (if p then q)
                and (x can bring it about that p)
                        → (in the absence of countervailing desires
                           or preferred strategies, x brings it
                           about that p)].

Instead of treating (1) as a contingent causal claim we might treat it as a normative one, according to which one *ought* to bring it about that p, when the conditions detailed in the antecedent obtain – we treat the arrow as deontic instead of causal. We may go on to hold that (1) is employed to explain actions by making them intelligible – by showing them to be obligatory under the circumstances in which they occur.

But, now let us ask, why does the obligation explain the event? The EMist can only reply that is it because people's prudential obligations usually cause their actions. To give any other answer would betray the basic empiricist strictures on explanation that motivate EM to begin with. But causation is to be analyzed in terms of regularities. So, if (1) is a prescription with explanatory force, then behind it stands another bit of FP, a causal claim of the form,

(2) $(x)(p)$ [if x is prudentially obliged to bring about p
                       → x brings about p]

If FP has the power to make actions intelligible, then it must embody causal claims after all. EM is committed to this conclusion as a fundamental principle. But this means that EM is committed to treating FP as a theory.

It is sometimes held that the generalizations of FP are definitions, and for this reason FP does not constitute a contingent theory that neuroscience must compete with. But this interpretation will not enable the EMist to maintain a dignified silence about the status of FP.

If the general statements of FP are definitions, the question still arises whether there is anything that satisfies these definitions, whether there are any desires, beliefs, and actions, and if there are, why psychology should turn its back on them. Besides, the supposed distinction between definitions and factual generalizations is irrelevant to their methodological role. We can treat FP as a body of stipulations, and this just shifts the empirical enquiry to the question of whether anything satisfies these definitions. Or we can treat FP as a body of contingent generalizations of mixed quantification. Either way it has the same bearing for explanation and prediction. A meth-odological distinction between theory and definition is just not one EMists can accept. So they cannot really decline to treat FP as a theory, no matter how convenient it would be to do so.

Watering down EM, so that it is just a methodological prescription, or changing the subject of FP so that EM need not be committed to its alleged failure as a theory, is not an acceptable means of dealing with EM's self-refutation problem. For EM is the product of fundamental metaphysical and epistemological principles that no EMist is willing to surrender.[9]

3.   Saving the Appearances of Folk Psychology

EM's conflict is with FP's generalizations, and its ontology. EM alleges that neither the existence claims – that there are intentional kinds – nor the "laws" – like (1) above – that FP assumes can be reconciled with neuroscience. But what of the singular causal judgments ex-pressed in the language of FP – statements like "I just turned on the radio because I wanted to listen to the news and I noticed it was 5:00"? In a sense these singular judgments constitute the data, the ap-pearances of FP. These singular judgments constitute the data of observation in a very literal sense. For we make many such claims every day, and credit their truth on the basis of introspection. In fact, their introspective warrant provides the strongest reason to pursue psychological theory in the spirit of FP. It is difficult to see how we can "save the appearances," that is, accommodate the introspective data, without following in the footsteps of FP. Of course, it is open to argue that the singular judgments we make about mental states, their causes and effects, are already imbued with a theory, and that introspection is suspect for well-known reasons. So EM need not and should not be reconciled with this theoretically tendentious description of the data. But to do this is simply to turn one's back on the incredibility problem sketched above.

However, if we can render the singular causal judgments consistent with EM's condemnation of FP, we can solve the incredibility problem. Perhaps such a reconciliation will also help EM to deal with the prob-lem of self-refutation.

What we need is an account of singular causal judgements about action and its causes that shows how they could on the one hand be true, or at any rate "true" in scare quotes, while, on the other hand, be hopelessly misleading about the basis of their truth.

The history of science provides a neat illustration of how singular causal claims may be true, even though they are highly misleading and appeal to theories that are scientific dead ends, quantifying over types of entities that do not exist. Interestingly, the illustration is to be found in phlogiston chemistry, a theory to which EMists frequently compare FP.[10]

It is beyond argument that phlogiston theory is false, and that there is no such thing as phlogiston. The egregious falsity of the former and its total failure to be preserved in the theories of combustion that succeeded it are the grounds for denying the existence of the latter. Since there is no such thing as phlogiston, there is also no such thing as calx, dephlogisticated air, or inflammable air. The reason is that calx is defined as the residue of a metal after it has emitted phlogiston, dephlogisticated air is defined as air from which phlogiston has been removed, and inflammable air is the result of producing a calx of iron by passing steam over iron. Paraphrasing the EMist, we deny the existence of phlogiston, calx, dephlogisticated and inflammable air because phlogiston theory "constitutes a radically false theory, a theory so fundamentally defective that both the principles and the ontology of that theory [were] eventually displaced, . . . by" oxygen theory.

And yet, despite the defects of phlogiston theory, chemists like Priestly and Cavendish made a number of claims that we would like to credit as true. Priestly noted that breathing dephlogisticated air made "his breast [feel] particularly light and easy for some time"[11] and Cavendish discovered that exploding a large quantity of dephlogisticated air with a small amount of inflammable air produces water.[12] How can we explain the truth of these claims while repudiating entirely the theory in which these terms figure? One answer we can rule out is that phlogiston theory is reducible to oxygen theory, or equivalently that the claims of Priestly and Cavendish can be uniformly translated into claims about oxygen, metallic oxides, proton donors, and hydrogen.[13] On the other hand, it is clear that the referents of the sentence tokens they emitted on those occasions in which they made true claims were samples of oxygen, iron oxide, proton donors, and hydrogen. The presence of these samples of real kinds provide a big part of what explains both why they made their claims and why the claims were true. But many other claims made by phlogiston theorists are false, and their falsity is to be explained in part by the fact that their sentence tokens fail to refer to samples of kinds, or for that matter to kinds themselves that actually exist. But how can "phlogiston" change its referent from occasion to occasion?

This is a question that has been addressed by Philip Kitcher.[14] His object in addressing this issue was to show how the intelligibility of scientific claims can be preserved through revolutions. His further aim was to undercut claims of relativism and noncumulation which often turn on the alleged incommensurability of theoretical paradigms. For reasons that will become obvious, we EMists should be happy to help ourselves to Kitcher's theory. After all, incommensurability is the greatest obstacle to the claim that what cannot be reduced (*e.g.*, FP) rationally ought to be junked (though incommensurability is also part of a tempting argument to the effect that what is not reducible will wrongly be stigmatized as unscientific).

Kitcher's suggestion is that what a token refers to is determined by the right explanation of its production. He introduces the notion of an *initiating event* in a chain leading to the tokening to be explained. This initiating event "is either an event in which the referent of the token is causally involved or an event which involves the singling out by description, of the referent of the token" (p. 537). Consider those tokenings of Priestly's and Cavendish's that we deem to express truths about, say the effects of breathing oxygen or mixing it with hydrogen. The explanation of what these theorists said will connect the tokenings with particular samples of these elements in fairly direct and obvious ways.

Before making the observations that led to these true claims, Priestly and Cavendish made many claims about "dephlogisticated air" whose reference was fixed by description, which connected it to the experiments of Stahl and Becher. These scientists originated the notion of phlogiston as the substance emitted in all cases of combustion. Since there is no substance emitted in all cases of combustion, neither earlier tokenings of "phlogiston" nor of "dephlogisticated" air secured reference at all.

Kitcher's theory absorbs the widely held causal or historical theory of reference. On his theory the initiating event that explains the things a speaker says is sometimes to be found in some baptismal act of the earliest user of the term. But sometimes this best explanation will not appeal to such an occasion. Rather the best explanation of what a person says involves reference fixed by description, or by particular observations and/or other acts of the speaker. In these cases the initiating event, which is part of the best explanation for the particular utterance in question, is not to be found in an act of baptism at the beginning of a causal chain. Stahl could never have baptized anything as a sample of phlogiston (otherwise, our denials of its existence would be incoherent), but Priestly using the same term sometimes successfully secured reference and sometimes did not.

Kitcher's approach accounts for all three utterances: Stahl's, and both of Priestly's.[15]

Can EMists avail themselves of this account or a suitable modification to preserve the truth of the many singular causal claims about human action we wish to preserve, and also eventually to explain how EM can be asserted, defended, argued for, and so forth, even though there is no such thing as assertion, defense, arguing, and so forth?

4. Folk Psychology and Phlogiston

Three potentially serious obstacles to such an approach present themselves. First, Kitcher's strategy saves a few of the appearances of phlogistic chemistry, whereas EM needs an approach that will underwrite vast numbers of first- and third-person causal claims about mental states and their effects. Second, Kitcher's strategy will not help in the case of FP if it does not work in the case of phlogiston. And it may be tempting to deny that anything Priestly or Cavendish said "about" phlogiston is true. If this is right, then Kitcher's approach can't help us explain away singular causal claims of FP as true. Third, even setting these problems aside, EM has nothing to match oxygen theory. Yet oxygen theory's ontology and laws are essential to explaining those utterances of Priestly's and Cavendish's we want to preserve as true. EM needs a neuroscientific ontology, and its associated generalizations, to make anything like the case Kitcher can make for the appearances of phlogiston theory.

I have little to say about the first two problems. It does not seem to me that in comparing these cases the much larger numbers of utterances preserved in the displacement of FP should count. We probably need an explanation for why FP took hold so much earlier, so much more widely, and so much more firmly among human beings than did phlogiston theory. But this explanation is fairly obvious and will help explain the differences in numbers. The second matter is trickier. If nothing Priestly and Cavendish said was true, then it will be argued that Kitcher may still have an interesting and important account of reference for scientific claims. For his aim is not to underwrite the truth of utterances about phlogiston, but to explain their rationality, intelligibility, and commensurability with the theory that replaced phlogistic chemistry. Will this be enough for EM? That is, will showing the rationality of FP's singular causal judgments be enough to deal with the incredibility problem? If it isn't, then EM will need a theory of approximate truth, or assertability, or some such supplement to accord the singular sentences of FP the dignity common sense demands for them. One reason this problem is not more disquieting to me is my belief that Kitcher needs such a supplement, too, as does anyone who embraces the notion that the insights of superseded theories are somehow worth preserving, that scientific theorizing makes cumulative progress, and that this progress needs explanation.[16]

This leaves the third obstacle to exploiting this approach: EMists have nothing to match oxygen theory. That is, although with hindsight we can explain the true tokenings of the phlogiston chemists by connecting them with samples of oxygen, hydrogen, iron oxide, and so on, we do not have the relevant neuroscientific theory to explain the true tokenings of intentional psychology. But perhaps it will suffice if we make one up. After all, our goal is not to establish EM, rather it is to show that EM is at least possible, thinkable, not self-refuting. To do this it suffices that a neuroscientific theory of the right sort be merely possible.

Assume we have a fully developed theory that accounts for movements of the body on the basis of a bottom-up theory about neural networks, afferent–efferent connections, the molecular biology of stimulus generalization and discrimination, nonintentional information storage, parallel processing, and all the other fashionable ideas of the latter-day noncomputational program in psychology, in short everything we need to replace FP. Our theory is powerful enough and well-enough confirmed to make us confident that there are no such things as discrete mental representations, propositional attitudes, and the rest of the ontology of FP. These notions will have gone the way of phlogiston, calx, and so forth. Can we nevertheless credit the utterance of singular causal judgments about the causes and effects of mental states with truth, or approximate truth, or warranted assertability, or otherwise say they are worth preserving?

Now consider the historian's tokening of "Chamberlain signed the Munich accords because he wanted peace." What is the best explanation of why the historian says this, and what initiating events give the referents of his token? In the light of completed neuroscience, the best explanation for the historian's utterance goes back, through diaries, letters, parliamentary speeches transcribed in *Hansard,* newsreel footage, and so on, to the brain states of Neville Chamberlain, during the years up to October 17, 1938, and to the displacement of his body on that date. These brain states, and this behavior, which our fully developed neuroscientific theory will have enabled us to identify, give the referents of the historian's token. Because they obtain and are causally related to the historian's utterance in the right way, they enable us to provide an explanation of what the historian says that makes it comprehensible, reasonable, appropriate, like Priestly's tokenings of the refreshing effects of dephlogisticated air. This explanation of why the historian tokened the sentence in question makes it more than tempting to conclude that what he said was true or somehow worth preserving in the light of completed neuroscience.

On the other hand, what initiating events figure in the best explanation of someone, say a philosopher in the thrall of FP, tokening an instance of (1) above? The most reasonable thing to suppose is that the initiating events involve the adoption of particular definitions and analyses of intentional states, like those of desire and belief. Since, according to EM, there is nothing that satisfies these definitions and analyses, (1) has no more theoretical role to play than the generalization that heating a metal in air produces a calx and releases phlogiston. Facts about the brain states and behavior of particular people, as reported in an adequate neuroscience, have no direct role in the explanation of why someone tokens (1) or any other generalization of FP. It is thus not at all tempting to credit anyone tokening (1) with making a true statement, by contrast with the historian's claim.

Here there is a parallel to Priestly's tokenings of "dephlogisticated air" in which the reference is fixed by description as the substance obtained when phlogiston is removed from the air. It will be far less reasonable to credit tokens in which the reference is thus fixed as expressing truths than ones in which the initiating event in the best explanation is the inadvertent isolation of a sample of oxygen.

Now, why can't almost everything we say in everyday contexts about the causes of our own and others' behavior, and about the effects of our own and others' brain states, be like Priestly's claims for the refreshing qualities of a sample of dephlogisticated air? Even if we decline to credit Priestly's claim with truth, it still reflects an important insight we wish to preserve. Mutatis mutandis for the singular causal claims couched in the terms of FP, thus we preserve all the singular causal judgments we want to save about "actions" and their causes. We can even segregate the ones worth preserving from those singular judgments not worth preserving, the ones common sense and FP would simply call false, sentences like "Chamberlain signed the Munich accords because he wanted to hasten the war and believed that appeasement was the way to do so." The best explanation for a particular tokening of this sentence would presumably not advert to Chamberlain's brain state on or before his behavior on that fateful day in the fall of 1938. It might well appeal to the brain states of the utterer, states that FP might have identified as the desire to make a joke, or be sarcastic, and so forth, but that have no place in humorless neuroscience.

5.   Have We Really Solved the Incredibility Problem?

In his discussion of a previous attempt of mine[17] to reconcile EM and the singular causal claims of FP, Alfred McKay writes:

Just imagine! Literally billions of singular, causal belief—desire—action claims, made since substantially before Plato's day, and ever since, by people of all races and climes, all employing concepts that not only do not fit but do not even come close, all operating at an explanatory level (individual human acts) where there are no (undiscovered) competing accounts, no causal laws of any sort, and *very many* of these singular, causal claims turning out to be true. Not perhaps impossible, but surely incredible. How did we manage to luck into these true claims, each of them . . . [referring] in mysterious ways to unknown causal factors operating in ways of which we are completely ignorant.[18]

McKay's claim is that reconciling the truth of these claims with EM is not just a matter of showing their logical compossibility; defenders of EM have to do more. They must show how we managed "to luck into" all these true claims.

There seem to me to be three views one can take of this demand. One is to deny that EM requires anything more than bare logical consistency with the truth of singular claims of FP. The trouble with this view is that it will not convince anyone not already besotted with EM. The second is to hold that McKay's demand cannot be satisfied until a good deal more is learned by neuroscience about the brain and behavior. If these singular claims are true, or assertable, or worth preserving, then neuroscience will eventually help explain why this is so. This response to McKay's problem is dangerous, however, for it moves EM perilously close to reducing FP, instead of displacing it. An explanation for the truth of large numbers of singular causal judgments that located their justification in some neurological facts common to all these cases would in effect provide the basis for some sort of at least partial reduction of the kinds of FP. But this would tend to vindicate them as less than "fundamentally defective" and would enable us to frame mixed explanatory generalizations, partially in the language of FP, and partially in that of neuroscience.[19]

The third response to McKay's challenge is to take it up. EMists need to show that all these singular causal judgments are not true by accident. Because they are causal claims, we assume too readily that they are factual ones, so that it's facts about the world — causal laws — that make them true. Well, if most such singular statements were vacuous to the point of being bereft of factual content, then our taking them for true would not be difficult to explain. EM could then go on to discredit them, in spite of their truth, both by appeal to the Kitcher account of reference, and by providing a neuroscientific explanation of why people find relief from explanatory puzzlement in utterances about them.

There is of course a large literature testifying to the difficulty of testing claims about mental states, their causes and effects. It usually focuses on the alleged analyticity of general statements like (1). The response to these charges has usually and correctly been that (1) is a central theoretical law, and is not tested by observations in isolation. This is a backhanded way of saying that by itself (1) is easy to defend as true, come what may. But because (1) is so easy to defend, so are its substitution instances. Notice how often a singular claim in the language of FP is defended against apparently countervailing first- or third-person evidence by saying the agent "really" wanted or "really" believed things that the agent denies believing or wanting.

FP individuates intentional states by their propositional content. But this sort of specificity is illusory. Even if we grant the existence of intentional states, they have nothing like the specificity of spoken and written statements. The illusion that they do is fostered by the fact that when we report on the causes of our own behavior and our hypotheses about the causes of the behavior of others, we do so in language, thus providing a false picture of specificity.

This indeterminacy of content becomes clear on the functional approach to content. If we individuate a state by reference to its functional role, it quickly becomes apparent that there is no such unique role. Rather, a state has efferent connections with a large number of outcomes, each more or less appropriate to one or another aspect of the immediate and mediate environment. And on the other hand, the outcomes never point back directly to any particular statement.

This indeterminacy is particularly clear in the case of animal behavior. When a dog lunges for a piece of steak, it is impossible precisely to identify the relevant "desire" because we cannot determine from behavior alone under what description the dog brings the object of desire: Is it T-bone, aged sirloin, beef, meat, protein-and-fat, food, nutrition, yummy stuff, prey, and so on? It is probably none of these. As Dennett says, why should the discriminations of our dictionaries and the dog's line up together?[20] One is tempted to say, if only the dog spoke a language we could translate into English, we could read the one right description – the content – of his linguistic tokens. In the absence of language, we cannot narrow the functional role of the relevant brain states of the dog beyond that of representation of object of desire, and desire for object represented.

Is the situation any better in the functional approach to organisms that do token sentences? Not really; the data of linguistic tokens still doesn't reach the level of giving us one particular sentence as the content of the functionally characterized state.[21] These limits on the naturalistic approach to content are recognized even by those who do not endorse EM. But they are steps on the slippery slope to EM.

For the indeterminacy of attribution not only makes FP predictively weak, as EMists are eager to emphasize, by the same token it makes FP's singular claims hard to refute. If neither environment nor behavior isolates any particular statement as the propositional content of an intentional state, it doesn't rule out very many of the coherent alternatives either. It is easy to see under the circumstances why we endorse vast numbers of these claims as true.

They are as near to vacuous as causal claims can get. How vacuous that is can easily be illustrated. Consider the claim that the sinking of the Titanic was the effect of the event that caused the Titanic to sink. Here is a true singular causal claim, in which distinct events are referred to, and which reports a contingent connection between them, but which is of little explanatory or predictive use. In fact it is as close to vacuous as such a statement can come. The singular causal claims of FP are rarely any more informative, and for the same reason. They are contingent, but only just, and roughly for reasons that Kitcher's approach to reference helps reveal: The explanation of what makes them contingently true involves initiating events in the brain, about which we are still quite ignorant. But it also involves the vagueness and the empirical slack in the connection between the causes and effects that commonsense reports in the language of FP.

Let us add to these facts what McKay calls the "anthropological reasons why we are inclined to view one another as agents," the fact that "morality, religion, law, etiquette, and social life generally require the use of concepts like belief and desire and action," and the fact that "the point" of many such singular causal claims "is given in terms of the moral/legal practices of assessing responsibility, laying the blame and fixing punishment."[22] Now it should no longer be surprising that we treat the vast majority of these singular judgments as true.

Here then is the disanalogy between phlogiston theory and FP. Those statements of Priestly's and Cavendish's that were true, or at least worth preserving, were few and far between, but they had considerable empirical content – phlogiston chemists could be sure that they had the means to produce water from gasses. The statements of

FP that are true and that we can preserve are legion; because they have so little content, they provide almost no assurance about anything specific beyond the occurrence of the states and events they report.

McKay writes, "it would require an elaborate pre-established harmony, extensive particular divine interventions on an ad hoc basis, a large number of small scale miracles, or something similar"[23] for all these singular statements to be true, in the absence of any laws of the sort FP requires. It would, if they had the character of most causal claims. But the singular claims of FP are crucially different. Revealing this difference goes a fair way to solving the problem of incredibility in the way McKay demands.

6.   Has EM Avoided Cognitive Suicide?

With something approaching a solution to the problem of incredibility let's turn to the first of our problems: the incoherence charge. Lynne Rudder Baker has detailed this charge against the coherence of EM in greatest detail, and concluded that it succumbs to the threat of cognitive suicide. Let's see how well the present account of the singular claims of FP deals with them.

According to Baker anyone who hopes to circumvent EM's incoherence problem must provide an alternative account of "justifiably accepting a proposition":

The skeptic [about FP] . . . must come up with a successor to the family that includes 'believes that', 'accepts that', and other such expressions, which will permit a distinction between say, "accepting" (or whatever the content-free successor of accepting is) one thing and "accepting" another *without adverting to content.*

. . . The successor concepts must allow both for a distinction between being "justified" in "accepting *p*" and not being so "justified" . . . without presupposing that there are contentful states. [*Saving Belief,* p. 135]

If the approach to defending EM above is right, then Baker's demands on it are too strong. She is right to insist that the successor theory and its terms can make no appeal to *intentional* content. Our suggestion honors this demand. The closest it gets to content is its admission that there are sentence tokens that express propositions, but do so in a way that is intention free. (See Section 1, Churchland's Gambit.) As for all those singular statements, their truth no more commits us to intentional states than do the true claims of the phlogiston theorists.

But Baker's demand for a type-for-type replacement of intentional concepts by nonintentional ones is too strong. All we really need are explanations for utterances that retrospectively illuminate them as tokening differing truths, or falsehoods for that matter.

Compare the situation between phlogiston theory and its successor. If oxygen theory could make all the same distinctions that phlogiston theory makes, so that every claim of phlogistic chemistry had a dual in oxygen chemistry, not only would the historian of science's claims about incommensurability be undercut, but phlogiston chemistry would be reducible or translatable into oxygen chemistry, and there would be no reason to deny the existence of phlogiston and the other kinds that figure in phlogiston chemistry. None of these things obtain, though the approach Kitcher develops holds out the hope nevertheless of trans-theoretical intelligibility of phlogistic claims and the ability to distinguish true ones from false ones on a case-by-case basis. The possibility of a similar case-by-case distinction between particular instances that FP would describe in its terminology is all we need to vindicate the intelligibility of EM.

The closest EM could come to meeting Baker's demand is a non-intentional substitute for FP and its intentional states like justified belief. The substitute theory would not be very interesting from the point of view of neuroscience, but it would answer to Baker's demand. And it would provide a substitute for those who think we need to replace FP with something at least predictively powerful.

We can begin by substituting a purely extensional state for the intentional state of believing. We could call this state 'acceptance', following terminology already introduced elsewhere,[24] but Baker has already claimed the term to describe a state with intentional content. Let us instead call the nonintentional state we substitute for belief 'registration',[25] and say that, whenever neuroscience deems to be "true" an FP claim that someone believes a certain statement, p, what is in fact the case is that the person registers p *and* every statement that can be derived from p by substituting coreferential terms and coextensive predicates in p. (Whether a term is coreferential and a predicate coextensive will require us to appeal to Kitcher's or some such theory that explains the utterances "inspired" by superseded theories.) Registrations will thus have no intentional content, though they will still have 'content', because they will be individuated by statements. It will be difficult to identify these statements with precision, because we will only be able to infer what they are from observation of behavior and environment. In this respect they will be like the contained statements of FP. For example, hold a piece of meat before a (normal) dog; it will register that piece of meat is before it, and it will register every statement derivable from the original one by substitution of coreferential terms for 'that piece of meat'.

When will a registration be "justified"? When it is the product of a process that produces true registrations or starts with true registrations and produces true registrations with at least some very high probability. Thus, vision produces mainly true registrations, so organisms are "justified" in registering statements about what they see. The transition from the registration that p & q to the registration that p preserves truth, thus the resulting registration is true every time the starting one is true. Every transition among registrations that mirrors deductive inference is justified.

This strategy also requires an equivalent content-free substitute for desires. Here there seems to be less difficulty. We can simply help ourselves to a biological notion like 'goal', which is already nonintentional in the required sense: In the attribution of goals to biological systems, free substitution of coreferring terms and coextensive predicates always preserves truth.[26]

Harnessing registrations together with goals will enable us to do anything the desire–belief combination can, though we will have to frame new generalizations linking registrations and goals to behavior, generalizations that will supplant (1) above. For example, it will turn out that individuals register far more incompatible statements than we are willing to credit them believing, and they are not nearly as efficient in attaining their goals as they seem to be in attaining their desires. The reasons are that individuals will register far more statements than they are supposed by FP to believe, and will have far more goals than desires. Both of these consequences obtain because of the permissibility of substitutions in the statements they "contain."

There is of course something highly artificial about this elaborate mechanism, whose only *current* purpose would seem to be that of satisfying Baker that something like justified acceptance without intentional content is possible. There is no reason to suppose that, in the long run, a nonintentional notion of acceptance or registration will supplant our current and convenient locutions, any more than the discovery of heliocentrism led to the abolition of talk about sunrises and sunsets. Nevertheless, intentional states will go the way of epicycles in scientific theorizing.

We may even expect that, perhaps as neuroscience develops and takes hold, the meaning of our ordinary terms will change to reflect this advance. As neuroscience identifies the neural structures that subserve direct visual registrations, the more central processes subserving aggregations of sensory registrations, and their inferential successors, we may start to use the term 'belief', to refer to registrations, and so deprive it of its intentional character, while of course radically revising our lists of what people 'believe' and our generalizations about the causes and effects of 'belief'.

In addition to providing an alternative for the notions of acceptance and justified acceptance, Baker also demands the EMist provide "some indication of how there can be assertion without belief" (p. 138). Without it, we cannot assert that there are no beliefs. The right response to this demand is the reply that, on the one hand, there is no such thing as assertion, in the sense of a kind intentionally characterized by its intentional causes – among them the desire to express a certain statement. On the other hand, there are 'assertions'. That is, neuroscience enables us to distinguish those events that token statements from those that don't, by differences in their (nonintentional) causal histories. And by Kitcher's strategy we will be able to credit the FP-inspired identification of these events with truth, like the truths Priestly advanced about phlogiston.

Baker claims that "it is difficult to guess how to specify the right causal history without attributing to the speaker some state with the content of what is asserted." But, as we have seen in Section 5, one of the motivations for EM is the difficulty FP faces in trying to do just that, attribute content to a state that causes the agent to make an assertion. More important, identifying the particular causal history of some EMist's utterance that "there are no beliefs" which shows the utterance could be truly described in the terms of FP as an assertion is a task with no systematic payoff for the explanation or prediction of behavior. It is therefore unreasonable to demand of neuroscience anything more than a sketch of how it is possible. To do otherwise is the equivalent of asking modern chemistry to show how the production of ozone, or some other form of oxygen unknown to Lavoisier, could be described in the language of phlogiston.

When I token "EM is reasonable," "FP's laws and ontology are radically defective," "there are no beliefs and desires," the causes of these tokenings are not beliefs that they are true and desires to communicate them. That means these tokenings are not actions. Nevertheless, the explanation for their production will involve nonintentional facts about my brain states, and these brain states' causal dependence on facts about the world that make for the truth of EM and the falsity of FP. By contrast, tokenings like "FP is true" will not have the same causal explanation: There will not be the appropriate causal connection to facts making for the truth of FP, because there are no such facts: FP isn't true. What is this "appropriate causal connection"? It is one whose full delineation must await the development of neuroscience which EM advocates. The trouble with such a promisory note, however, is this: Once neuroscience has developed to the extent envisioned by EMists, the full delineation of the "appropriate causal connection" will be an exercise of purely retrospective interest, without any payoff for the future of psychology.

NOTES

1. Paul Churchland, "Eliminative Materialism and the Propositional Attitudes," *Journal of Philosophy,* 78 (1981): 67.
2. Arguments to this effect are to be found in Norman Malcolm, "The Conceivability of Mechanism," *Philosophical Review,* 77 (1968): 45–72; and, more recently, in Lynne Rudder Baker, *Saving Belief: A Critique of Physicalism,* Princeton, Princeton University Press, 1988, Chapter 7. Malcolm's argument was directed against a psychophysical identity theory, and its force as an objection to materialism is much weakened by the fact that, *pace* Malcolm, most noneliminative materialisms are compatible with commonsense psychology. Malcolm's argument, however, still has considerable force against eliminative materialism, a thesis whose origins Malcolm's paper antedates by a few years. I discuss Baker's objections in detail in Section 6. Page references to Baker hereafter are to this volume.
3. Indeed, some of the most extended arguments for EM not only do not respond to it, they are silent about its existence. See for example, Steven Stich, *From Folk Psychology to Cognitive Science: The Case against Belief,* Cambridge, Mass., Bradford Books, 1983.
4. *Sociobiology and the Preemption of Social Science,* Baltimore, Johns Hopkins University Press, 1981; and "If Economics Is Not a Science, What Is It?," *Philosophical Forum,* 14 (1983); 296–314.
5. Churchland, p. 89.
6. In fact, elsewhere I have argued that it requires a theory, and, if general enough a prescription, it requires a philosophical theory. "Methodology, Theory and the Philosophy of Science," *Pacific Philosophical Quarterly,* 66 (1985): 377–93.
7. Exemplified in what Davidson has called the "tide of little red books," from Routledge and Kegan Paul, published in the late 1950s and early 1960s, R. S. Peters, *Concept of Motivation;* A. I. Meldin, *Free Action;* Peter Winch, *The Idea of a Social Science;* as well as other works like A. R. Louch, *The Explanation of Human Action;* C. Taylor, *The Explanation of Behavior;* and S. Hampshire, *Thought and Action.*
8. See Donald Davidson, "Actions, Reasons, and Causes," *Journal of Philosophy,* 60 (1963): 685–700.
9. Among these principles are the following: Explanations for contingent occurrences are fundamentally causal or nomological; to be is to be the

value of a variable in a true theory; a theory is most strongly confirmed by its explanatory and predictive employment; science seeks to unify theories, especially in cognate and adjacent areas; a predicate that has no place in a well-confirmed empirically progressive scientific theory is not a "natural kind," does not reflect any fundamental or derivative ontological category, and should not figure in a scientifically accurate description of the world. For a discussion of how these principles bear on EM see Paul Churchland, *Scientific Realism and the Plasticity of Mind,* Cambridge, Cambridge University Press, 1979. It is worth noting that it is these last two principles, about the demands on scientific unification and the nature of natural kinds, that prevent the EMist from adopting a token-materialist or anomalous-materialist position. The incoherence and incredibility problems do not arise for this view because it allows for the autonomy of psychological laws and the reality of nomologically dangling kinds. The EMist considers these allowances too great a price to pay for reconciling FP and neuroscience.

10. Cf. Churchland, p. 89, and Rosenberg, Chapter 7.

11. Priestly, *Experiments and Observations on Different Kinds of Air,* Vol. 2, New York, Kraus Reprint, 1970, p. 161, quoted in Philip Kitcher, "Theories, Theorists, and Theoretical Change," *Philosophical Review,* 87 (1978), 519–47, 533.

12. Cavendish, *Experiments on Air,* Edinburgh, Alembic Reprints, No. 3, 1961 p. 19, quoted in Kitcher, p. 533.

13. Anyone tempted to identify dephlogisticated air with oxygen and inflammable air with hydrogen should read Kitcher's paper carefully. Much of my discussion, both of phlogiston theory and of how a singular causal statement can be true though thoroughly misleading, depends heavily on this important paper. Part of the explanation for this untranslatability has to do with the unsettled state of phlogiston theory throughout its existence. See Kuhn, *Structure of Scientific Revolutions,* Chicago, University of Chicago Press, 1962, Chapter 7, and especially p. 70. EMists will point to the same disagreements in FP, of course.

14. Op. cit.

15. Kitcher summarizes his approach as follows:

> . . . we identify the initiating event as the event such that the hypothesis that our subject is referring to the entity involved in that event best explains why he says the things he does. In some cases, our search for the initiating event may lead us back through events involving other speakers to some primal act of baptism by the first user of the term. However, when we are concerned with the utterances of scientists who are developing particular theories and using vocabulary peculiar to those theories, I think that different explanations will often be appropriate. We may find, for example, that a scientist's argument presupposes that the referent of a term satisfies a particular description, and [we may] best explain his utterances by hypothesizing that they are initiated by an event in which the referent of the term is fixed by that description. Or, as in the case of Priestly, we may find reports which are prompted by particular observations and account for the scientist's judgements by taking tokens he pro-

duces to be initiated by those observations. "Historical explanation" accounts of reference often paint the picture of a single chain connecting tokens of a term to the object singled out on the first occasion of its use. I am suggesting a rival picture in which the connections of terms to the world are often extended in subsequent uses. This picture appears to accord better with the continued reapplication and redefinition which is typical of scientific usage, and of which the case of Priestly furnishes a striking example. (pp. 538–9)

16. See Kitcher, p. 519, "Historians of science are interested in discovering what Priestly was talking about and how much of what he said is true."

17. Rosenberg, *Sociobiology and the Preemption of Social Science*, Chapter 7.

18. Alfred McKay, "The Incredibility of Rejecting Belief–Desire–Action Explanations," *PSA 1982*, Vol. 2, East Lansing, Mich., Philosophy of Science Association, p. 121.

19. In effect, the kinds of FP would end up methodologically on a par with the Mendelian gene, a concept now superseded in many contexts by the molecular gene, but that nevertheless retains important explanatory, pedagogic, and practical functions in genetics. The theory in which it figures is certainly not fundamentally defective, like phlogiston theory, nor has it been displaced. Whether it has or can be reduced, however, is a vexed question. See Rosenberg, *The Structure of Biological Science*, Cambridge, England, Cambridge University Press, 1984, Chapter 4.

20. *Content and Consciousness*, London, Routledge and Kegan Paul, 1969, p. 85.

21. The possibilities FP would describe as insincerity, confusion, ignorance of the language, not to mention indeterminacy of homophonic translation, all undercut facile inferences from linguistic tokens to the content, if any, of their causes. See, Steven Stich, *From Folk Psychology to Cognitive Science*, Cambridge, Bradford Books, 1983, especially Chapters 4 and 5.

22. McKay, p. 123.

23. McKay, p. 121.

24. See for example, L. J. Cohen, "Belief and Acceptance," *Mind*, 98 (1989): 367–90.

25. The term is introduced in Jonathan Bennett, *Linguistic Behavior*, Cambridge, England, Cambridge University Press, 1976, in Bennett's attempt to construct a naturalistic functional account of belief. The "trouble" with registrations is that they turn out to be referentially transparent, and allow free substitution of coextensive predicates, as I argue in "Intentional Psychology and Evolutionary Biology: Part 1," *Behaviorism*, 14 (1987): 15–28. For the EMists' purposes, this of course is no defect.

26. Cf. my *Structure of Biological Sciences*, Cambridge, England, Cambridge University Press, 1984, Chapter 3; and Bennett, op. cit., Note 24, Chapter 3.

8

The Long Past and the Short History

KATHLEEN V. WILKES

1. Introduction

Is commonsense psychology a scientific theory? It seems accepted dogma today that it is, even if many regard it as a rudimentary or fledgling scientific theory, or as a very inadequate or degenerating theory, one that needs to be rejected and supplanted.

The dogma sets up a broad trichotomy amongst those who share it. There are those who think that commonsense psychology is basically all right, but that it could and should be improved, tightened up, made respectable; there are those who think that it can never attain the status of a "proper" theory, but that we are stuck with it; and finally there are those who ask us to reject it root and branch – to "eliminate" it – and to opt instead for something quite different: maybe a pot of gold at the end of a future neuroscientific rainbow. To illustrate the first, Fodor wrote recently: "We have no reason to doubt that it is possible to have a scientific psychology that vindicates commonsense belief/desire explanation" (1987, p. 16); for Fodor, commonsense psychology, improved and strengthened, could become respectable. Scholars such as Davidson, however, have hefty reservations about its scientific possibilities. And third, both the Churchlands seem to regard commonsense psychology as the main albatross around the necks of those trying to develop a science of cognition and behaviour.

In several places[1] I have tried to argue against this dogma. I do not want to repeat these arguments, except where a brief recap is unavoidable; and so in this paper I shall instead attempt to underline the differences between commonsense psychology and scientific psychology by means of historical observations. When we take note of a few features in the development of the science of psychology, the gross divergences and contrasts between the aims and ambitions of the two – in my judgement – simply show themselves and scarcely need to be spelled out. I shall not of course be offering here a potted history of psychology. Psychology's past, both in its lay and its scientific versions, is simply used as a source of arguments and illustrations. From a selection of the abundant material, we shall see that commonsense and scientific psychology do and must coexist, and that they are not rivals in the same game.

Since they are not rivals, and since scientific psychology is struggling hard to build genuine theories of the behaviour and cognition of humans and other animals, it seems to me dangerously misleading to call commonsense psychology a "theory" – if by theory we mean the sort of thing that the philosophy of science describes and assesses. And I would ask the reader to note that this is much more than a terminological point. The reason that it is not "merely terminological" is that those who regard commonsense psychology as a "theory" inevitably confuse it with the products of research done in laboratories and white coats, and end up attempting to defend, refine, redefine, or attack it by means of standards appropriate only to the sciences.

One more terminological point, and this time a fairly (but not wholly) trivial one. Despite prevalent fashion, I shall resist the label 'folk psychology'. This, for two reasons: First, it begs the question in favour of the critics of commonsense psychology by suggesting folksiness, tweenness, homeliness, even simplemindedness – and yet commonsense psychology can be astonishingly sophisticated, penetrating, and profound. Second, the title 'folk psychology' has a deserved historical home of its own, in Wundt's *Völkerpsychologie* (1900–9). But Wundt was not, with the term *Völkerpsychologie*, talking about commonsense psychology. His *Völkerpsychologie* concerned "these mental products which are created by a community of human life and are, therefore, inexplicable in terms merely of human consciousness" (1916 edition and translation, p. 3). This is not the 'folk psychology' that has been discussed recently in the literature.

2. The Long Past

The title of my paper is of course derived from the famous comment of Ebbinghaus: "Psychology has a long past but a short history." The long past is, I shall claim, commonsense psychology; the short history dates maybe from James's somewhat hesitant remark in 1867: "It seems to me that perhaps the time has come for psychology to begin to be a science" (in James 1920, p. 263); or, more firmly, from Wundt in 1873–4: "The work I here present to the public [*Principles of Physiological Psychology*] is an attempt to mark out a new domain of science" (1904 edition and translation, Preface). Naturally, the science of psychology did not spring unheralded into existence in the 1860s or

1870s; but it was round about then that it started seriously to cast off or to rethink the shackles that had hitherto bound it so tightly to physiology, or to philosophy, or to both, and it was round about then that it began on its own autonomous existence.

The long past needs relatively little said about it, since it is fully familiar to all readers. Indeed, it is fully familiar to all normal adults, whether they realise this or not; for it is the psychology of the street, the tacit know-how that allows us to cope with our conspecifics. By 'cope with', though, I do not mean 'describe and explain'. Indeed, we use it for that purpose, from time to time – primarily to describe or explain the activities of individual agents, with particular histories, in specific contexts and circumstances; and those to whom we explain are audiences with their own idiosyncratic background knowledge of the agents and the circumstances, and with their own unique puzzles concerning the behaviour they want explained. But in any case describing and explaining individual bits of behaviour are a *small* part of the story: Far more importantly, we deploy it to rule, warn, woo, win over, threaten, cajole, placate, encourage, educate, hint, sneer, assess, recommend, blame, joke . . . and *countless* more tasks besides. Humans are, as Aristotle noted, *social* animals; and we have a massive cranial capacity and encephalization quotient.[2] Unlike sheep, then – which are also social animals, but which are relatively birdbrained – our world, our needs and interests, and our possibilities are rich and multifaceted. The complexities of survival and success in such a world include essentially the demand to predict, handle, assess, and react to the behaviour (linguistic and nonlinguistic) of our conspecifics. Along with – and of course interlocking with – the development of the capacity to manufacture and deploy tools, and to use language, came our mastery of commonsense psychology.

The result is that from the earliest records we possess we find a rich, penetrating, and profound understanding of human character and motivation. One can verify this for oneself by, say, reading Homer, Sophocles, or Euripides; but we should not forget that generals at the battle of Marathon needed just as subtle an assessment of the designs of the Persian generals and of the morale of their own and the opposing forces as are needed by any commanders in twentieth-century wars. The point is that we can all exploit commonsense psychology, and often with immense detail and profundity – *but* we have needed to do this for millennia. The proper study of humanity not only is, but has to be, humans. It just so happens that a few (Euripides, Chaucer, Shakespeare, Dostoyevski, Proust, Henry James) are better than most at writing this down.

We needed commonsense psychology in the past; and we need it no less now. This I take to be so obvious as to need no argument. All I need to do in this section is to stress five points in particular that arise inevitably from this admission, and which will serve to underline further its divergence from scientific psychology.

First, the conceptual apparatus of commonsense psychology is intoxicatingly *rich* and *subtle*. Masses of everyday terms overlap to some extent, but have different nuances and connotations when used in particular contexts; consider the different implications that can be conveyed by the choice of 'believes', 'knows', 'thinks', 'understands', 'assumes', 'realises', 'takes for granted', 'has the prejudice that', and more; or by the choice of 'wants', 'desires', 'longs for', 'hopes', 'expects', 'thinks it his duty', 'lusts after', and again more. These are not readily definable terms or phrases – but then hardly any terms of common sense (except boring ones such as 'bachelor', or 'unemployed', or 'square') have sharp definition: Even the boring term 'chair' does not. The fuzziness of the terms in question is eliminated by the context, almost always a highly individual and idiosyncratic context, of their use. *Within* such a context, subtle and detailed shades of meaning can be captured by, say, commenting "he did that because he knew that *p*," rather than "he did that because he thought that *p*." The rich and nuance-ridden nature of the conceptual apparatus is what explains the richness *and the precision* of our mastery of common sense know-how; and this is not a paradox.

Second, commonsense psychology has few if any links with the biological (physiological or neurophysiological) sciences. It matters to our understanding of Euripides not at all that he (probably) agreed with Aristotle that the brain was there to cool the blood – any more than it matters to our understanding of fairy tales that wooden Pinocchios, or rabbits in waistcoats, are unlikely to have a rich mental life. The person in the street generally believes, vaguely, that the brain is the centre of mental functioning, just as Aristotle believed (without complete commitment: See *Metaphysics* 1035^{b}26–7) that this role was played by the heart. It is hard to think of any neuroscientific discovery that could make a major difference to actions and reactions in commonsense psychologising. This, as we shall soon see, explains one of the fundamental splits between the psychology of the long past, and that of the short history. There are of course areas within which scientific psychology and neuroscience have infected and coloured our views, and the implications for action of such views; but these, for reasons that will follow, are generally in the domain of abnormal behaviour. Such reasons follow immediately.

This is the *third* main point to make about the long past. Commonsense psychology is notoriously poor at understanding abnormal, aberrant, or irrational behaviour. Some of the longest-running – and still unsolved – problems in the philosophy of mind (a discipline that seems to me to be the study of the spaghetti-like complexity of commonsense psychology) are after all *akrasia* and self-deception. The reason for this failure, which is an important failure, is that commonsense psychology makes actions and thoughts understandable *by showing how, in the circumstances, they are rationally intelligible.* Since it does and must explain in this way, abnormal and irrational behaviours are evidently problems for it.

Historically it has attempted to cope with this in two main ways. One was to appeal to nonhuman, but still 'rational', factors. Thus, for example, we find Homer explaining abnormal behaviour on the part of his heroes via a 'higher' rationality: The gods – who took sides in the Greek/Trojan battle – had intelligible reasons for assisting their protegés by beclouding the judgement of their opponents. Similarly, odd behaviour in the Middle Ages and often later was ascribed to the malign or benign, but rationally intelligible, effect of witches, warlocks, and their spells and potions. In the 1990s we are no longer content with the Homeric pantheon, nor with witches and demons. So nowadays, when confronted by bizarre and apparently irrational behaviour, we may resort to something like Freudian psychoanalytic theory – but note the extent to which Freud's explanations make substantial appeal to the rational intelligibility of the behaviour of postulates such as ego, id, and superego. Put another way, there are occasions of behaviour that cannot be understood by everyday commonsense psychology alone, but for which external rational agencies (whether these be gods and demons, or the factors cited by psychological theories) are called in.

The other main strategy for coping with behaviour we find unintelligible is to abandon commonsense psychology for nonrational (not *ir*rational) explanation; or at least to supplement it from these sources. Thus in the past we abandoned anthropomorphic (or rather deomorphic) accounts of the weather, in favour of causal–mechanical meteorological accounts. In a similar vein we may now find that deficiency of catecholamine in the limbic system is a better explanation of some forms of depression than are psychological explanations; only neuroscience can handle the fascinating and extraordinary phenomenon of pure alexia.[3] Very crudely, when reason-giving explanation fails, we often resile towards causal explanations.

The central point is that commonsense psychology per se requires, and is built around, the assumption of rationality: It attempts to understand how behaviour can be seen as rationally intelligible in the context. (This is of course related to what has been called the principle of charity, or the principle of humanity.) Insofar as we depart from this assumption, to that extent we depart from commonsense psychology.

The *fourth* main point is led into by the fact that commonsense psychology is often supplemented by theories external to it (whether theological or scientific–psychological or causal–mechanical), and it is one that will not take long to defend. When attempting to distinguish commonsense from scientific psychology, I am not drawing a sharp and exclusive line. They are on a continuum, just as everyday beliefs about what happens when you throw a brick at a window, and full-blooded physics, are on a continuum. But there is nothing "wrong with" continua. Differences of degree can be colossal *or* slight. Noticing that one's octogenarian great-aunt has difficulty in remembering over the short term is an observation potentially relevant to science, just as is noticing that water boils at a different temperature at high altitudes; wondering why one's daughter prefers this pop group to that is rather far removed, as is the idle speculation about just what atomic lattice structure this particular screwdriver may have. The mere fact that all continua have grey areas (when does a hill become a mountain?) does not jeopardise the distinction. The mere fact shows only that there will be topics and matters of concern that engage both the layperson and the scientist.

Fifth, I have claimed already that it is unhelpful to regard commonsense psychology as a "theory." For similar reasons we should not think of it as employing or exploiting "laws." There is, it is true, massive generality in commonsense psychology. But the generality derives from our mastery of a subtle and sophisticated language, enriched and bewitched by the "holism of the mental," combined with the context relativity of our assessments and reactions to the behaviour of others. We know, for instance, that if X is watching O, he sees O. (Trivial.) He is likely to be interested in O. (Less trivial; often false.) If he is described as "sadistic," there are certain courses of action we might *expect* him to pursue. (Iffy, often false, but occasionally perceptive.) We have 'know-how' much more than 'know-that', in this elaborate and rich network; our mastery cannot be reduced to laws (*e.g.*, "If X fears that p, and X discovers that not-p, then X is pleased") because such alleged laws depend entirely upon the *ceteris paribus* – sometimes *ceteris absentibus* – clauses which are indeterminate, unspecific, highly context-dependent, and which do all the work. For instance, suppose that our X is a child about to go on a roller coaster. Then he may be afraid, but may very much want the feared event to happen. It is in highly specific and context-dependent individual circumstances that the apparatus of commonsense psychology really comes into its own. But when it does, the alleged invocation of "laws" looks merely silly.

Moreover, laws – in any substantial sense of the term 'law' – hold between phenomena that are systematically fruitful *explananda* and *explanantia*. Since commonsense psychology is used for countless purposes other than description and explanation, and since even when it is used to describe and explain it is only rarely and peripherally interested in *systematic* explanation, and since the richness of its conceptual apparatus precludes any search for economical systematicity anyway, it is scarcely surprising that it serenely abjures the attempt to identify and define such systematically fruitful *explananda* and *explanantia*. Hence, for this reason too, there are few if any 'laws' exploited in common sense.

[*Parenthesis:* This gives a reason, tangential to those he provides, for agreeing with Davidson that 'the mental' is *anomalous* – that there are no psychophysical laws. But the reason holds for commonsense psychology; not, as we shall see, for the scientific version. There is a further reason too; as Davidson writes, "too much happens to affect the mental that is not itself a systematic part of the mental" (1970, p. 99); mental holism is not just *mental* holism, at least not if we consider the turmoil involved in everyday coping-with-conspecifics. (What people are likely to do, and how they react, will depend on, for instance, what professional deadlines they must meet; the weather; British Rail timetables; their bank accounts; earthquakes; plane crashes; AIDS or a cold in the head; their dogs' distemper; Alzheimer's syndrome . . . and the list could continue indefinitely.)]

3. The Short History

If we accept that psychology took off (at least in Germany) in the 1860s and 1870s, then one fact about the great German founders stands out: the number of them who came to the "new science" from physiology, anatomy, medicine, or neuroscience. Wundt is merely the greatest of these, Freud (admittedly an Austrian) perhaps the most notorious. This is of course no accident. Physiology, under the guidance of such giants as Helmholtz, was extremely prestigious throughout Germany at the time. And it was one of Helmholtz's mentors, Johannes Müller, who resoundingly declared "*nemo psychologus nisi physiologus.*" Many (before Wundt) regarded themselves as physiologists engaged in work that was indifferently "physiological" or "psychological." Wundt – who had studied with Helmholtz in 1858, and who had tried hard but unsuccessfully to get one of the rare chairs in physiology – called his early lectures (in 1867) "physiological psychology."

But physiology in its turn owed its success in large part to its links with the physical sciences; and it is of course the physical sciences which, then and now, set the standards for any would-be science, whether biological or psychological. It is hard to exaggerate the impact of Newtonian physics on all Newton's successors up to the twentieth century; for Hume, Newton was "the greatest and rarest genius that ever arose for the ornament and instruction of the species." This had massive impact for the development of psychology, both ontologically and methodologically.

Ontologically: Newton had provided a picture of the physical world as consisting of simple atomic elements combining under the laws of motion. It is no accident that the British empiricists and their successors (Hume famously wanted to be the "Newton of the moral sciences") developed a picture of simple mental items ('perceptions', or impressions and ideas; later, 'sensations'; perhaps qualia, or sense data; most recently 'representations') combining under laws of association: three for Hume, one for Hartley, twelve for Brown, one for Hamilton, one for James Mill, four for John Stuart Mill. Later we find Wundt writing about the "threefold task" of psychology:

The *first* is the *analysis* of composite processes; the *second* is the *demonstration of the combinations* into which the elements discovered by analysis enter; the *third* is the *investigation of the laws* that are operative in the formation of such combinations (1897; 1907, p. 28).

His student Titchener calculated that there were 44,435 elementary sensations: "Each one of these forty thousand qualities is a conscious element, distinct from all the rest, and altogether simple and unanalyzable" (1896; 1902, p. 75).

Physics changes its ontology from time to time; it is no accident that the psychologists adapted to that, as the prestige 'superego' subject supplied different models and metaphors for the emerging one. For example, Köhler studied with Max Planck in Berlin, and acquired there an interest in field physics. The force field was one of the metaphors that inspired and set off the Gestalt school (see Wertheimer's classic paper of 1912), and was especially conspicuous when Gestalt moved from Frankfurt to Berlin; to choose just one example, the law of Prägnanz, fundamental to the Gestalt theory, exploited heavily the tendency of force fields to simplify themselves. The analogy with field physics was explicitly recognised, and pressed:

Anybody familiar with the elements of physics will be reminded of the behaviour of forces . . . the behaviour of vectors in motivational situations is the same as the behaviour of forces in nature (Köhler, 1959, p. 730).

Physics, and the physics-influenced physiology of the nineteenth century, had another ontological impact; they equally coloured every psychologist's attitude to the mind–body relation. Not all welcomed the staunch reductionism of Helmholtz, who had studied both physics and the biological sciences, and who had no doubt but that the latter could be grounded in the former. But the early psychologists either assumed that physical reduction was an achievable goal, agreeing with such as Johannes Müller, Helmholtz, and the Freud (early – 1895) of the "Project"; or, if not that, they agreed with the *later* Freud that, although such a reduction would not be achieved in their lifetime, the claims of psychology are ultimately hostage to validation or disproof from future biology; or, if not that, at least that the physical and psychological worlds could be reduced to one, for which the laws of physics could be adopted (as with Fechner's panpsychist monism); or, if not that, at least that there would be a strong psychophysical parallelism, as stressed of course by Wundt: "every elementary process on the psychical side has a corresponding elementary process on the physical side" (1897; 1907, p. 364); or, if not that, then the weakest position, that the structure of the laws governing the physical world would serve also to explain the psychological (as we find with Lotze at Göttingen).

Virtually all positions on the mind–brain relation could be and were occupied; it is, however, often unclear which of the battery of modern labels ('parallelist', 'eliminativist', 'monist', 'reductionist', 'epiphenomenalist', 'emergentist', 'functionalist', 'type identity theorist', 'token identity theorist', etc., etc.) to pin on them. Wundt for example talked of "the bodily *substrates* of mental life"; but he also as we have seen defended a thesis of point-by-point psychophysical *parallelism*. In either case, though, a belief in 'substrates', or in such a detailed parallelism, evidently helped determine the nature of the psychological ontology: The conjectural description of the physiological goings-on prescribed in part the sorts of psychological processes and capacities to which they were claimed to be parallel or of which they were the 'substrates'. The same point can be made with Freud too. His (changing) ambitions for solving the mind–brain relation show us someone who believed all his life in the principle *that* psychological phenomena must be explicable in terms of biological theory; but after the early "Project" (1895) he gave up most attempts to realise this hope.[4] That he never abandoned the principle, though, is clear from a remark of

1914: "all our provisional ideas in psychology will presumably some day be based on an organic substructure" (*S.E., xxiii*, p. 282); and, from 1920, another telling remark: "Biology . . . may . . . blow away the whole of our artificial structure of hypotheses" (*S.E., xviii*, p. 60). With Freud, too, we can even see the influence reversed:

The phenomena with which we are dealing do not belong to psychology alone; they have an organic and biological side as well, and accordingly in the course of our efforts at building up psychoanalysis we have also made some important biological discoveries and have not been able to avoid framing new biological hypotheses (*S.E., xxiii*, p. 195).

So on the one hand we have Wundt, whose physiological conjectures helped determine his psychological ontology; on the other Freud, who was no parallelist, but who was forced to abandon the hope that biology could as yet have much direct bearing on his psychology. These two (deliberately chosen to exemplify scientists working in widely disparate regions of psychology) show how from the start of the science psychology and the physiological sciences were seen as inextricably interlocked, albeit in highly subtle ways. (Just such a could easily be made by reference to others – including others working earlier in the nineteenth century, and indeed also in the eighteenth.) The impact of the biological sciences, and through them physics, runs so deep that, although entertaining, "it is forbidding to speculate about what might have happened had psychology had to start its career against a background of modern quantum theory" (Oldfield 1960, p. 33).

But the influence of physics, and the physiological training of the early scientific psychologists, reached further than this ontological input. *Methodologically* the impact ran even deeper. R. I. Watson expresses the point colourfully:

The rejected child of drab philosophy and lowborn physiology, [psychology] has sometimes persuaded itself that actually it was the child of highborn physics. It identified with the aspirations of the physical sciences, and, consequently, acquired an idealized version of the parental image as a super-ego, especially concerning scientific morality, *i.e.*, the "right" way for a scientist to behave (R. I. Watson 1973, p. 20).

It is this methodological emphasis that tends increasingly to distinguish the *philosophical* study of mind from the *scientific* study. For instance, Locke and Hume emphatically belong in the history both of philosophy and of psychology. But Hartley, Thomas Brown, de la Mettrie, and de Condillac are among the many who illustrate the growing gap in the eighteenth century between empirical and a priori approaches to the subject matter; and they belong more centrally to the history of psychology. De Condillac in particular was well schooled in the physical and mathematical sciences of the day, and insisted that their rigorous and successful canons of precision, economy, experimental purity be adopted for the study of mind, the whole to be structured by a formal mathematicological system. Then, in the Contents section of his *A System of Logic*, we find Mill introducing and summarising his Book 6 ("On the Logic of the Moral Sciences") with the comment: "[t]he backward state of the Moral Sciences can only be remedied by applying to them the methods of Physical Science, duly extended and generalised" (1862; 1906, p. *xv*). And a little later Wundt revealingly writes:

Physiological psychology is . . . first of all psychology . . . It is not a province of physiology . . . the adjective 'physiological' implies simply that our psychology will avail itself to the full of the means that modern physiology puts at its disposal . . . it is clear that physiology is, in the very nature of the case, qualified to assist psychology on the side of *method;* thus rendering the same help to psychology that it itself received from physics. . . . There are thus two problems which are suggested by the title 'physiological psychology': the problem of *method,* which involves the application of experiment, and the problem of a psychophysical *supplement,* which involves a knowledge of the bodily substrates of the mental life. For psychology itself, the former is more essential (1873–4; 1904, Preface).

We saw this in action (the quotation on p. 151) as he illustrated the "threefold task" of psychology.

Let us once again set Freud up along and against Wundt. The scientific status of Freud's psychoanalytic theories is of course much disputed. What is not in dispute – or should not be – is that Freud, with his long training in biology and neuroscience, knew very well what was required of a 'real', or 'hard', science and struggled to make his theory so. As late as 1938, one year before he died, he wrote: "[p]sychology, too, is a natural science. What else can it be?" (*S.E., xxiii,* p. 282). And, to jump to quite another extreme – someone who is as far removed from Wundt and Freud as are either of those two from each other – consider John B. Watson (who was particularly influenced by the positivist movement in the physical sciences); his concluding remark is as we have seen coincidentally echoed by Freud fourteen years later:

[The behaviorists] saw their brother-scientists making progress in medicine, in chemistry, in physics. Every new discovery in those fields was of prime importance; every new element isolated in one laboratory could be isolated in some other laboratory . . . the behaviorist asks: Why don't we make what we can *observe* the real field of psychology? . . . You will find, then, the behaviorist working like any other scientist. His sole object is to gather facts about behavior – verify his data – subject them both to logic and mathematics (the tools of every scientist). . . . Experimental technique, the accumulation of facts by that technique, occasional tentative consolidation of these facts into a theory or an hypothesis describe our procedure in science. Judged on this basis, behaviorism is a true natural science (1924; 1961, pp. 5*ff*.).

The dominance of the physical sciences as a "superego" for psychology did not go unchallenged. But William James, by his very complaint of 1890, illustrates how far it had spread in Germany:

. . . what one may call a microscopic psychology has arisen in Germany, carried on by experimental methods, asking of course every moment for introspective data, but eliminating their uncertainty by operating on a large scale and taking statistical means. This method taxes patience to the utmost, and could hardly have arisen in a country whose natives can be *bored*. Such Germans as Weber, Fechner, Vierlordt, and Wundt obviously cannot . . . (1890, p. 192).

(But remember that Newton described himself – however inadequate we find the description – as one of those he called the "dry calculators and drudges"; and he revolutionized the field.) Ebbinghaus too criticized the dominance of physics as the methodological superego; more recently, Lipsey has complained that when psychology emulates the physical sciences, it "resembles the duck that has imprinted on the football" (1974, p. 409). Maybe. But the German strategy coloured the rise of the subject in the United States and elsewhere, for two reasons: First, almost every early American psychologist of note studied in Germany before returning to establish the subject in his home country; second, because of the diaspora of German scientists before and after the second world war.

The moral of all this is clear enough. The ontologies and the methodologies of the emerging science of psychology are determined in large part by factors that have nothing whatsoever to do with the factors that colour and explain the commonsense framework.

A study of the mind that is self-consciously setting out to be a "proper" science evidently aims at theories – in a full-blooded sense of the term – and laws. To do so, as I have suggested already when contrasting commonsense psychology, it evidently needs to frame a systematic, economical, and well-defined conceptual apparatus, and to identify systematically fruitful *explananda* and *explanantia*. This was not, and is not still, an easy task. Few scientific psychologists agree about the content, and the concepts, for their work. And even in the age of the great "schools" of the early part of the century, between say 1890 and 1920, this bedeviled the science:

. . . we have the voluntaristic system of Wundt with its emphasis on will, the act psychology of Brentano stressing the basic importance of the intensionalism of psychic acts, the structuralistic psychology of Titchener glorifying sensation as the key to mental life, the psychoanalytic psychology of Freud elevating the unconscious wish to similar status, the hormic psychology of McDougall organized around the concept of instinct or innate propensity, the behaviouristic system of Watson with its focus on reflexes and conditioning, and still other systems based upon such varied central ideas as that of the principle of association or the concept of self or the notion of a Gestalt (Klein 1970, pp. 222*f.*).

It proves an interesting exercise to rewrite this paragraph in the context of the 1990s; we have at least as many clashing ontologies and theories now as Klein describes for the early history of the subject. The central point, though, is that the fight is about what should be the pivotal concepts in terms of which to suggest hypotheses and laws, to construct theories with an economical basis, to offer *systematic* explanation; and that this fight, then as now, has no bearing on the adequacy or inadequacy of commonsense psychology, nor vice versa.

4. So Why the Confusion?

So why, then, the confusion between the two? This is a topic that would need an extensive and separate treatment in its own right; for now I just want to draw attention to the role of philosophy.

I emphasised earlier that the difference between common sense and science was one of degree – sometimes a vast degree, sometimes a small one. Almost all sciences have used commonsense generalizations and observations as *springboards* for the development of science, from which they bounce more or less far from what common sense can provide. And philosophy has always (*inter alia*) examined the structure and content of language and thought. So, in Hume and Locke for instance, we can judge with hindsight which bits of their discussions of human nature are more 'psychological', and which more 'philosophical'; and it is of course no accident that the 'philosophical' bits are found more important today than the 'psychological' bits. (One example: Hume's *first* – philosophical – definition of causality has cast a far longer shadow than his *second* – psychological – one, even though he was himself undoubtedly more interested in the latter.)

However, the most weighty impact of philosophy was certainly Cartesian. Here we see centrally philosophical issues (of epistemology) determining a metaphysics for the mind, because of the threat of the Cartesian sceptic: an ontology of incorrigibly knowable, consciously immediate 'ideas', for which introspection was the single access route. Consciousness, and introspection, were the twin parameters within which most subsequent work laboured for centuries. Titchener makes this very clear:

Psychological observation is observation by each man of his own experience, of mental processes which lie open to him but to no one else . . . psychological observation is *introspection,* the looking *inward* into oneself (1899, p. 291).

What could be introspected, at least until the experimental techniques developed at Leipzig and Würzburg, and later Cornell, were naturally the commonsense contents of the layperson's mind. Indeed, *that* introspection seemed the only source of psychological knowledge is clearly seen when we look at the start of comparative psychology; we can't ask nonhuman animals to introspect, but introspection is the source of psychological data; so we have to work with analogy from our own introspective capacities:

. . . starting from what I know subjectively of the operations of my own individual mind, and of the activities which in my own organism these operations seem to prompt, I proceed by analogy to infer from the observable activities displayed by other organisms, the fact that certain mental operations underlie or accompany these activities (Romanes 1884; 1969, p. 16).

This illustrates, with a vengeance, how introspectable commonsense "data," which were inevitably *conscious* data, determined the categories within which psychology – human or nonhuman – must proceed. As early as 1898 Thorndike complained:

[Descartes's] physiological theories have all been sloughed off by science long ago. No one ever quotes him as an authority in morphology or physiology. . . . Yet his theory of the nature of the mind is still upheld by not a few, and the differences between his doctrines of imagination, memory, and of the emotions, and those of many present-day psychological books, are comparatively unimportant (Thorndike 1898; unpublished papers).

Against such a background, the overreaction of Watson's behaviourism could only act as a healthy counterpoint: Maybe, by expelling not only consciousness but also the rest of 'the mental', he kicked too much out of the domain of psychology – but he helped the emerging science to cut itself free of its second parent, philosophy.

As I have tried to argue, the emergence of the *experimental* method, quite soon after Hume recommended it, started to distinguish the a priori, "armchair" study of the mind from that of the scientists. James, as a philosopher–psychologist, thought as we have seen that "[t]his method taxes patience to the utmost, and could hardly have arisen in a country whose natives can be *bored*"; but his colleagues and successors in the United States were more prepared to join Newton as one of the "dry calculators and drudges." Yet for a long time each claimed to be studying the same subject matter: It was John Stuart Mill who defined *philosophy* as "the scientific study of the mind." (This was, indeed, why Wundt resisted Külpe's idea that psychologists should detach themselves from their homes in philosophy departments: *What* is studied is the same, even if the methods differ in the degree of systematicity.)

Philosophy has a lot to answer for.

5. Conclusion

And *this*, I claim, is the legacy that is with us yet. Although we have to some extent eased up on the idea that the psychological is coextensive with the conscious; although most of us are highly sceptical about the methodological adequacy of introspection; although almost all "cognitive scientists" would agree that the traditional 'philosophical' approach to the mind is a priori, and thus can be distinguished from the work of those in laboratories and white coats . . . despite all this, far too few acknowledge that the ambitions and scope, the subject matter, the conceptual framework, the role (or lack of it) of theories and laws divide commonsense psychology from scientific psychology just as clearly as does the acknowledged methodological difference. Hence the confusion of the two.

There is a lot of room for 'traditional' philosophical studies of the conceptual apparatus of common sense: of notions of time and space, of persons and minds, of rights and duties, of knowledge and belief, of truth and meaning, of goodness and beauty, and so on and so forth. In 'traditional' philosophy of this kind concerning psychological concepts, the label 'philosophy of mind' seems appropriate. There is also a lot of room for study of theories in physics, in psychology, and in all other sciences. Where such work concerns scientific psychology, the label 'philosophy of psychology' seems appropriate. There are certainly extensive grey areas where it is neither clear nor important whether one should rather be described as working in 'ordinary-language' philosophy, or as working in the philosophy of science or theoretical science.[5] The main point is that philosophy's role with respect to psychology is in every important respect the same as it is with mathematics, physics, chemistry, astronomy, medicine, biology, and so on. For (*a*) in all sciences there are detailed studies of scientific theories and methodologies; (*b*) in all there are examinations of 'everyday' concepts; (*c*) in all there are large swathes where (*a*) and (*b*) come together. With (*a*) and (*c*), we would hope to hear from people adequately trained both in the science in question, and in philosophy. The mistake I am trying to pinpoint as far as psychology is concerned is the assimilation of (*a*) and (*b*) – which these days tends to be captured by the pseudotag, 'philosophical psychology'. This tag is no better justified than would be 'philosophical physics'.

Labels and tags do not of course matter. (Their main role today is bureaucratic; we need to know in which building to find our own offices.) But insofar as they stand for principled views about the complex and convoluted relation between philosophy and psychology, then perhaps it does indeed matter that we should identify and assess those views.

NOTES

1. Primarily in *Inquiry* 27 (1984), 339–61; then in *Inquiry* 29 (1986), 169–85; then in J. Russell (ed.), *Philosophical Perspectives on Developmental Psychology* (Oxford: Blackwell, 1987), 3–16.
2. The "encephalization quotient" (EQ) juggles brain weight and body weight in an ill-disguised attempt to find a formula that brings humans out ahead of, say, whales or elephants (which would win on brain-weight calculations), and ahead of the lowly mouse (which would score above us on brain-to-body weight calculations). Thus $EQ = E_t/kP^a$; where E_t is the real brain size, P is body weight, and k and a are constants.
3. Pure alexia is a condition such that patients can write, but cannot read (although sometimes they can read numerals); they can recognise almost all other objects presented visually, except colours – that is, although they can accurately sort (say) orange and red colour chips, and can say *that* the sky is blue, blood is red, etc., they cannot name a colour on sight. This, I contend, is unintelligible to commonsense psychology, but is readily explicable if we resort to neuroscience.
4. He gave up *most* attempts. But he never forgot the role of biology; to take just one example, chosen at random, he wrote in 1923 that psychoanalysis was "obliged to seek a basis for the theory of instincts in biology" (S.E. *xxiii*, p. 195).
5. It is impossible to overstate the claim that there are "extensive grey areas." Quite a different example concerns epistemology – the very heart of philosophy. If Quine and others are right, the future of epistemology lies with the 'naturalized epistemologist'; and, if they are right, his research project is one that belongs to scientific psychology rather than to philosophy.

REFERENCES

Aristotle, *Metaphysics*, W. D. Ross (ed.) (Oxford: Clarendon Press, 1924).

Davidson, D., "Mental Events," in L. Foster and J. W. Swanson (eds.), *Experience and Theory* (Amherst: University of Massachusetts Press, 1970), 79–101.

Fodor, J. A., *Psychosemantics* (Cambridge, MA: MIT Press, 1987).

Freud – *see* Strachey.

James, H. (ed.), *The Letters of William James*, Vol. 1 (Boston: Atlantic Monthly Press, 1920).

James, W., *The Principles of Psychology*, Vol. 1 (New York: Henry Holt, 1890).

Klein, D. B., *A History of Scientific Psychology* (London: Routledge and Kegan Paul, 1970).

Köhler, W., "Gestalt Psychology Today," *American Psychologist* (1959) 14, 727–34.

Lipsey, M. W., "Psychology: Preparadigmatic, Postparadigmatic, or Misparadigmatic?" *Science Studies* (1974) 4, 406–10.

Mill, J. S., *A System of Logic Ratiocinative and Inductive*, 8th edition (London: Longmans, Green, and Co., 1862; 1906).

Oldfield, R. C., "Experiment in Psychology – a Centenary and an Outlook," *Advancement of Science* (1960) 17.

Romanes, G. J., *Mental Evolution in Animals* (New York: AMS Press, 1884; 1969).

Strachey, J. (ed.), *The Standard Edition of the Complete Psychological Works of Sigmund Freud*, 24 vols. (London: Hogarth Press, 1963).

Thorndike, E. L., "The Psychology of Descartes," unpublished Thorndike papers, 1898.

Titchener, E. B., *An Outline of Psychology*, 2nd edition (New York: Macmillan, 1896; 1902).

"Discussion: Structural and Functional Psychology," *Philosophical Review* (1899) 8, 290–9.

Watson, J. B., *Behaviorism* (Chicago: University of Chicago Press, 1924; 1961).

Watson, R. I., "Psychology: A Prescriptive Science," in M. Henle, J. Jaynes, and J. J. Sullivan (eds.), *Historical Conceptions of Psychology* (New York: Springer Publishing Co., Inc., 1973), pp. 13–28.

Wertheimer, M., "Experimentelle Studien über das Sehen von Bewegung," *Zeitschrift für Psychologie* (1912) 61, 161–265.

Wundt, W. M., *Principles of Physiological Psychology*, 5th edition (London: Swan Sonnenschein, 1873–4; 1904).

Outlines of Psychology, 7th edition (Leipzig: Engelmann, 1897; 1907).

Völkerpsychologie: Eine Untersuchung der Entwicklungsgesetze von Sprache, Mythus and Sitte, 2 vols. (Leipzig: Engelmann, 1900–9).

9

Common Sense Naturalized:
The Practical Stance

RADU J. BOGDAN

If commonsense psychology is the solution, what was the problem?

1. Introduction

Almost everybody believes, but nobody has conclusively shown, that commonsense psychology is a descriptive body of knowledge about the mind, the way physics is about elementary particles or medicine about bodily conditions. Of course, commonsense psychology helps itself to many notions about the mind. This does not show that commonsense psychology is about the mind. Physics also helps itself to plenty of mathematical notions, without being about mathematical entities and relations. Employment of notions about the mind does not by itself establish the nature and business of commonsense psychology. To find out what the latter's notions are *about* requires finding out what they are *for*. To find out what they are for, we should start by asking *who* employs them in *what contexts* and for *what reasons*. If we consider seriously these questions, we should not be too surprised to find out that:

1 A *subject* is an agent busily pursuing his worldly interests. In the process, he encodes, operates on, can be read for, and often deliberately conveys information about his current as well as past or future cognitive and behavioral states, and about the world around him, as it was, is, and could be.

2 A *sense maker* is also a busy agent. To pursue her worldly interests, she needs the subject as a source of information about himself and the world around him. The subject is an *information tool* that the sense maker uses for her own aims. To this end, the sense maker must select and conceptualize the information relations at a subject in a form in which, and to an extent to which, they are practically relevant and useful.

If these propositions are plausible, so are the next two:

3 Such practically motivated and information-sensitive notions provide the sense maker with the cognitive means, not only to get
data about, and thus predict or retrodict, the subject's cognition
and behavior (the primary function), but also to interpret, explain, and rationalize him (the secondary function).
4 As a result, making sense of a subject (applying commonsense
psychology) is not likely to be a theoretical pursuit aimed at producing a descriptively accurate map of mind in terms of explanatory kinds and laws. Motivated by biosocial and practical pressures, commonsense making is primarily an enterprise of extracting information from conspecifics in a context, so it must be a
psycho*praxis,* not a psychologos.

These are the basic theses of this essay. Its basic argument is mostly
programmatic: I am more interested at this stage to sketch a principled position on what commonsense psychology is, and is not, rather
than attending to the details of its conceptual mechanics and operation in particular cases. But there will be enough examples and details, I hope, to lubricate and validate the argument.

I begin in Part 2 with the critical claim that commonsense psychology is not a logos of the psyche. 'Psychology' is therefore a misnomer,
for there is no logos in common sense. This is why I will be talking
mostly of commonsense *making.* ('Making' is closer to the idea of
practice which I associate with the use of commonsense notions.) Not
being a logos, common sense does not have the conceptual functions
we attribute to a logos, namely to explain and predict from the nature
and the laws of the entities and processes in its domain. I then suggest, in Part 3, a naturalization strategy in terms of which commonsense making is shown to be a specialized cognitive competence whose
original and essential function must have been to read the intelligent
psyche of our conspecifics for the information useful in contexts of
action, cooperation, and conflict. Part 4 puts this psychoinformational
hypothesis to work. Examples are considered and implications are
drawn to the effect that, with respect to content, commonsense concepts are not about data structures (or representations) and other
internal conditions of a subject but rather about the information that
a subject's psyche conveys about the world and/or self in a context.
This is why I call the concepts of common sense *psychoinformational.* In
Part 5 commonsense explanations are shown to be parasitic on infor-
mation-providing predictions and retrodictions; and even when

intended as genuine explanations, they utilize notions that are psychoinformational, not descriptive of the mind.

The argument of this essay assumes a sharp distinction between intentionality and content. The former is an objective property of the functional design and operation of our cognition, a matter about which I have nothing to say here (but see Bogdan 1988a). Content, as understood by common sense, is quite another animal. To attribute content, common sense relies on the intentionality or aboutness of cognition, just as it relies on various properties of the world and of behavior. But 'reliance on' does not mean 'theory of' or even 'concept of'. To do its job, common sense need not have a theory of the intentionality of cognition; and, not surprisingly, it doesn't have any. As a result, its notion of content need not be, and is not, explicative of that of intentionality. Nor, conversely, is the notion of intentionality (which may end up being elucidated by the sciences of cognition or by metascientific reflection on them) explicative of that of content. The naturalization of content, and of its paradigm, commonsense psychology, is an enterprise quite distinct from the naturalization of intentionality and mental causation. This paper is concerned only with the former enterprise.

When used *philosophically*, our mentalist vocabulary is nevertheless torn between intentionality and content. Endemic confusion of the two is not the only culprit. Current philosophy of mind and language has the programmatic objective of analyzing intentionality in terms of content, and vice versa. This is a misguided effort. The result is tension (intuitions fighting each other) and frustration (no solution). The tension is absent in the *normal* use of mentalist words which is eminently geared to content, and is calculated to appeal to cognitive representations and *their* aboutness only to the extent to which they contribute to content fixation in a context. My use of mentalist words in this paper follows common sense (as diagnosed) and is normal. In this sense, I assume that, for example, the commonsense notion of belief picks up a token representation, having *its* aboutness for a subject, and places it in a network of content-constituting (or information-fixing) relations, relative to a sense maker, in a context; and I deny that the network in question, specified for a sense maker, can possibly define a genuine and causally efficacious *type* of internal mental states of a subject.

Themes of this essay are present in some recent philosophical and psychological works. Although I learned from and relied on them, I do not want to imply that their authors would agree with either my account or the way I put their insights to work for my theses. To locate

my approach on this friendly map and pay respects, while also anticipating differences, let me mention a few key points of reference. The
recent literature on animal psychology (Premack and Woodruff 1978;
Griffin 1984; Dennett 1987) has brought home the realization that
animals may be attributing to each other cognitive and conative states
as they read each other for information and try to predict the other's
next moves. It does not make much sense to assume that animals
engage in such attributions for explanatory reasons. What they need
is the information their conspecifics and others may provide. If animals do it, humans do it too, for they are animals who depend informationally on their conspecifics. The animal connection suggests a
competence for cognitive and conative attributions that has adaptive
benefits (Fodor 1987).

Frege may have been the first to note that our interest in the reference of words betrays an interest in how the world is. Field (1978),
Loar (1981), and Schiffer (1981) have developed this insight by arguing that we generally exploit mind–world relations to gain information about the world, and that this exploitation has a lot to do with our
content attributions and the semantic constructs we devise for this
purpose. Their position is that the fact of someone believing something can be construed as reliable information about how the world is.
My account looks at the same relation from the other direction: The
fact that one needs another to supply one with information about the
world is reason to construe the other as believing something about
the world. Both the content and the attitude attributed are commonsense constructs posited in order to secure and conceptualize the
information of interest.

Putnam's and Burge's well-known puzzles, and diagnoses thereof,
have prompted and spread the realization that attributions of mental
states have at least two, and often incongruous, objectives, one, to
explain behavior, the other, to identify and evaluate the semantic relations between mental states and the world. This is how the dual-track,
or two-factors, theories of propositional attitudes construe our ordinary psychological notions (Field 1978; Loar 1981; McGinn 1982). I
agree with the standard diagnosis that what is semantically evaluable
cannot also be explanatory. But I seriously disagree with the explanatory role foisted on the internal or cognitive track of our content
attributions. This is the logos myth coming back through the window.

Although not dedicated specifically to the story of commonsense
making, Barwise and Perry's book on situation semantics (1983) contains perhaps the most elaborate treatment of how sense makers utilize subjects, particularly as speakers, for getting the information they

need. The notion that commonsense making is a practice concerned with particular contexts, rather than a protoscientific theory in search of general patterns and laws in human psychology, has been defended by Morton (1980) and Wilkes (1981), among others. This line of analysis has been anticipated by some early ordinary-language analyses of Wittgenstein, Austin, and Urmson. From a logos stance, Stich (1983) has also provided insights into the pragmatic and contextual workings of commonsense psychology.

Finally, should you be reading what follows as another exercise in eliminativism? You should, if your thought on the matter is characterized by the following two assumptions: (*i*) the commonsense notions have the function to pick up types of internal states; *and* (*ii*) the types in question are posited for logos or theoretically explanatory reasons. If you do not buy these assumptions, and at the same time hold that commonsense making has quite a different domain of application, and hence has integrity, conceptual autonomy, and an important business to do, and moreover is not false of *its* genuine domain, is not in competition with science, and cannot therefore be eliminated by (or for that matter, reduced to) any science, then you are with me, and we definitely are not eliminativists. When I mention eliminativism in what follows I have in mind logos eliminativism (of the Churchland sort) which foists the wrong ontology of intrinsic cognitive types on commonsense making. If I am eliminating anything, it is this wrong ontology, not a wise body of practical knowledge.

2. The Logos Impasse

A Puzzle

Commonsense psychology finds itself at the tender and elusive center of our understanding of the mind, which is why people are passionate about it. For its defenders, commonsense psychology has a unique and privileged hold on how the mind works. For its proscientific defenders, this folkloric wisdom must be absorbed by the sciences of cognition if they are to be successful. For the antiscientific defenders of common sense, the principled failure of science to accommodate our folk wisdom about the mind is a reaffirmation of the mind(folklore)–body(science) dualism. For its detractors, however, commonsense psychology has no hold on what the mind is and how it works. What common sense offers is simply a conceptual myth, often practically useful for limited purposes, but in general a troublemaker because attractive yet ultimately false.

Both the pro and con positions face a puzzle. On the one hand, it looks as though no matter what domain of facts common sense is wise about, it is a superficial wisdom, bound to be wrong, ultimately and fundamentally. This expectation is grounded both in reflection on the nature of common sense and on the historical record of its accomplishments. Nobody expects folk physics or folk biology to be ultimately and fundamentally true of matter or life. On the other hand, as friend and foe acknowledge, common sense is not only good at figuring out minds and behaviors but indispensable. It offers a conceptual scheme about the mind that we simply cannot do without. This fact presents foes and friends with a vexing question. For the foes, the question is one of success and indispensability based on falsity. If commonsense psychology is ontological nonsense, in that it refers to no genuine and causally active properties of the mind, how can it succeed and be indispensable in explaining and predicting what people think, want, and do? For the friends, the vexing question is what sort of truth common sense has access to that would explain its success and indispensability. If common sense is good at figuring out what people think, want, and do, it must know something important about minds; what could that be?

The Logos Fallacy

Both friend and foe attempt to explain (or explain away) the apparent success of commonsense psychology from the wrong premise. I call it the *logos thesis*. It says that in making psychological sense of our conspecifics we employ a logos, a theory, with principled types (beliefs, thoughts, desires, etc.) and generalizations (if belief and desire, then intention; if intention, then action; and the like) whose business is to explain and predict from true representations of how things are in its domain, essentially, or in virtue of the nature of the things. A scientific logos is indeed expected to deliver types, generalizations, and hence explanations which appeal to the *nature* of things in its domain. I will call these *N-types, N-generalizations,* and *N-explanations.* Because it N-explains from N-types and generalizations, common sense must be a genuine theory, a *logos:* and because it explains cognition and behavior, it must be a logos of the *psyche.* The logos thesis about common sense is compatible with several versions of N-explanation, from the deductive nomological to functional and even interpretational. In what follows, I will have in mind mostly the first two.

The reasoning behind the logos thesis seems to be based on the principle that the success of a theory points to its essential function which in turn points to its ontology. Commonsense psychology is successful at explanation; what it is successful at must indicate its essential function, to explain; and since what is being explained by common sense concerns cognition and behavior, commonsense making must be about some N-types and N-regularities of cognition and behavior. This reasoning starts from a good premise but ends in a fallacy.

The good premise connects the essential function of a body of knowledge with its ontology.[1] This premise is justified by the general observation that whenever structures have functions, the latter can be thought of as constraining the former in the sense that (over time) the structures do not get organized that way, or selected and preserved if already organized, unless they perform the desired functions. If we *further* assume that N-explanation is the essential function of common sense, then we can infer that, in order to be properly served, N-explanation is bound to constrain (select, shape, or favor) concepts that can do an N-job. This would mean that the commonsense concepts are N-explanatory the way (say) the concepts of force and gravitation are N-explanatory in physics: they are posited to represent the basic entities and properties in the domain which, together with laws governing them, allow us to N-explain various events in the domain.

This is how the commonsense psychological concepts end up as N-explanatory in different guises: They are assimilated to either relations to syntactic forms in a language of thought, or to dispositions to behave, or to neural states of some sort, or to phenomenal experiences, depending on which theoretical paradigm one adopts as true of the nature of cognition. On either paradigm, though, the N-explanatory role that is foisted on the commonsense concepts is dictated by an antecedent theoretical ontology of "cognitive natures." Thus, for cognitivism, belief is a computational relation to a syntactic form because (antecedently) syntactic form and computational relation are N-explanatory types (cognitive natures) in the cognitivist ontology; or belief is assimilated to the notion of disposition to behave upon stimulus registration because (antecedently) disposition, behavior, and stimulus are N-explanatory types in the behaviorist ontology; and so on. For eliminativists, the commonsense notions are theoretical fictions precisely because they cannot be assimilated to the N-explanatory types (be they syntactic forms, neural states, connectionist networks, or whatever) antecedently accepted in the ontology of the neurosciences.

If our commonsense wisdom is N-theoretical and N-explanatory, then comparing it with science is both inevitable and instructive. For, when construed as genuine logoi of the mind, both common sense and the cognitive sciences appear to be in the business of conceptualizing the way the mind is *in order to* N-explain cognition and behavior. The common sense concepts then are either about N-explanatory types, in which case the sciences of cognition ought to adopt and refine them (the somewhat friendly reductionist position), or are about no such types, in which case the sciences of cognition ought to eliminate and replace them with its own (the definitely unfriendly eliminativist position).

Now the fallacy itself. It is all right to reason from the essential function of a body of knowledge to its ontology. (I will use this principle later in my own argument. So it must be all right.) But it is not all right, since fallacious, to reason *from* the success of a body of knowledge at explanation *to* the notion that N-explanation is the essential function of that body of knowledge, and hence *to* the notion that the latter is a logos about the nature of things. This fallacy, alas, is quite endemic. Friends and foes of folk have all-too-blindly jumped to the conclusion that common sense is essentially in the business of N-explanation because it is *good at* explanation (or, more exactly, at something that looks like explanation).

Many concepts can be used successfully to explain something or other, in some manner or another. This does not mean that their essential business is explanation, nor that the explanation they are capable of is particularly of the N-sort. My concept of table (together with other facts) enables me to explain why, and predict that, objects on the table will not fall to the ground (because the top is solid and will hold things not too heavy) and other such things, in some intuitive form of explanation and prediction. Yet, as far as I can tell, my concept of table was not formed *in order to* explain these profound verities, nor was it formed to explain them the N-way, in terms of some deep and natural facts and laws. My concept of table is a practical concept whose business is to enable me to recognize as well as to physically handle tables. The concept also helps me to explain and predict a number of things, in a rather degenerate way, but it does this on the side, as it were, without reaching too far into the nature of tables, if there is one.

In general, concepts are formed, changed, or abandoned under constraints reflecting some essential function, even though they can and do perform other less essential functions, on the side. [One can keep the fire alive with a philosophy book or two but this is not what (most) philosophy books are essentially for.] If the constraints on concepts are N-explanatory, then we have one sort of concepts (the scientific sort), whatever other things we may do with them. When the constraints reflect functions essentially other than N-explanation, then success in explanation must originate in an ontology posited for other than N-theoretical reasons, and be measured by criteria other than N-theoretical.

Another way of reaching the same conclusion is to note that the constraints on scientific explanation make N-concepts and N-theories unable to discharge the functions of commonsense making. This ought to suggest that common sense would be foolish to imitate science, even if it could. It is rational for commonsense making *not* to be about what science is about, and *not* to operate the way science does. Consider two major constraints on psychological explanation, methodological solipsism and methodological individualism (Fodor 1987, Chapter 2). The former urges that psychological states be type individuated without respect to their semantic relations, while the latter urges that those states be type individuated with respect to their causal powers. Both recommendations favor internal structures as N-explanantia. Methodological individualism favors internal structures because they alone have the causal powers to drive cognition and behavior; unless the input is internally tokened in some structure, it has no causal efficacy. Methodological solipsism favors a nonsemantic reading of the internal structures because their causal powers do not have access to their semantic relations. Internal structures cause in virtue of their being the right sort of structures (syntactic, neural, whatever), not in virtue of their being semantically pregnant structures. Yet common sense not only needs data structures that are semantically evaluable; it needs the very information relations that invite semantic evaluation. Both these needs make the N-explanation inappropriate for common sense. Moreover, as I am going to argue later, the need that common sense has for information and semantic relations should also alert us that its explanations cannot be of a truly causal form.

3. The Praxis Alternative

The Naturalization

To find out what commonsense making is all about, I suggest we ask some basic questions about its origins and rationale. Common sense must have biosocial roots which developed into a specialized skill or competence underlying our mastery and use of sense-making concepts and attributions. The competence can be construed as a design solution to the practical problems posed by treating a conspecific's psyche as an information tool.

If making sense of one another is a cognitive competence, it matters how we approach the competence. Here is an analogy. Vision and language processing are now rather well-understood cognitive competences precisely because their more recent theories have started from basic questions and have not been fooled (as earlier philosophical and psychological theories all too often have been) by the superficial effects and uses of visual and linguistic outputs. The innovative approaches of Noam Chomsky and David Marr to the study of language processing and vision, respectively, owe very much to their methodological insight of asking first questions about the rationale for, and function of, a cognitive competence *before* asking more technical questions about design, implementation, and performance.

To answer the fundamental questions, What is a cognitive competence *for?*, What is its *essential function?*, we must begin by asking, What is the *original* or *ur problem* that the competence itself is a solution to? What is the rationale for having such a competence?[2] Once we have the answers to these questions, we can ask the more technical questions about the conditions of the exercise of the competence. The first technical question to ask is, Given the conditions in which the sense-making competence must be exercised, what are the *problems* faced by its exercise? Then we can consider the cognitive *means* (concepts, programs, formalisms, attribution, and interpretation strategies, etc.) by which these problems are solved. It is only at this point that we should concern ourselves with the ways in which the solutions are actually *implemented,* implicitly by architecture and explicitly by representation.

Let us compare for a moment this methodology with the one still popular in the analysis of propositional attitudes and content ascriptions. We note, with David Marr, that cognitive representations and algorithms can be better understood in terms of the nature of the problem being solved than in terms of the mechanism and the hardware in which they are embodied. For our discussion, think of 'representations' as commonsense judgments (attributions and evaluations), of 'algorithms' as rules and recipes under which such judgments are formed, and of 'mechanisms' as the (typically language-bound) means by which the 'algorithms' are applied, and the judgments made. The 'mechanisms' would include logical forms, grammatical constructions, semantic relations (reference, etc.) and artifacts (propositions, etc.), and so on.

While few philosophers would recommend a study of human hardware in order to understand our commonsense concepts and judgments, a long, distinguished, and very influential tradition initiated by Frege has regarded the logical, semantic, and grammatical 'mechanisms' operating in language as providing the key to the nature of these concepts and judgments (or 'representations'). If the thesis of this essay is right, such analyses of 'mechanisms' must come late in our study of commonsense making, rather than being its starting point.

Methodologically, then, the Fregean tradition has got things upside down when it comes to understanding commonsense making. I call the phenomenon "the Fregean inversion." The reason it is an inversion is that analyses of 'mechanisms' can only tell us how (by what means) commonsense concepts are applied, and commonsense judgments are formed, but not what these concepts and judgments are for, and why they operate the way they do. The logos thesis has conspired with the Fregean inversion, in ways that I cannot detail here, to shape our philosophical intuitions about commonsense making. In so doing, it has obscured the latter's nature and functions.

The methodological policy I am suggesting is meant to free us from this unholy coalition. The policy can be formulated in four steps:

(*i*) *ur* problem ⇒ function and domain of the competence
(*ii*) function + conditions of execution in the domain ⇒ problems
(*iii*) problems ⇒ types of solutions
(*iv*) implementation of the solutions: (*a*) explicit, by representations
    (*b*) implicit, by architectural assumptions

(*i*) to (*iv*) implicitly approximate what I mean by *naturalization* in this chapter, for they point to a disciplined method of answering the question: What is the nature of commonsense making? What I am talking about is a *design* or functional naturalization, as opposed to the much more popular notion of naturalization as ontological reduction constrained by some truth of science. I do not think we should *begin* with an ontological or reductive analysis of commonsense notions, for we do not yet know what the analysanda (belief, desire, thought) are. And we do not know that because we do not yet know what their ontology is; to determine the latter we must first figure the essential function of commonsense making. The questions I begin with are about commonsense *making*, the enterprise itself. They are questions about its function, design, and *raison d'être*. The answers will tell us what the business of the enterprise is, and hence what its domain of operation or ontology is. Only when we know the latter can we fruitfully ask analytic or reductive questions about the constitutive notions (belief, desire) and the sort of entities or relations these notions represent.

This chapter is exclusively about step (*i*), with rare intimations of (*ii*) and (*iii*) here and there. Although we get to identify the general ontology of commonsense making, I will have nothing specific to say about how the commonsense notions concretely engage and operate in this ontology. As a result, my discussion is going to be very much unlike most in the current literature. The knowledgeable reader is warned that the familiar logical and semantic problems of commonsense ascriptions and evaluations belong to steps (*iii*) and (*iv*), on which I will keep extremely mum. I know I will be losing readers when this sentence is over, but that's naturalization, incremental, modest, and slow.

The Competence

The psychological facts about commonsense making point to a cognitive competence that is specieswide and transcultural. We all make sense of our conspecifics in roughly the same ways, beginning at about the same age, without much effort, unreflectively, fairly quickly, and a good deal of the time successfully. Neither culture nor age nor talent nor education nor tribal affiliation seem to contribute much, either positively or negatively, to the basic exercise of this competence. We communicate to each other the results of our making-sense efforts much better than those of other intellectual efforts. Artists, advertisers, German-accented shrinks, political manipulators, and generally sensitive and thoughtful people are often said to be better sense makers than the rest of us. This may well be true, but we are talking here of meat and potatoes sense making, not of French cuisine.

There are also familiar historical and biological facts which indicate that the competence is robust, deeply ingrained and durable, and possibly innate.[3] Historically, commonsense making does not appear to have significantly evolved, if at all. This fact tells some logos people (for example, eliminativists such as Churchland 1979, or Stich 1983) that there is something wrong with commonsense psychology. It would indeed be, if the latter were an explanatory logos. But it isn't. As a matter of fact, its very lack of intellectual evolution ought to warn us that the exercise of the competence does not have grandiose epistemic objectives and hence is not, and is not meant to be, an evolving body of theoretical knowledge. This, in turn, is a sign that commonsense making is likely to be immune to empirical falsification. I construe the historically proven conservatism of common sense as evidence that the competence at work is a psychological answer to some permanent practical features of our existential situation.

The biological data, still tentative and incomplete, seem nevertheless to suggest that common sense may have an animal pedigree of sorts.[4] That could possibly point to a competence somewhat incrementally shaped by evolution, as opposed to one accidentally and uniquely ours. A number of advanced species seem to have their members sizing each other up, psychologically, before improvising an appropriate course of action, or engaging in deception, or doing other such intelligent things. The animal story offers a delicate balance between the need for making sense of conspecifics (which is obviously there) and the cognitive resources needed to do the job (which most often are not). We are still guessing where to draw the line.

The ur Problem

Why make sense of the others? Why such a competence? Because others are a good, often the only, information source about themselves and their environment. Consider animals first. If you are a rabbit in the forest, you must be able to establish whether the fox is full and unlikely to be aggressive in the near future, or whether the lady rabbit is in the mood, or whether the dog has noticed you, or other such pleasant or unpleasant things. Animals face such problems constantly. Many animal species also engage in more complex activities such as traveling and hunting together, caring together for the young, playing together, gathering information, signaling danger, communicating various other things, or building a home – activities that all have a social and often cooperative character. To engage in such activities, animals must have ways of figuring out and anticipating each other's behavioral states as well as those of the world, present as well as future. A scared rabbit tells another rabbit that the fox or the dog or the hunter or some other danger is not far away. A rabbit seeing another rabbit running by, scared, finds out how the world was and still is, for the other, and how it will soon be for itself. (It is a damn scary world.)

It is often said that superior animals are "natural psychologists," that some even have a "theory of mind" which allows them to make attributions of cognitive and conative states to conspecifics and humans as well. Simple organisms have a few vital goals, not much else, and are likely to be innately attuned to the vital goals of other organisms, conspecific or not. The rabbit is a natural fox psychologist! It has no problems knowing the fox's obsessive goals. It has to sweat a bit to figure out the cognitive and motivational states of the fox. If not wired already, some simple associative learning will teach the rabbit a few helpful truths. This would not be much different from how the rabbit learns that barking correlates with dogs, dogs with being chased, being chased with having to run, and having to run with running.

Being a social animal may be necessary but not sufficient for developing a sense-making competence. Bees cooperate by sharing incomplete but cumulative information, yet they need not make much sense of each other. They are wired to access and share the collective information. Beavers cooperate in building shelters, and dolphins in saving a sick companion, yet even these remarkable cooperative accomplishments are still compatible with genetic readiness or simple associative learning. Whatever such social animals learn about conspecifics and, through them, about the world is likely to be more attuned to the vagaries of the context rather than to the vagaries of the conspecifics to be made sense of.

It is this very last difference that holds an important *cognitive* clue to the nature of common sense. Making sense of a human subject, or of the world as represented by a human subject, is not so much a matter of being intelligent in general (which dolphins and chimps are, to some extent), as of being intelligent about the subject's *psyche*. Common sense requires intelligence about another intelligence. This is the *psychoinformational* half of the *ur* problem to which commonsense making is an answer: How to read and tap an intelligent psyche for the information of interest? This is part of the question to which the competence for commonsense making is an answer.

Intelligence about Intelligence

Intelligence being a notoriously tricky notion, I will simplify it to coincide with the capacity for problem solving and means–ends reasoning. An organism is deemed intelligent if it can achieve its ends by flexible and often novel means attuned to changing circumstances. Intelligence thus requires individual improvisation, as opposed to species adaptation. The former is at work on an ad hoc and short-term basis, the latter requires structural changes whose benefits (if any) are only long term. Intelligence makes individual cognition adaptive. Animals are tested for intelligence in terms of their ability to solve (new) problems before reaching their goals. Köhler's chimp Sultan, for example, was famous for having taken a branch off a bushy tree in his cage in order to recover a banana lying beyond the bars of the cage.

Why is Sultan said to be intelligent? Because he solves a means–ends problem in a novel and constructive way. He projects an interim goal (to find a way to reach the banana) and perceives something (the branch) as the means to get him to the final goal (the banana). To satisfy the interim goal Sultan projects an even more proximal goal (get a tool in the form of a branch) and perceives an action (breaking off the branch) as getting him to satisfy the latter goal. Both the successive projections of interim goals and the perceptions that guide the actions toward the satisfaction of these goals are newly formed to fit the circumstances. The branch itself is perceived as a tool for getting an interim result. Treating things as means to solve problems to achieve ends is a mark of intelligence.

Suppose now that the other chimps around Sultan often go about their business handling things the way Sultan handled the branch and the banana. The chimps are intelligent problem solvers. Suppose also that they share some goals, and solve a number of problems by social cooperation. Their practical intelligence acquires a social dimension. Suppose, finally, that these intelligent problem-solving chimps constantly inform each other about themselves and the world in order to pursue their individual and communal activities. To do that, they must not only form concepts and make judgments and inferences about their intelligent conspecifics, in order to obtain the information of interest (the psychoinformational problem). They must also codify and regiment the concepts and judgments in question, if the latter are to be socially useful and recognizable. This is the other, *social,* half of the *ur* problem facing common sense. This is the half about which I will have nothing important to say in this paper.

Why is intelligence relevant to understanding commonsense making? Because there are key features of commonsense making that are best explained by the hypothesis that commonsense making is an intelligent practice of extracting information from intelligent subjects. The fact that the subject is intelligent creates operational problems for the exercise of the sense-making competence [problems that a full account must specify at step (*ii*)], which in turn influence the solutions [to be envisaged at step (*iii*)] that the commonsense notions and judgments embody [step (*iv*)]. The beginning of the story could go as follows.

Intelligent cognition can be individualized and creative (in Chomsky's sense) in how it computes and encodes its data, and hence innovative in how the data convey the information of potential interest to a sense maker. It takes intelligence to register, track, and figure out another intelligence. Simple associative concepts that animals can form, or architectural assumptions they are wired to have, are not going to work when it comes to dealing with an intelligent psyche as informant. Common sense must be geared to these properties of intelligent cognition to be successful; and it documentably is (Morton 1980; Wilkes 1981; Bogdan 1986a). As a result, the commonsense explanandum (*e.g.*, a particular intention formed, or a specific action performed) is unique in an *essential* way – unlike the scientific explanandum (*e.g.*, a body falling to the ground, or a cell dividing) which is uniform, average, generic, and unique only inessentially (*i.e.*, with respect to space, time, and other boundary conditions) (Bogdan 1988b). Having such an essentially unique explanandum, the commonsense explanation is bound to be baroque, improvisational, reconstructional, and heavily ceteris paribus. Since intelligence is cognitively penetrable and has holistic access to information, there are many ways in which an intelligent agent can structure his data and thus inform on a situation. The sense maker is therefore bound to make guesses and engage in reconstruction, which she can discipline and keep under control only by simplifications and ceteris paribus assumptions. The role of the latter is to exploit context and experience to eliminate most of the possible routes to representation and action that intelligence allows.

Intelligence provides us with one important instance where the logos view gets things wrong. To say, with the logos people, that commonsense explanations simply premise beliefs and desires to infer actions is to emphasize the trivial while missing the essential. Of course, any organism acts on its data and its needs; and almost any organism (even simpler ones) must be aware of this truism in some form or another when it reacts to another. We would not worry so much about common sense if that were *all* its wisdom about cognition and behavior. The real logistical problem for common sense is not that intelligent organisms act on data and needs. The real problem is how their intelligence allows them to *represent* their data and needs – representations that a sense maker must identify if she is to track the information of interest. Commonsense attributions and inferences are hard for the analyst of common sense to understand, not because they premise data and needs, but because those attributions and inferences encapsulate ways of tracking the subject's intelligently utilized data and needs for the information relevant to a sense maker.

4. Psychoinformation

If the psyche of a subject is primarily an information tool, how does a sense maker utilize it to get the information she wants? I am going to begin with some simple and intuitive examples. The emphasis is on content, not attitude, that is, on the information that a subject's representations or data structures convey to a sense maker, not the causal efficacy of those representations. I use the notions of representation or data structure in the technical sense of explicit displays of mental symbols, such as images, linguistic forms, and so on, in an internal data space, perhaps a short-term memory. The point I will be trying to get across is that such data structures do not generally *encode* the contents (beliefs, thoughts, desires) that common sense is attributing in sentences of the form '*S* believes that *p*'. The *p* in the content clause is generally type individuated in relational or psychoinformational terms, not in internal representational or datal terms. The *p* that *S* believes, according to the commonsense attribution, is not the data structure he encodes in his cognitive data space.

The psychoinformational type individuation of content is a result of *practical reconstruction*. It is practical because, normally, both the sense maker and the subject are agents going about their businesses. The information the subject provides the sense maker must be relevant to the latter's goals and agency, or else why would a busy agent want to be a sense maker? To get this information, the sense maker must engage in reconstruction. At some time and in some context, out of the subject's many cognitive and behavioral conditions pregnant with information, the sense maker selects and reconstructs only those which provide her with the information needed, in the form needed. The world can also be an informant about an agent, or itself. But again, the world is big, stuffed with information, whereas the sense maker is small, busy, confined by current interests and with limited time on her hands.

Cases of Sense Making

Suppose you ascribe to me the belief that it is going to rain on the basis of the fact that I am walking faster, looking at the sky, and reaching for my umbrella. You are right to make this belief ascription. But, let me tell you, I am doing many other mental and behavioral things at the same time, things that you may not know about. In fact, I am so routinized about rain in this damp and frivolous city that I have

"compiled" the information and no longer form any explicit representation of it. I keep my data space free for more worthy items of
interest. So I simply walk faster and reach for the umbrella automatically, while *at the same time* doing many other things: worrying about
the force of this very example in the economy of my argument, hearing various noises and inferring to their uncivilized sources, seeing
various objects and events, remembering something else, and so on.
The belief you are ascribing to me (the information that explains my
behavior) and its form (the very proposition attributed) are the result
of *your* reconstruction from bits and pieces I and the world offer. You
simplify, amalgamate, and summarize a whole lot. I certainly do not
encode my data *in the form* of information assumed by your ascription.
I am only an information tool in your hands.

In the other direction (world to mind), you could have used the fact
that it is going to rain to anticipate a belief I am likely to form and the
behavior it is likely to cause. You now use the world as an information
base to identify my internal conditions, representational as well as
physical. The belief you ascribe (that it will rain) need not match the
form of any of my current representations. I might not explicitly
represent anything to that effect. Your belief ascription reconstructs
and summarizes something about me (my internal conditions) on the
basis of something about the world (external facts) in a fashion that is
suitable for sense making (getting the desired information).

Let us now change your interest but keep me, as an informant, and
the context the same. Suppose you are now interested in some cause
of my behavior (the sudden change to a faster pace), and are satisfied
to establish that I must have noticed something (no matter what). To
get this result, you only have to attribute to me the perception that
something happened by inferring (on the basis of some behavioral
evidence) to no more than my tokening a representation caused by an
external event. The attribution allows you to obtain information
about the presence of an external cause from the evidence of its effect
in me. The *form* of the information *you* thus reconstruct is not propositional anymore, although the representation *I* encode cannot fail to
be propositional since it is about some fact or another. But since you
are interested only in an unspecified event, you do not care to reconstruct my representations in propositional form. You reconstruct only
the *causal* form of the information relation I have with the world, for,
as mere effect, my representations (not what they represent, just their
physical tokening) suffice to indicate the physical presence of some
causing event. You could have exercised other attribution options as
well, if your interests demanded it.

Things do not change much when the information is deliberately communicated. People communicate to achieve goals. If I am telling you that it is getting late and we should hurry, you, as sense maker, get more than what is literally said. You not only determine my belief that it is getting late and we should hurry, and also the conditional belief that if it is getting late, one should hurry; if, to change the context of your interest but not what is said, you are worried about me, you may take the utterance to inform on my impatience. You may do so on the evidence of what I say or how I say it. I am a versatile informant, and so is everybody else. A speaker's utterance can be the tip of an iceberg or the whole iceberg. It depends on what and how much information the sense maker needs, in what form, and for what purpose.

Here is a collective case of sense making (inspired by Dennett 1987, pp. 56–7). Imagine different people in different places doing their different cognitive and behavioral things and to whom a (type) similar belief is attributed. Imagine that, at a specific time period $t1$, I ascribe to them the belief that urban ugliness breeds confused and erratic thinking and behavior; I abbreviate the belief as p. Not only are the hardware configurations of these people different at $t1$, but so is almost everything else in and around them, in particular the information flows they are part of, and hence the cognitive and conative data structures they currently token. Suppose their beliefs that p are *virtual* in the sense that they are only entailed or suggested by a variety of other explicit data structures our subjects encode but do not share. It takes a reconstruction to isolate and lift the belief that p out of the many data structures among which it is implicatively buried in different brains busy doing different things in different environments. Their belief that p is the summary of such a reconstruction, not a literally realistic description of their data structures. This is, by the way, how we often attribute political beliefs to people, not from the literal expressions of their representations, but rather, by way of summary, from reconstructing such beliefs from bits and pieces of what people say or even how they say it.

My Data, Your Information

The most important thing these examples are calculated to show is that it is the sense maker's information that determines what counts as the *content* of the subject's belief. What you construe as my belief that it rains is the outcome of utilizing a frame or grid that you impose on my psyche's relation to the world to fix the information you need in a context. The belief you ascribe to me (that it rains) is formulated as a fact you are interested in. Neither the event (raining) nor my internal representation of it (whatever that is) need have the format (factive construction), the degree of abstraction (ignoring other events involved in raining as well as in my representation of raining), and the implications (logical, functional) of the attitude report in which you summarize the information in question. This is not a claim about the particulars of the case but rather about how the sense maker uses the conceptual resources at her disposal in this case and others.

If you were to represent me in another attitude report as *perceiving* that it rains, you would use the same content sentence (that it rains). Yet obviously what I am said to perceive and believe, when it comes to raining or anything else, come in vastly different forms of internal representation with respect to format (images may be analog, hence nonfactive, beliefs are factive and digital), degree of abstraction (images take in a lot of detail, beliefs don't), and implications (beliefs interact inferentially with other beliefs and desires, images don't; beliefs often need linguistic encoding, images don't; and so on). Obviously you don't care about these *internal* differences in encoding. You are not a psycho*logist*. You are not interested in how my head works or what it literally contains, except to the limited, superficial and pragmatic extent to which it tells you something interesting about the world or about myself. You are a psychopractician, not a theorist.

Your abstractive moves (what to consider, in what form, and what to disregard) in portraying me, first as believing that p and then as perceiving that p, can be best explained by the hypothesis that what you, as a sense maker, are after is information about a condition of the world (that it is p) or of me (that I represent p), relative to the condition of the other relatum. What other reason could there be to use the same sentence to specify such vastly different internal cognitive conditions of the subject as those involved in perceiving and believing? The same could be said, by the way, about belief and desire. We represent them in the same content descriptions (I believe that p; I desire that p) but the internal data structures involved must be vastly different from a psychological point of view. Our content formulations therefore must envisage something other than just the internal representations associated with beliefs and desires.

We should also remember that our ordinary language is rich enough to allow all sorts of constructions when the need arises. Consider perception. If I want to describe the *proximal input* of your perception of a fact, as opposed to a *fact* you perceive (via the input), I can say something like, "it appears to you, as you visualize the scene in front of you, that there is a patch of color which. . . ." The sense-data terminology would indeed have a point *if* the content descriptions were calculated to pick up features of the stimulus or indeed of the image it causes. Yet even a sense-data description cannot fail to be psychoinformational, albeit at a closer remove, as it singles out (narrower) informational covariations between data structures and stimuli, and describes the former in terms that inform on the latter.

The examples also show how the same content sentence can be used by the sense maker to find out how the subject or the world are, will be, have been, or could be, possibly or even counterfactually. If you take me to believe that it rains, you not only find out how the world is right now and in the near future (rainy) but also, as a future event, how I am likely to behave (walk faster, mutter some harsh words), how I came to be in this cognitive condition (by noticing clouds, seeing agitated birds), and hence how the world was a while ago (cloudy, full of agitation). Your belief attribution allows you to access these various pieces of information about all sorts of conditions with which I am, was, or could be correlated in different ways, but which I do not explicitly represent at the moment.

The psychoinformational story can handle intelligibly and plausibly such a variety of uses of information relations intersecting at a subject. It tells us that the sense maker's interest is neither in the subject's internal data structures per se nor in the world's intrinsic condition (at some level of N-theoretical description) but rather in a partial and pragmatic reconstruction of the commerce between the two, to the extent to which, and in a format in which, it can deliver the useful information.

The subject's *data* are the functionally efficacious structures tokened in his head and processed in various forms (inference, decision, storage). The structures are said to be *datal* because they (*a*) explicitly represent conditions of the world, and (*b*) causally drive as well as guide cognition and action in virtue of what and how they represent. I assume that the datal structures and processes can be taxonomized in terms of internal types by the sciences of cognition. This taxonomy is a logos business. I have also assumed that the datal structures are intrinsically intentional. They covary with aspects of the world that have biological and cognitive importance to us, and these covariations are constrained by various functional and behavioral obligations that the data structures have in our cognitive economy. I happen to believe that the ultimate constraints on covariations and hence on the intrinsic intentionality of cognition must receive a teleological account; up to a point, such an account is likely to be part of our logos understanding of cognition (Bogdan 1988a). But this is not the issue now. The issue is that the intrinsic intentionality of our representations is not for common sense to clarify and explain. The contents that common sense attributes *assume* the intentionality of our datal structures and processes, and go on to exploit it to corner the information of interest.

That *information,* the sense maker's, is the relation between the subject's internal conditions (datal, hence intentional, as well as physiological and behavioral, hence nonintentional) and the world around him. Information is a relation, a data structure only an element of it, a relatum. The psychoinformational types are relation sensitive, not relatum sensitive. The commonsense notion of content is informational, not datal, for it picks up and summarizes what the sense maker needs to know, given the subject's (mostly) datal encounters with the world. This claim is about what the commonsense notion of content is designed to represent, as part of the sense-making competence, hence about its objective constraints and limitations. It is very important to see that it is a claim about common sense *competence,* not about performance. It is not a claim about how commonsense concepts are intended to be used or indeed are used in particular situations by particular people. I may want to use commonsense psychological concepts to study the mind or the table or the universe. I may even make some progress. Yet this is not what these concepts *are for.*

Suppose I intend to describe your visual image of a scene. I have two choices. Either I describe the image (as data) in the theoretical vocabulary of vision, in which case I cannot commonsensically describe what you see, as content, or else I describe the latter, in which case I cannot theoretically describe your image. And, as far as I can tell, *tertium non datur.* I explain this dilemma a few paragraphs from here. Right now I want to extend this point about perception to more central forms of cognition, such as thinking or planning, in order to consider a serious and popular alternative to my account. Either we describe the datal outputs of higher cognition in some N-theoretical vocabulary (of, say, cognitive psychology), or else commonsensically, as contents. In the former case, we type individuate the outputs by internal criteria of form and function, in the latter case, by relational psychoinformational criteria. These two sorts of individuation criteria do not pick up the same entities from two different perspectives; nor do they pick up various properties or relations of the same entities, which is why the following friendly and reasonable compromise is not acceptable.

The compromise suggestion, of a dual-track spirit, is this. What about having the two candidates for content, data and information, join forces in the sense that an internal data structure qualifies as (attitudinal) content *only if* it informs in relation to the world? This suggestion saves the apparently ineliminable intuition that contents are in the head because encoded by data structures there; and at the same time, acknowledges that contents matter publicly to common sense only to the extent to which they inform. The suggestion also trades on the often visible isomorphism between the content attributed (say, that p) by the sense maker and the very data structure encoded by the subject (the same p). This is a matter on which I will have more to say later. Since, as I have assumed, both the content attribution and the subject's encoding are intrinsically intentional because they are both cognitive representations, they must be about the same fact. The content, then, must be in the subject's head, notwithstanding the fact that it is type individuated in semantic or psychoinformational terms.

Why not say, then, in this ecumenical spirit, that a belief is a reliable datal informant about how the world is? A number of philosophers (Field, Loar, Schiffer, Barwise, and Perry) hold that beliefs and other cognitive states should be construed informationally while others (Stampe, Dretske, Stalnaker, Fodor) analyze this informational construal in terms of regular covariations between a state of the world p and one's datal state that p, under some normality conditions. A regular covariation is, after all, the metaphysical soul of an information relation. This suggestion places beliefs and other attitudinized contents back in the head, *as internal types* of data structures, but requires that their type individuation be informational.

The trouble with this suggestion is that what is informational on one proposal need not be covariational on the other, and vice versa. To assume otherwise is to assume, quite implausibly, that there are internal types of data structures which are determined by the external, psychoinformational criteria of common sense. The assumption becomes even more implausible when we ask how the internal datal tokens of those externally determined types could be causally efficacious in cognition and behavior *in virtue of the functional laws* ranging over those types. How does common sense get these magical results? How does it carve up the mind at exactly the joints which both inform the sense maker interestingly and flexibly about the world, *and* internally constrain the subject's cognition and guide his behavior in that world? How can common sense get the internal functional laws of cognition and behavior to range exactly over types determined by factors outside the subject's head? (Preestablished harmony?) These puzzling questions have been asked by the dual-tracks theorists and by their critics, and their answers generally tell us that semantic relations do not mesh well with internal functional roles, and hence cannot be construed as criteria which taxonomize the latter (for a survey and spirited discussion of the matter, see Fodor 1987).

Yet my reluctance to buy the suggested compromise goes deeper than the implausibility of a miraculous coordination between the information needed by common sense and the inner workings of cognition. I think that such a coordination is virtually impossible because the properties in virtue of which a cognitive state informs a sense maker are not necessarily, and are not likely to be, the properties in virtue of which a cognitive state either covaries with the world or causes other cognitive and behavioral states or both. What I am saying is that the intrinsic intentionality of a cognitive state of the subject is quite unlikely ever to overlap, typewise, with the information needed by a sense maker; what the former state represents is not the same as what the content description encoding the latter information represents.

Consider vision. Methodological individualism allows for an analysis that acknowledges the intrinsic intentionality of vision. This means that the analysis can taxonomize visual data structures which systematically covary with features of the input and of the external world, and whose covariations have further functional roles in cognition. Such a taxonomy is intentional. Yet the intentionality of vision is beyond common sense. It is hard to imagine that commonsense attributions of perceptual contents could possibly capture a subject's visual data structures. One cannot be said, commonsensically, to perceive that p if the intended analysis is to the effect that (i) one's visual structures covary, via input, with the scene perceived; and (ii) the clause 'that p' describes what one's visual structures or images covary with. (ii) is simply false.

Visual images covary with (proximal) light intensities, and through them, with (distal) edges, boundaries, textures, surfaces, shapes, motions, forms, and such. The latter are not what the content clause 'that p' represents, as far as common sense is concerned. Suppose I take you to see that p, where p is 'the table is to the left of the wall'. There isn't any visual image of that scene that can be said (in the principled vocabulary of a theory of vision) to covary with what p represents, *according to common sense.* The commonsense content attribution not only appeals to concepts (table, left of, wall) that do not belong to the principled vocabulary of vision but it selects very little from the richness of the visual image on grounds that have nothing to do with that image's covariations.

If we were to try to translate p into the scientific vocabulary of vision, we would lose track of what the commonsense content judgment represents. And if we want to do justice to the latter, we must abandon the language of, and the constraints on, the covariations involved in vision. I see no way out of this dilemma. This conclusion is independent of the assumption, which I entered earlier, that common sense exploits the intrinsic intentionality of the cognitive states it exploits as informants. Needless to add, common sense does not and cannot have the foggiest idea of what visual structures are, and how they covary with proximal light and distal features; nor does it appear too embarassed by this limitation.

In further support of the distinction between the subject's data and the sense maker's information, and of the claim that the latter cannot be taken to taxonomize the former, there is the obvious observation that commonsense attributions of content depend on the manner of content specification. We talk, for instance, of *de re* and *de dicto* individuations of perception or belief or thought, and also of direct object individuation of contents (*e.g.,* I see the landing plane) as opposed to fact-centered or propositional individuation of contents (I see that the plane is landing). We cannot plausibly believe that these distinctions are datal, that is, internal to cognition. We have no evidence, for example, that vision is specialized in object as well as propositional representation (a submodule for facts and another for objects?). Yet this is what we ought to conclude if the commonsense attribution of perceptual content were to taxonomize internal types of visual data. Similarly, if beliefs were types of internal data structures, then we ought to conclude that we have *de re* and *de dicto* types of doxastic data structures. But neither conclusion makes much sense, as I have argued elsewhere (Bogdan 1986b).

So we seem to have a *reductio:* If, in general, contents are individuated *de re* or *de dicto,* in terms of either objects or facts, then the contents envisaged by common sense cannot be datal, for there are no intrinsic features of our data structures that reflect these forms of content individuation. On the psychoinformational account, the latter specify not types of internal data structures but rather the *relata* in terms of which an information relation is identified. These relata can be worldly items (*de re* readings) or datal ones (*de dicto* readings); with an eye to the worldly items they inform about, the datal relata can in turn be described in a direct-object or propositional format. If this suggestion is true of such various specifications of content, why not say that it is true of *any* commonsense specification of content? Or, simply, of content? What else is there to content but its commonsense specification?

This last suggestion and the examples considered a section ago do

indicate, however, that common sense individuates *token* datal configurations in a context, relative to their informational importance, either in terms of their manifest expressions (linguistic, behavioral) or
of their worldly correlata. Common sense also individuates token actions in terms of their immediate effects or distant repercussions,
without the implication that a behavior becomes *type* identical with its
effects or repercussions. (What I am denying, again, is that common
sense can or cares to individuate datal configurations in virtue of their
being tokens of internal types with causal powers under functional
laws.) Common sense reaches inside the head for data structures but
only in their *particular* or token configurations which are then taxonomized in terms of their psychoinformational significance. How
common sense accomplishes such individuations of token data configurations is a complicated matter that concerns the methodological
steps that I said I will not consider in this essay. (There are a number
of proposals around which I briefly survey in the introductory paper
to this volume.)

Self-Informant: Language, Consciousness, and Mental Causation

Having reached this point in our argument, we must dispose of a few
stubborn and reactionary intuitions which may obscure the truth we
are after. They cluster around the first-person perspective we all have
on our cognition and that of others. I have so far portrayed the sense-
making game as eminently social. I think that this is how the game
originated and how it is typically played. I think its motivation is
social, which is why its concepts reflect the common denominators of
our inevitably partial, often idiosyncratic, and almost always publicly
inaccessible representations. Yet the game is also played privately.
There is self-sense making.

It is consciousness and language that make common as well as self-
sense making possible and at the same time obscure it. I consider
conciousness first. For the purpose of our discussion, let us construe
consciousness as awareness or internal access of some sort. The conscious self-access is phenomenal, more direct and surefooted than the
access we have to others. Yet, I want to suggest, what we are tracking
consciously is only the *evidence* for applying the commonsense concepts to ourselves. When we consciously inspect and talk about our
own THOUGHTS, BELIEFS, and ACTIONS, *as publicly and commonsensically
categorized in these terms,* we either explicitly treat ourselves as informants (subjects) or else exploit the conceptual resources we have as
common sense makers. In either case, we apply psychoinformational

concepts to ourselves. The difference between social and private sense making is in the nature of the evidence for applying the concepts, not in what the concepts are objectively about.

When one self-attributes the concept of belief (takes oneself to believe something), one takes one's experiences, or consciously accessed data structures, such as images, memories, and the like, and other conditions, such as feels, to guide the application of the psychoinformational concept that common sense has taught one to use in the social case. Without the commonsense concept one would not know what the internal evidence is evidence for. A visual image may move me to action (just as it can move an animal) but I would not know to treat its information as a content I BELIEVE, *so categorized commonsensically*, unless I had the conceptual means to treat it this way (which the animal does not). There is no private ontology of types of internal experiences that the commonsense concepts of content naturally spring from and represent.

I happen to think that even the attitudes (believing, desiring) cannot be fully taxonomized by introspection. But the discussion here is about contents, not attitudes. I fail to see how one can taxonomize contents just introspectively. Since this failure is likely to upset a lot of introspective folks, I give them a choice: Either we discuss the issue in terms of commonsense concepts, in which case they had better come up with a competitive account of these concepts, commensurate with an alleged introspective grasp; or else we avoid commonsense discourse altogether and try to capture, if we can, the phenomenal passing show in terms of suitably private and introspective descriptions. Since you know my position on common sense, let me tell you what's happening privately inside me when I describe myself as believing or thinking something.

The data structures I internally experience come in all sorts of forms and shapes such as vivid images, faded images, cartoonish sketches, fragments of utterances in sotto voce or aloud in some language or another, occasionally an aria or a chanson, even mixtures of all of the above, vaguely and intermittently sampled linguistically. Short of imposing a commonsense content taxonomy, I fail to see any shared internal types or even vaguer family resemblances within this variety of experienced data structures. If I describe the latter structurally (*i.e.*, with respect to their form), then they have very little, if anything, in common that I am aware of. If I describe and group them with respect to what they represent or are about, then how can I avoid the commonsense scheme of individuation? (The experienced data structures do have an intrinsic intentionality, as the earlier discussion of vision was meant to suggest, but it is inaccessible for examination and analysis to both introspection and common sense.)

If it looks to us that what we encode and process datally is what we say we PERCEIVE or BELIEVE, *conceptualized in these very terms,* it is because we must formulate our cognition to ourselves in commonsense terms. I am not merely saying that we must formulate what is going on in us in a public language (what other choice is there?). I am also denying that it is the intrinsic representational and functional features of our datal structures and processes that we taxonomize with the help of the notions of perception, belief, and the like. I do not think we can do that even if we wanted it.

I hasten to add that the *epistemology* of the self-attribution and self-evaluation (the fact that, in a strong sense, I know when I believe, and how strongly I believe, but do not know when and how strongly another person believes) has nothing to do with the point I am belaboring here to the effect that in both social and self-attribution and -evaluation I owe my grasp of the content types to the commonsense paradigm. The epistemology of attitude attribution and evaluation has to do only with the *evidence* for the particular conditions in which the commonsense concepts are applied.

A subject can cooperate with a sense maker by volunteering 'I believe that *p*' to indicate either how the world is or was (in a *p* condition), or how the registered condition of the world might affect the subject's subsequent cognition and behavior, or both. It may well be that this is how we learn self attribution. When I am telling myself (or simply thinking) that I believe that *p,* I am surely telling myself something about a condition of the world (that it is *p*), and perhaps implicitly how I got the information about it (say, by perception); and I am also telling myself how the information about the condition of the world could later be treated in my cognition and behavior (I may confidently infer something from it, or act on it). This is of course a bit artificial (I may not talk to myself, or not talk to myself in English, or not explicitly think about my beliefs) but I am not interested in how we *describe* a self-attribution; I am only interested in what it objectively amounts to, as an application of commonsense concepts. Common sense is with me, inside the skull. I am a self-ascriber and evaluator (a self-interpreter) because on so many occasions I am a self-informant.

What about natural *language?* Doesn't it collapse the distinction I am making between the sense maker's information and the subject's data structures, particularly when the two are one and the same person? Aren't many of the subject's data encoded in a natural language? Doesn't a natural language (like English) provide the means to encode our higher-level datal outputs (thoughts, beliefs, plans)? And isn't this the very same language in which we also make sense of others and ourselves? If so, can't the content that the sense maker attributes, say, that p, be the very linguistic structure the subject relates to internally when he is described as thinking that p? Isn't this even clearer in the case of self-attribution? If I form and attitudinize the sentence p *as a data structure* in my head and do something internally with it, I can surely take the data structure to be the very *content* I am self-attributing. Well, you guessed, it is not so simple.

My first move is to challenge the assumption, implicit in some of the above questions, that a natural language is a typical code of cognition and a primary form of encoding its data structures. The primary code may well be a computational mentalese or connectionist neuralese or something similarly antecedent to, more basic than, and possibly responsible for, our natural language competence. A natural language may be used to recode and make sense of the *outputs* of cognition in the primary code. My thinking that p (in English) may well be such a recoding. If the data structures that run our cognition are in some primary code, they must be inaccessible to common sense, in which case the linguistic episodes, such as my thinking that p, are artifacts by means of which we recode, sample, and summarize the datal outputs (in the primary code) in an accessible natural language fragment.

One important function of the natural language recoding and sampling is indeed that of self-sense making. My thought that p may be a self-directed commonsense summary of my (deeper) cognitive encodings and processes in a primary code. The linguistic summary is an internal datal encoding but it does not causally drive (and explain) my cognition and behavior; it just reidentifies and makes sense of structures in the primary code which do the real representational and functional chores. My thought that p is the common sense's kibitzer on the scene, in which case 'that p' indeed identifies an internal encoding of data (a linguistic structure) but only with respect to its instantiating a thought content whose type is taxonomized by common sense. As a content description, the linguistic structure is an instance of a type (the thought content) which does not characterize the internal workings of the mind.

Even outside sense-making contexts, the natural language recodings and summaries of primary (mentalese or neuralese) cognition can be active functionally, as data, *without* doing a representational or functional job. In which case, again, the linguistic data we encode may coincide with a content ascribed and yet fail to taxonomize the cognitive properties responsible for representation and mental causation. It follows that a linguistically explicit self-attribution cannot pick up cognitive N-types of the representational or functional sort, even though it picks up a functionally active data structure.

Here is an example of what I have in mind, which also brings the general matter of mental causation into sharper focus. Suppose I hear an utterance and come to encode an active (not kibitzing) linguistic structure to the effect that p. I am faced with a serious situation, p is my information about it, so I must think, infer, and decide in terms of p; yet p is not the data structure doing the real cognitive work. Let p be 'that dog is getting vicious'. Its key concepts are 'dog' and 'vicious'. A concept (we may assume) contains a list of features, some encoded as prototypes, some as visual stereotypes, others as activators of, or links to, other concepts (lists). Doghood and viciousness mean nothing to me unless I access and open up the right conceptual files in my head. Those files have linguistic labels, nowadays in English, but what they contain is neither linguistic nor particularly English. They are mostly imagistic and cartoonish (I have that kind of mind). It is these pro-totypical and stereotypical encodings in my mental files which do the representing and also cause other states in virtue of what they repre-sent. (Relative to the situation described, it is my mental files which are intrinsically intentional.) The words 'dog' and 'vicious' help me access and open the files. This is an internal function of the sentence containing these words but is not the representational function that steers my cognition and behavior. The words in question also have the function of aligning my perhaps idiosyncratic files to the public con-cepts. This is how I am able to map the heard utterance onto my mental files.

The sentence 'that dog is getting vicious' does not only inform me about the world. It can *also* be used, for making-sense purposes, to identify a belief of mine with that content. But now it looks as though the very same sentence both describes a belief content (the common-sense role) and plays a functional, file-activating role, in my mind (the cognitive role), and moreover plays the latter role in virtue of what it describes, contentwise. This must collapse my distinction between data and content, for the sentence 'that dog is getting vicious' is now both. Yes, but it is not the *right* kind of data. Neither the belief content ascribed to me nor the sentence that describes that content nor indeed the initial utterance that alerted me to the vicious dog are in my mental files. My mental representation and causation originate in the latter, when activated by some input. If I use the sentence 'that dog is getting vicious' to self-ascribe a belief, I am using an internal kibitzer (the content description) which also happens to have a functional (file-activating) role. The coincidence between the linguistic input with the latter role and the content description with the former role is not grounded in how my mind works, representationally and functionally, but rather in how linguistic communication and commonsense making are coordinated.

We communicate in terms in which we make sense of others and ourselves. If we ask what the belief content is in the case described, the answer is that it is what the sentence 'that dog is getting vicious' describes. That is precisely what a sense maker, myself or someone else, would need to know about the world and myself when I activate my mental files and pick up the stereotypical and prototypical representations with which I register the situation and do something about it. The sentence in question is a public and informative summary of which items in my mental files will be doing the relevant representational and causal work in me relative to which publicly identifiable aspects of the environment. In the first-person case the same sentence not only allows for self-sense making, but also has the functional role of a file activator. In neither position, however, is the sentence an instance of an intrinsic representational or intentional type with functional role.

Needless to say, the causal story told by this example is just one of many. A worldly fact can activate my mental files without my having to hear or utter myself, and thus encode, a sentence to that effect as explicit data. Nor is sense making in the datal form of a content sentence needed for such file activation. Moreover, even when an utterance plays the role of an informative input, it may not only open mental files but also incrementally coordinate with other linguistic and nonlinguistic data structures already tokened in my internal data space, and cause in virtue of such coordination (Bogdan 1986a, 1988b).

In all these cases the commonsense content ascriptions pick up token datal configurations (the items in my mental files, other linguistic tokens, etc.) which must be considered from two distinct perspectives: On the one hand, these datal configurations inform on the world and myself, and are thus part of a relational triangle (subject–world–sense maker) whose taxonomy is psychoinformational and commonsensical; on the other hand, the very same token datal configurations belong to internal types (concept, mental file, stereotype, language forms, etc.) whose intrinsic intentionality and functions are or can be, to a vast extent, N-taxonomized by the sciences of cognition.

5. Explanation It Ain't

The moral of what follows is that, in more ways than one, common-sense explanation is not what it seems to be. In the opening sections of this essay, I was endeavoring to puncture the logos thesis by showing that common sense does not and cannot explain from the nature (essential properties and laws) of things in its domain. In later sections I have attempted to show that the main function of commonsense making is psychoinformational. Yet common sense does a lot of explaining and predicting, and a good deal of it appears to be based on causes. We are said to believe because we perceive, and perceive because we interact with the world; we also act because we believe and desire; and so on. The 'because' is very often that of causality. If commonsense explanations and predictions are often causal and successful, aren't they successful *because* causal? In which case, isn't the relation between causality and success telling evidence that common sense carves up the mind at essential and lawful N-joints? How else could it use causes to explain successfully? Isn't then common sense a sort of N-theory of cognition and behavior, as the logos thesis claims? And if it isn't, as I claim, what exactly is going on? Let us proceed incrementally and from several directions. The reluctant reader needs a lot of softening up.

False Theories Can Explain Successfully. We all know about Ptolemy's astronomy and Newton's physics. Great stuff, often good for explanation, but plain false. Scientific theories do not have to be true to explain. This goes to show that even if a theory misses the N-joints of its domain, it may still explain successfully. The implication I need for our discussion is that being true of N-joints is not essential to successful (causal) explanation. This implication gives our thesis some elbow room. For it suggests that there need be no incompatibility between commonsense making not being about the N-joints of cognition and behavior, and its explanations of cognition and behavior being causal and successful. But I am not maintaining that commonsense psychology is a false theory of the mind (as eliminativism claims), for it is not a theory at all, and is not about the mind.

The fact that false, or N-indifferent, theories can explain may have a number of reasons. Nature may "cooperate," as it were, by organizing itself in ways in which many properties are causal without revealing the ultimate N-texture (fundamental properties and laws) of things. This is what functionalism appears to claim about nature. It is also possible and indeed likely that what *we* consider a satisfactory explanation is not always and not irremediably tied to the true N-story of the world. It may even be the case – as van Fraassen (1980) and Cartwright (1983) have argued – that truth is not only independent of, but in some sense may be an obstacle to, explanation. Or it may be that what we think is explanation is not. These explosive thoughts originate in an important distinction.

Explanation Is Quite Different from Explaining; and the Satisfactoriness of the Former Can Often Be Found Only in the Modus Operandi of the Latter. Explaining is answering a why (or how) question, whereas an explanation is a regimented and simplified representation of the answer. The former is a complex and ramified question/answer structure, the latter the public summary of the answer. In the sciences, an explanation is said to take the form of an argument from laws (or mechanisms, or capacities) plus boundary conditions, in a deductive or inductive format. The logical format of the explanation argument, which is determined *methodologically* by requirements of justification or theory construction or theory application, may have nothing to do with the strategies of explaining which are determined by such *pragmatic* factors as uncertainty, curiosity, novelty, available evidence, alternative hypotheses, and so on.

Since explaining is answering some question, it is a request *for information*. Our spontaneous inferences and cogitations have been long recognized as displaying the general features of question answering or problem solving: activated or generated by some uncertainty, problem, or issue in a context, they move from a data basis and some background knowledge to the selection of a solution or answer out of several possible candidates, under suitable constraints and measures of plausibility, relevance, and usefulness. Let us call the entire process, subject to such pragmatic constraints, *mental induction*. As recent work has shown, mental induction serves a variety of cognitive enterprises, from inference and belief fixation to decision making and communication. It also operates in scientific explanation (van Fraassen 1980; Garfinkel 1981).

Now, if mental induction (*a*) is a form of answering questions and providing the information of interest in a context, and (*b*) is so pervasive in our cognition, it ought to follow that (*c*) in our natural cognitive condition we explain the way we normally cogitate or think, by mental induction. And the way we normally think is the way to get the right information about whatever bothers us at the moment in a context. This is why commonsense explain*ing* comes so easily and naturally: It is a normal way of thinking about a particular sort of topic, namely, a subject informing on himself or the world in a context. This is also why we are *satisfied* with what and how we are explaining in the same way we are satisfied with what and how we are thinking or deciding or communicating, namely, by getting the right answer to a question in a context, or forming the right plan for action, or conveying the right information in a conversation. In all these cases, the criteria and measure of a satisfactory solution or answer are determined relative to the pragmatic parameters of the question/answer structure (context, data base, alternative solutions, relevance relations, and the like).

If an explanation satisfies, it does so, not because its official summary specifies intrinsic reasons for the explanation to be satisfactory, in the sense that the premises refer to basic entities and laws in the domain, the boundary conditions fix their range of application, and, presto, we have an explanation because we have a nice deduction. The explanation satisfies because its official summary condenses and regiments an answer found pragmatically satisfactory relative to an *antecedent* question/answer structure. In other words, an explanation is satisfactory because it answers a question by providing the right information.

Making Sense Is (Mostly) Explaining. The distinction between explaining and explanation also operates in common sense making. A common sense *explanation* may have the regimented logical form of an argument of the sort ⟨attitude report and attitude report entail action report⟩, an instance of which would be "He did it because he wanted to get there and thought this is the way to do it"; or ⟨attitude report and attitude report entails another attitude report⟩, an instance of which could be "She believed him because she saw the event and remembered how he reacted." This is how we phrase the *outcome* of explaining, and how we *publicly* indicate or recognize that an explanation is offered. Yet, as in the scientific case, the argument form of the answer is different from how the answer was mentally arrived at, what question it addresses, and why it is satisfactory.

Here are some supporting considerations. Most analyses of commonsense making overlook the fact that ordinarily we do NOT use the argument forms of explanation – unless we have to summarize in order to convince, justify, look clever, or for other such rhetorical reasons. We explain ordinarily by answering why (and other) questions after going through the mentally inductive moves identified earlier. Likewise, we normally understand what, and how, other people explain by following or reconstructing their mental induction.

Even when we step aside from the flow of reasoning or communication, and turn to an argument form of explanation, the goodness of the explanation still depends on how good an answer it provides to the initial why question; and the goodness of the answer is going to be implicit in the mentally inductive moves we made to come up with the answer.

This is not to deny that we often make explicit attitude reports and link them logically in some form of explanation. But in normal contexts of cogitation, communication, or learned discourse, attitude reports and explanations appear for what they are, namely, convenient summaries of underlying or preceding or even suppressed but reconstructible chains of mental inductions – the logical tips of the less visible, more baroque, question-and-information icebergs. As in science, the reasons for resorting to the summarizing argument forms (the explanations) are rhetorical or epistemic or methodological rather than strictly cognitive.

Let us press this point a little further, and ask: Why should a scientific explanation be (say) deductive? And why deductive from laws? Why should a deduction from laws explain anything? Suppose I ask why x is P, and am told that all members of the set to which x belongs are P. This answer tells us that the explanation *is deductive*, not that it *is an explanation*. The answer is explanatorily satisfactory (if it ever is) for reasons that need not reside in the semantic or logical dimensions of its public summary form (*i.e.*, what the latter's law and initial conditions statements are about or how they are logically organized). The logical form of scientific explanation is convenient for testing, theory application, justification, formalization, and other such epistemic, methodological, and rhetorical objectives. By contrast, the cognitive value of a scientific explanation typically accrues elsewhere, in the mentally inductive processes that produce it.

The contrast between the logical skin and the pragmatic entrails of explanation is also visible in the specific case of *causal* explanation. And this matters to our discussion. The first fact to note is that the logical skin of explanation often bears few, if any, traces of causality. The causal relations that an explanation invokes are rarely made explicit by its logically regimented summary. Consider the law subsumptive (D-N) type of explanation. Fundamental laws have no causal potency by themselves. It is the structures and mechanisms these laws animate that instantiate events and thus cause what they do. When we come to consider the causally potent structures and mechanisms, and the events they instantiate, we are bound to consider the messiness of the real world, where causes interact and combine with, or cancel, each other – not the formal purity of the fundamental laws. And the messiness of the world, in which causes are active and push things around, can only be handled by empirical or "phenomenological" (*i.e.*, superficial and limited, as opposed to fundamental) laws, ceteris paribus provisions, and other methodological compromises (Cartwright 1983).

I am rehearsing these familiar observations to indicate that quite often the fundamental laws which figure in the official scientific explanation arguments are not necessarily the real causal workers. Finding the latter requires a rather laborious pragmatic process of mental induction, one that scientists do not always care (or even know how) to describe publicly, logically, and crisply. When it comes to the right framework for individuating causes, it should be that of explaining, rather than of explanation, that we must examine.

The same, I submit, is true of commonsense making. We *say* we explain causally in terms of beliefs, desires, intentions, and other such attitudes, but we cannot possibly *mean* it, if what we are saying is that it is the public attitude reports that explain causally *by capturing structures with causal potency* under suitable generalizations. True, we publicly formulate our commonsense explanations as arguments in the regimented terms of attitudes and action reports. An attitude report contains an attitude description (say, believing) and a content description or sentence (say, that *p*). An action report contains a behavior description and often some further parameter (the behavior's object, or relation to environment, or effect, or cause). I have suggested earlier that attitude and action reports are regimented summaries of the information of interest to a sense maker in a context. The suggestion now is that the attitude reports and their generalizations (belief and desire lead to intention; intention to action; and the like) by themselves do not and cannot identify the causally efficacious structures and processes which do the explaining.

I must be dogmatically short about the defense of this claim, and rely on points made earlier in this essay as well as on work done elsewhere. We have already seen one argument (about vicious dogs and mental files) in the previous section showing the causal impotence of what the attitude reports linguistically represent. I have provided elsewhere arguments to the effect that semantically construed content sentences rarely if ever capture the genuine datal configurations that animate an agent's cognition (Bogdan 1988b, 1989). There are also more familiar arguments in the literature about methodological solipsism and the dual-track theory of content which show that semantically construed content descriptions fail to account for mental causation. So much for the causal potency of what content reports report.

We can move on to commonsense generalizations. They logically connect attitude and action reports. To say that a belief and a desire explain an action is to mean that they do so ceteris paribus. To say ceteris paribus is to mean that other competing or interfering data and needs of the agent have been considered and set aside by the sense maker, that some normality assumptions about the agent have been duly made, and so on. We have a situation parallel to that in science. The official formulation of the commonsense generalizations is just a public facade. From a strictly causal standpoint, it explains little. When ceteris paribus considerations are brought into the picture, we move behind the logically luminous facade into the darker rooms of explaining, or reconstructing, where most of the cognitively causal action is likely to be visible. The surface argument form of our commonsense explanations is not the right framework in which to see, analyze, and understand why and how attitude reports explain causally and often successfully (several decades of furious philosophizing at the surface level notwithstanding). The right framework is that of *explaining*. Admitting this is a step forward. The question now is whether it is a step in the right direction.

Explaining by Other Means. Many analysts take commonsense making to be essentially an explanatory enterprise (the logos thesis). Yet, as we just saw, the model of explanation they have in mind (arguments from attitude and actions reports under appropriate generalizations) is not likely to identify the causal factors at work in cognition. To find the causal factors the analysts of common sense should attend to how the sense maker *herself* engages in explaining by mental induction. Explaining from causes is parasitic therefore on getting the right information by mental induction. But is this *explaining* from causes anymore? Probably not, at least not in a deliberate and explicit sense. So we have a paradox: The commonsense explanations, as summarizing arguments from attitude reports and generalizations, are not very causal, while the mentally inductive reconstructions to, and inferences from, causes do not look like explanations anymore.

Causes are not essential for commonsense making unless they help deliver the right information. As a result, the explanatory derivations from causes are by-products, *not* objectives, of the mental induction in search of the right information. To understand why this is so, we should recall that prediction and retrodiction can be seen as forms of *tensed* explanation. If you have an explanation such as "the earth rotates around the sun because (such and so)," then you can temporally index it to predict that "the earth will rotate tomorrow because (same such and so)" or retrodict that "the earth was rotating in 1448, when the Ottoman Turks had a jolly good time, because (same such and so)."

Common sense, however, is more likely to have it the other way around. It can explain because it *wants* to predict or retrodict. And it wants the latter, much more than the former, because it is interested in information about particular events and conditions in the world and the subject, as they occur in time, rather than in deep and time-less mechanisms and laws. Common sense manages to explain caus-ally to the extent to which, in predicting or retrodicting, it considers or exploits conditions that are informationally pregnant and useful, and that *also* happen to have a hand on causation. Commonsense causal explanation is a by-product of information-hungry prediction and retrodiction.

What makes this suggestion plausible is that we *can* predict or retro-dict without having to explain causally; we do this quite often. (It is this very possibility, by the way, that generates the problem of induc-tion: We can induce successfully without necessarily having adequate causal justification. Explanation is most often nothing but causal justi-fication.) I can, for example, predict that Babeau will sing tomorrow morning because he has done so in the past, without fail. The fact that he has done so in the past is no *causal* explanation of (and no con-clusive justification for) what he will do tomorrow. My prediction cites no causal conditions and mechanisms, although (I guess) some are at work; it only informs on future conditions relative to past conditions.

To take another example, suppose I want to know why some fellow is nervous. It appears that this is the 'why' of causal explanation. But (I suggest) it isn't – at least not in my frame of interest now. What I want to know, and need information about, are antecedent conditions, of his and the world around him, that are relevant to his current (nervous) condition. I need to retrodict to his immediate past. I may find out that he worked too much and was tired, or that the hot weather was too much for him, or that he thought that all this interest in commonsense psychology is getting out of hand (another anthology?). None of the antecedent conditions are explicitly causal, and only the second comes close to redescribing a chain of causal conditions, while the first and the third are too superficial summaries of too many things to allow any easy reconstruction of underlying causal conditions (if any). The ante-cedent conditions are construed, summarized, phrased, and communi-cated with an eye to their psychoinformational, not explanatory, duties.

As a sense maker, I find the antecedent conditions plausible candidates because they supply the information I need in daily life, not because they help me understand the deeper causes. I call them explanations in the commonsense parlance, but on further reflection I know they aren't, at least not in a causal sense. If I were a physician, I would be looking for those antecedent conditions that instantiate causes and mechanisms of nervousness, not those that only tell me how the world and the patient were some time ago, although some of the two sorts of conditions may well overlap.

To round it up, let us consider an example discussed by Garfinkel (1981). When Willie Sutton was asked why he robbed banks, he is said to have answered that that's where the money is. (Still true.) The commonsense maker smiles and is satisfied, the social scientist (a priest in the real story) doesn't and isn't. The latter would like to subsume and represent Sutton's behavior under some deep generalizations, such as poor and uneducated people, maltreated by society, tend to rob, and the like. (Notice, again, that the generalizations point to no causal mechanisms. Being poor or uneducated cannot, strictly speaking, be a cause of robbing or of anything else, for that matter.) Why does common sense smile? Because it is alert to the underlying pragmatic frame of explaining that is made visible by Sutton's answer. (Jokes also trade on the punch line making visible, quickly and unexpectedly, an underlying infrastructure of assumptions and inferences.) Here are a few elements of that frame. The presupposition is obvious (people need money and robbing is a way of getting it); there are several solutions for Sutton's problem, compatible with the presupposition (banks versus other moneyed places such as mattresses, pockets, or *USA TODAY* machines); there is also a faint suggestion of an evaluation criterion (risks and effort versus benefit); and so on.

Why does Sutton's answer appear satisfactory in the context? Because, we are often told, it is opaque in the sense that it portrays the situation from his angle. True enough. His answer does summarize some of his thought processes and motivations, and thus tells how he sees the matter. Commonsense explanations are said to be intensional in that they are true in virtue of the way the agent represents his situation and his actions. It is also said that the agent's representations cause his other representations and actions. As a result, we are also told, explaining intensionally amounts to explaining from internal causes. It is this conclusion that I resist.

We have already seen that content descriptions, even in an intensional tone, do not necessarily capture the subject's data structures that do the causal work. And even when they do, they capture only token data structures, not their types. How do we get such a token handle on datal internal causes? When a content description appears to explain causally what Sutton did, it does so by allowing us to reconstruct his mental induction and in this way close in on some of his datal conditions responsible for both his public reports and his actions. This reconstruction is still psychoinformationally motivated but it ends up opening up some of Sutton's mental files where the token datal causes are. Suppose, to press our search for the datal causes, we ask Sutton, Why rob at all? And he may answer, Why not? Or he may answer, What do you want me to do? Teach philosophy? Become a tenured zombie? Or he may become autobiographical, or whatever.

Are these answers more explanatory, causally? Hardly. All we get is further information about still earlier conditions of Sutton and his milieu. These conditions may be relevant to what happened later or could happen next; they predict and even appear to explain. By elimination and reconstruction, they may succeed in sampling some of Sutton's causally effective representations in his mental files. At that point the search for information has come up with some genuine internal causes. The means and hence the taxonomic types that the sense maker uses to characterize these token causes are psychoinformational. The commonsense inference from such causes may look like explaining. But it surely is not a deduction (or induction or analogy) from internal *types* of causal mechanisms and their *laws*, so it is not much of an explanation, really.

6. Practicalities

As a pretext for review and anticipation, I am going to conclude with a few remarks about what makes commonsense making a practice, and why the practice is successful. We know what it is for a scientific theory to be successful: It must be true of the N-joints (types and laws) of its domain or ontology. We also know, at the other extreme, what it is for a behavioral skill (such as writing or riding a bike) to be successful: It must engage its domain (movements, things to move, relations to surrounding things, etc.) at the causal joints where the right performance produces the desired effects.

Commonsense making is neither theory nor behavioral skill. Unlike other skill-based practices (such as driving a car), commonsense making appears to rely on explicitly encoded knowledge (its concepts and axioms), and also results in explicit representations (the commonsense judgments). But then, isn't the success of common sense based on a *truth* about its domain, and isn't it therefore a *theory* of that domain?

Let us begin with the outputs. The commonsense judgments are explicitly represented and truth valuable. What these judgments are mostly about is, as we saw, a sort of trilateral informational pattern ranging over internal conditions of a subject, external conditions of the world, and the sense maker's own cognitive condition (curiosity, interest). It is these "triangles" that specify the truth conditions of our commonsense judgments. To put it crudely, the ontology of common-sense making is made of such triangles and combinations thereof. This does not make commonsense making a *theory* of psychoinforma-tional triangles, notwithstanding the fact that its outputs are explicit representations of the triangles. One reason for this is that the psy-choinformational triangles have *no fixed natures* (in the form of essen-tial properties and laws) that the commonsense concepts could invari-ably and reliably pick up and represent truly. Another reason is that the competence for commonsense making can be thought of in terms of *rules and instructions* to construct specific representations (common-sense judgments) about the situation at hand; it is hard to think of such rules and instructions as strictly descriptive, hence true, of any-thing. The two reasons are related. If the psychoinformational tri-angles have no fixed nature, then there is nothing specific in them for the commonsense concepts (in the form of rules and instructions) to represent.

I begin with the latter reason. It is possible, although I do not know how likely, that our commonsense knowledge is deep-down pro-cedural in that it contains rules and instructions that are not them-selves explicitly encoded somewhere (*e.g.,* in memory) – and hence are not consulted *as text* when the occasion arises. This reminds one of the controversial matter of how our grammatical knowledge is en-coded. Is it a text somewhere, ready for consultation, or is it accessible in some other form, say, compiled or wired in? The grammatical outputs, like those of commonsense making, are explicitly encoded but the grammatical knowledge that produces them need not be. There are some reasons to push this proceduralist line of thought. As we saw, there are features of commonsense making, such as innate-ness, smooth and unreflective operation, immunity to education, culture, and sophistication, which may point to something like an inexplicit, possibly architectural set of rules and instructions. If this were true, then it would be hard to see what such rules and instruc-tions could possibly be about, or true of, strictly speaking. Rules and instructions can, when applied, produce events and structures, in-cluding representational structures, without having to be about these events or structures; this is true not only of grammatical but also of genetic instructions and traffic rules as well.

How do the commonsense-making rules work? This is a matter to be taken up in the later stages of the naturalization of common sense. By way of anticipation, here is a useful metaphor. We saw that a content ascription is a representation of a psychoinformational triangle in which, given her curiosity and interests, the sense maker positions herself relative to a subject and a portion of the world. I am looking for a notion that intuitively approximates this script, something like 'informational triangulation by representation under appropriate rules'. *Triangulation,* says the dictionary, is the location of an unknown point by forming a triangle having the unknown point and two known points as vertices. Triangulation is very much used in navigation. And that, you remember, was our *ur* problem, how to navigate through life with the help of conspecifics. We must triangulate them, the world, and us in a context. Since the conspecifics are intelligent, and the triangles vary with context, no fixed representation of triangles will do. What we need are rules to apply flexibly and contextually, as well as sequentially (chains of triangles) and compositionally (using various combinations), not mere associative concepts that we can learn in a context and generalize over other similar contexts.

I am going to hijack therefore the concept of triangulation for our purposes. If a sense maker knows (or has evidence for, or does a ceteris paribus with respect to) any two of the angles, she can in principle triangulate the third. A sense maker can be said to *apply* the concept of content if she can generate a representation of the psychoinformational triangle of interest in a context, under appropriate rules, evidential clues, and ceteris paribus assumptions. To make or understand a content ascription is to know how to apply the representation in question and triangulate the information of interest. To *have,* antecedently, the very concept of content is to know the rules that generate the representation in the first place. The truth conditions of a content ascription reflect a triangulation by some representation under rules. This is to look only in the direction of the solutions to the psychoinformational problems. There are also, as I have indicated, social coordination problems that we have not even touched here.

We have now material enough to tackle the other reason why I do not think that our commonsense competence *is true of* the nature of its ontology (the triangulation domain). The reason is that psychoinformational triangles have no fixed nature, which is why the basic concepts of commonsense making are essentially practical. Here is an important analogy. Think of practices that involve tools, of which sense making is an instance, since it treats conspecifics as information tools. Most tools have no essential natures. None of the physical or geometrical properties of tables are essential to tablehood. Play with these properties and you will see. What material is typical of tablehood? Wood, iron, plastic? How many legs for a table? Four, twenty, one hundred? How tall the legs? One meter, two, twenty? No legs at all? Just the top? All right. How thick? Half a meter? One centimeter? Aluminum foil thickness? The game is obvious. It leads nowhere if essential nature is our destination. All that matters is the *function* of tables, which is to eat and write and put things on. The physical and geometrical properties fit the tablehood type relative to how well they serve the assigned function.

The concept of table is *functional* in that it enables its possessor to recognize properties and relations of candidate objects to the extent to which they satisfy the functional conditions of tablehood. It is the function that selects the properties that get into the extension of the concept. This makes for a tight (analytic?) connection between what a table is for, and what a table is, as a type – an indication that what counts as a table is a matter of interest and decision, not of objective correspondence to some fixed type of external facts. The connection between function and type is tight notwithstanding the fact that the type tablehood is inherently fuzzy. If one meets a borderline case and does not know whether the concept applies (the top, made of dry baguettes and supported by huge champagne bottles, extends from Cannes to La Napoule, and everybody eats there in the evening, facing the sea and singing Trenet's "La Mer"), it is because the function allows for and indeed encourages such indeterminacy. If one knows the function, and hence has the concept of table, one cannot be too wrong about an object being or not being a table. It is the function–type conspiracy that makes the concept of table so successful. When the function is in addition *practical,* the conspiracy almost guarantees success. This is what I think happens with our commonsense-making concepts.

The concept of table can again help to clarify the point. The concept is not only functional but also practical. The difference is the following. Items in the extension of a functional concept have functions in virtue of their nature or design; those in the extension of a practical concept have functions in virtue of being designed for practical uses. Hearts have the function of pumping blood because so designed (arrived at) by evolution; knives or tables are designed to have practical uses. The practical concepts are more flexible and versatile than the functional ones, as they are meant to adjust to the needs and the dimensions of the practice itself. Simple functions may be fixed forever (pumping blood is all that hearts do, which is just as well). The functions in the service of a practice are context-sensitive and adjustable. The functional properties of a table adapt to various conditions in which tables are put to some practical use. The concept of table reflects this adaptive character. Our concepts of tools are practical in this sense, and so are those of commonsense making.

The commonsense triangulation of psychoinformational patterns is not unlike constructing (or recognizing) tables to fit particular situations, needs, and possibilities. Imagine we are in a forest. Lunchtime; no table in sight, so we must improvise one. Although we may each have a (perhaps) visual prototype of a table, as a control representation, we still must deploy *further* "tablehood rules" flexibly, compositionally, and contextually, to take account of the conditions around us: How many we are, how informal we want to be, how tall we are, standing or sitting, what we want to eat, what material is available, and so forth. No prototype or any other explicit representation can take care of all these contingencies.

Notice two things about this example. First, all I have said about tables and their construction (or recognition) does not make the concept of table less referential in a robust realist sense. The concept is about real things with real properties. It is, however, applied under practical constraints which determine what properties in what relations get into its extension. That varies from context to context. A table prototype may invariantly refer to a common denominator but that still is only a fixed part (the control part) of our more versatile practical knowledge of tables. Second, with the latter knowledge, one cannot be too wrong about what counts as a table. How could one? The success criterion is built into the practical functions. Once the latter are known, not only anything will do that serves the function, but often the context of the practice can further liberalize the range of the concept. One can of course misidentify a table for something else. This is a matter of concept *application.* Yet one is not likely to have a *concept* of table (the type) that does not refer to tables and does not license successful representations of, or predictions about, tables.

I want to say pretty much the same about our commonsense-making concepts (qua rules). Attributing a belief (*e.g.,* triangulating someone's cognitive state from the way the world is and how he behaves, relative to what the sense maker needs to know) is not unlike improvising a table in the forest. The concept of belief has robust application: Its triangulation rules focus on and pick up real aspects and relations in the subject and the world, in a regular pattern. These aspects and relations are variables whose values can be fixed only in a context. Given the practical functions of a belief attribution, which is to provide the sense maker with a representation of the information of interest, how could the sense maker be wrong about having rules with which to corner and fix the information of interest? She surely could be wrong in *applying* the rules and, for example, misread the evidence and fail to determine a cognitive state or an action of the subject. That happens quite frequently, and makes commonsense judgments empirically truth valuable. But this is different from saying that the commonsense *rules* for psychoinformational triangulation systematically misapply, or do not apply at all. The latter failure does not make much sense, unless of course we take commonsense making to be in a totally different business, with a totally different ontology.

The commonsense concepts apply successfully because they serve a practice of tracking information and sharing it socially. The very conditions of the practice ensure that the concepts apply. This plot should warn us that commonsense making cannot possibly be an empirical theory of anything, let alone of the most frustratingly complex systems imaginable, our own minds. If commonsense making were sensible, it would have constituted itself as an information-tracking practice, not as an empirical theory of the mind. Its historical survival and efficacy show that it is sensible. So it must be such a practice.[5]

NOTES

1. This is not an instrumentalist axiom. The fact that explanation and prediction constrain the concepts they use does not imply that the concepts fail to have real extensions; it only implies that which properties and relations matter and are included in the extension, at what level of abstraction, is largely determined by the need of explanation and prediction.
2. I am not suggesting that a cognitive competence is created or evolves for a reason. I am suggesting that, no matter what pedigree it has, such a competence does not get selected, reinforced, and improved unless (normally) it does a job for the organism and enables it to solve some major bioexistential problem. Such a solution then constitutes the (evolutionary) rationale for the competence.
3. See Fodor, 1987, pp. 129–33. Dennett talks of commonsense psychology as a "vernacular social technology, a craft" which we know the way we know the grammar of our native tongue (originally in "Three Kinds of Intentional Psychology," 1981, reprinted in his 1987, p. 46). The literature on animal psychology (next note) points in the same direction.
4. See Premack and Woodruff (1978); Griffin (1984).
5. I want to thank the regulars of the Tulane Seminar on Current Research for criticisms and suggestions.

BIBLIOGRAPHY

Barwise, Jon and Perry, John (1983): *Situations and Attitudes*. The MIT Press/Bradford Books, Cambridge, MA.

Bogdan, Radu (1986a): "The Manufacture of Belief," in Bogdan (ed.), *Belief*. Oxford University Press, Oxford.

(1986b): "The Objects of Perception," in Bogdan (ed.), *Roderick Chisholm*. Reidel, Dordrecht, The Netherlands.

(1988a): "Information and Semantic Cognition," *Mind and Language*. 3, 81–122.

(1988b): "Mental Attitudes and Common Sense Psychology," *Nous*. 22, 369–98.

(1989): "Does Semantics Run the Psyche?," *Philosophy and Phenomenological Research. XLIX*, 687–700.

Cartwright, Nancy (1983): *How the Laws of Physics Lie*. Oxford University Press, Oxford.

Churchland, Paul (1979): *Scientific Materialism and the Plasticity of Mind*. Cambridge University Press, Cambridge, England.

Dennett, Daniel (1978): *Brainstorms*. The MIT Press/Bradford Books, Cambridge, MA.

(1987): *The Intentional Stance*. The MIT Press/Bradford Books, Cambridge, MA.

Field, Hartry (1978): "Mental Representation," *Erkenntnis*. 13, 9–16.

Fodor, Jerry (1987): *Psychosemantics*. The MIT Press/Bradford Books, Cambridge, MA.

Garfinkel, Alan (1981): *Forms of Explanation*. Yale University Press, New Haven, CT.

Griffin, Donald (1984): *Animal Thinking*. Harvard University Press, Cambridge, MA.

Loar, Brian (1981): *Mind and Meaning*. Cambridge University Press, Cambridge, England.

McGinn, Colin (1982): "The Structure of Content," in A. Woodfield (ed.), *Thought and Object*. Oxford University Press, Oxford.

Morton, Adam (1980): *Frames of Mind*. Oxford University Press, Oxford.

Premack, David and Woodruff, G. (1978): "Does the Chimpanzee Have a Theory of Mind?," *Behavioral and Brain Sciences*. 1, 515–26.

Schiffer, Stephen (1981): "Truth and the Theory of Content," in Parrett and Bouveresse (eds.), *Meaning and Understanding*. de Gruyter, Amsterdam.

Stich, Stephen (1983): *From Folk Psychology to Cognitive Science*. The MIT Press/Bradford Books, Cambridge, MA.

van Fraassen, Bas C. (1980): *The Scientific Image*. Oxford University Press, Oxford.

Wilkes, Kathleen (1981); "Functionalism, Psychology, and the Philosophy of Mind," *Philosophical Topics*. 12, 147–68.

Index

P.156

a Connection between common sense and science.